MACHIAVELLI: A DISSE

Also by Sydney Anglo

THE GREAT TOURNAMENT ROLL OF WESTMINSTER
SPECTACLE, PAGEANTRY AND EARLY TUDOR POLICY
THE RECEPTION OF MACHIAVELLI IN TUDOR ENGLAND

Sydney Anglo

MACHIAVELLI
A DISSECTION

Harcourt, Brace & World, Inc.

New York

Copyright © 1969 by Sidney Anglo

Library of Congress Catalog Card Number: 75-100503

Printed in the United States of America

Contents

Introduction

AT TEN O'CLOCK on the morning of 3 May 1869, the municipal dignitaries of Florence, together with a large group of scholars, representing learned institutions throughout Italy, assembled about the tomb of Niccolò Machiavelli in Santa Croce, and solemnly read two telegrams—one from the Società Dante Alighieri of Turin, and the other from the Municipality of Forlì—expressing deep admiration for the Florentine Secretary whose *virtù* had pointed the way to Italian independence. The celebrations of the four hundredth anniversary of Machiavelli's birth were under way.[1]

Exactly one hour later, the entourage marched to the house where Machiavelli had lived and died: and, to the martial strains of the band of the National Guard, they unveiled an inscription:

A Niccolò Machiavelli
dell'unità nazionale
Precorritore audace e indovino
E d'armi proprie e non avventizie
Primo istitutore e maestro
L'Italia una e armata
pose
il 3 maggio 1869
quarto di lui centenario.

Later, after lunch, in the neighbourhood of the Rucellai Gardens—where Machiavelli had once engaged in animated conversation with his friends—a "literary reunion" was held. Atto Vanucci addressed the assembly on Machiavelli's achievements; the savants announced a grand project for the study of the life, times, and works, of their national hero; a cantata was performed; and the band of the National Guard played a variety of symphonic works. Throughout the afternoon a public exhibition of Machiavellian manuscripts and books was on display; while in the evening there was more music, and Machiavelli's translation of Terence's *Andria* was produced. The whole affair went off brilliantly, and served as the centre-piece for a series of similar demonstrations—with lectures, verses, and even dramatic works—perpetrated throughout Italy. And the occasion was commemorated, in true Renaissance style, by a special Machiavelli medal, so that time might not dim the fame of these celebrations.

Amidst the plethora of patriotic activity, sparked off by this anniversary, there appeared a volume of prose and verse by students of the University of Padua, who contributed essays on Machiavelli's character, times, and ideas, together with lugubrious verses on Machiavelli's tomb, and a more fanciful cradle song put into the poetical mouth of his mother. But the most interesting contribution was by Alessandro Marin, who wrote of the "necessity of writing a life of Machiavelli". Just as the Florentine congress had opined—it was about time that somebody set the life of Machiavelli in its proper context, sorted out the fact from the fiction, and put the record straight.[2]

Within a decade Nourisson's important *Machiavel* had appeared, closely followed by the writings of Amico, Nitti, Triantafillis, and the first volumes of Pasquale Villari's *Niccolò Machiavelli e i suoi tempi*—long to be regarded as the standard biography. The rest of Villari soon followed, as did the first cyclopean instalment of Oreste Tommasini's *La vita e gli scritti di Niccolò Machiavelli*—a work used, abused, insulted and plundered by subsequent generations of Machiavelli students. The dykes—to employ a favourite Machiavelli metaphor—were breached, and a flood of scholarship, pseudo-scholarship, popularisation, and vulgarisation has been pouring forth unabated for a further hundred years.

Though Machiavelli is rarely regarded now as the founder of Italian unity, almost every other interpretation of his life and works may still be encountered; and many of them are quite as subjective and fantastic as the nationalistic projections of the nineteenth century. For Machiavelli has become a typical victim of modern evaluative criticism: of the research industry which invests his every utterance with significance; and which regards his every completed work as a masterpiece, his every saying as a subtlety, and his every literary mannerism as a stylistic felicity. The indiscriminate abuse commonly hurled at Machiavelli during the sixteenth and seventeenth centuries is scarcely more extraordinary than this kind of uncritical admiration. It seemed worthwhile, therefore, to celebrate Machiavelli's five hundredth birthday by taking a fresh look at his work—as far as possible without the preconceptions which still blur so much Machiavelli study.

I begin with a rapid survey of Machiavelli's early career—as recorded in his official correspondence—noting the political experiences which helped shape his thought; and continue with a consideration of each of his major works to establish the circumstances in which they were conceived, their purpose and structure, and the likely sources and precedents for their principal ideas. I end with a more thematic treatment of Machiavelli's writings; examining the realism which is generally regarded as his hallmark, and setting this in the context of earlier notions of political expediency—particularly the separation of public from private morality, and the relationship between ends and means. The recurrent use of the words *Virtù* and *Fortuna* is studied, and the consequences of Machiavelli's limited political vocabulary are assessed. And finally I attempt an analysis of Machiavelli's method and style where I am concerned not merely with the obvious idea of historical repetition and the lessons to be learned therefrom, but rather with Machiavelli's mode of presenting evidence and of constructing an argument; the extent to which his dialectical procedure might be termed inductive; the consequences of his disjunctive style in composition and thought; his love of aphorism and hyperbole; and his frequent sacrifice of reason to emotion.

Machiavelli himself, as we shall see, could not resist disjunctive sentences and disjunctive ideas; and many of his most striking opinions were expressed in terms of extreme polarities. His posthumous reputation was of a like kind; though we no longer need subscribe to an extreme view of his achievement. The Machiavelli who emerges from the present analysis is neither the impious monster who stalked the Elizabethan and Jacobean stage; nor the patriotic hero celebrated with fervour by the Risorgimento; nor, yet again, the super-intellect and universal genius lauded by so much modern scholarship. But he is, I hope, a good deal more credible and just as well worth reading.

As far as possible I have let Machiavelli speak for himself, and most citations are in my own translation from the editions listed in the bibliography and notes at the end of this book. I have, of course, also referred to the translations mentioned there, and have made especial use of A. H. Gilbert's accurate version of Machiavelli's private correspondence, and C. E. Detmold's less accurate version of the official correspondence. I quote from these last mentioned translations with such amendments as seemed necessary; and have also followed Peter Whitehorne's rendering of the *Art of War* whenever referring to that work. I would especially like to thank Professor Gilbert and the Duke University Press for kindly allowing me to use the material cited in the course of this study.

I

Machiavelli's Political Experience

ON 1 AND 2 MARCH 1498 Girolamo Savonarola, that dangerous combination of political demagogue and religious firebrand, preached at San Marco in Florence. The friar was a great orator and could be relied upon to move his audience deeply. But there was one observer in the church—a certain obscure young Florentine by the name of Niccolò Machiavelli—who was not at all favourably impressed, and he said as much in a letter to a friend. In his view, Savonarola was a mere power seeker, inflaming the populace with "great terrors" and arguments convincing only for those "who did not examine them". The friar "changed his cloak" as occasion demanded—arguing humility when he feared Papal retribution, and advocating positive action when he thought that the Florentine Signory would support him. "Thus," wrote Machiavelli, "according to my judgement he keeps on working with the times and making his lies plausible."[1]

Two months later, on 23 May, Savonarola ended his career, serving as the *pièce de résistance* of a public bonfire; and on 19 June Machiavelli began his when he was elected Secretary to the second Chancery. It is hardly likely that Machiavelli would have been appointed to a responsible, if subordinate, executive position without having already given some evidence of his capacity. But there is a curious gap in the sources for Machiavelli's life, extending from his birth on 3 May 1469 to the end of 1497 when his first surviving letter, concerning a family business matter, was written.[2] Of the years between we know scarcely anything. A diary kept by his father, Bernardo Machiavelli, has been desperately squeezed for information, but, not surprisingly, it yields much on Bernardo and little on Niccolò.[3] The other scattered scraps of information thus far dredged from diverse sources only stand upright when cemented together by words such as *presumably, probably, possibly, if, perhaps, likely*, and *unlikely*, and phrases such as *may have been, it is reasonable to assume,* and *granted that*.[4] The cutting description of Savonarola, with its cynical assessment of political realities, written amidst civic hysteria, is a more valuable starting-point for a consideration of Machiavelli's thought than any attempt to establish the role his great-grandfather might have played in Florentine politics.

The situation in Italy at this period, and more especially Florence's part therein, may be succinctly introduced by Machiavelli himself who, in 1504, wrote a verse narrative—the *Decennale Primo*—recording the previous ten years of Florentine history. It was, he said, in the fateful year 1494 that Italy opened the way for the French

and suffered herself to be trampled upon by barbarian peoples. And because your city was not ready to follow, he who held her bridle tasted the blows of their rage. So all Tuscany was thrown into confusion; so you lost Pisa and those states the Medici family gave to them (the French). Thus you could not rejoice, as you ought, at being dragged from under the burden that for sixty years had been weighing you down, because you saw your state laid waste; you saw your city in great peril, and the pride and ostentation of the French.[5]

Machiavelli was but one of many who saw the descent of the French into Italy as a turning-point in the history of the Peninsula. It became a truism that the "barbarians" were a veritable "flame and a plague" which overthrew states and changed "their forms of government and the methods of warfare".[6] Guicciardini, Machiavelli's younger contemporary, in a famous passage in his *History of Florence* expressed a widely-accepted attitude towards the effect of the invasion. Hitherto, he wrote, Italy had been divided into five principal states—the Papacy, Naples, Venice, Milan, and Florence—each looking to its own interests, and guarding against the slightest increase in the power of its rivals: "and when matters came to war, the support on both sides was so balanced and the infantry and artillery so slow in operations and movements, that the taking of one castle by siege occupied nearly a whole summer, so that wars were very long and battles commonly ended with few or no casualties". The French changed all that. Everything was turned upside down as if by a sudden storm: the unity of Italy was broken; states were conquered in less time than it used to take to occupy a villa; cities were taken not in months but in days and hours; battles became savage and bloody; and "states were now saved or ruined, given and taken, not by plans made in the chancery but by feats of arms in the field".[7]

The French were only the beginning of Italy's rude awakening from years of self-gratulation, elaborate but parochial political machinations, and chessboard warfare waged by treacherous mercenary captains and their untrustworthy troops. Charles VIII descended into the Peninsula in pursuit of his mad dream of conquering Naples. Within a few years Ferdinand of Aragon had intervened, and Italy became a battleground for the major European powers. France and Spain, and the Empire too—aided, abetted, or opposed, by the formidable Swiss infantry, or by the scarcely less dreaded Germans—struggled for an impossible mastery in Italy: and the natives could only look on in despair, or try to secure some trifling and transient advantage over their traditional flyweight rivals by offering support to the invaders.

As Machiavelli pointed out, the Medici family, dominant in Florence since 1434, had succumbed to the stresses produced in Italian politics by the French invasion; and the city was left to struggle with variously unsuccessful constitutional experiments, and to expend much of its energy and a large proportion of its wealth, over the next fifteen years, directing powder-puff blows at recalcitrant Pisa whose submission was deemed vital for the healthy resumption of Florentine trade. However, Florence itself was a good deal more vulnerable to French or Spanish power, than Pisa was to Florentine: and the city, with its government clinging reluctantly and with much vacillation to a traditional pro-French policy, was in constant danger. The restoration of the

Medici was a weapon readily available to all who sought either to injure or to gain some concession from the republic: and it was all the more perilous since there was always, within the city, a party of Medici sympathisers, which grew as the republican régime under the Gonfalonier, Piero Soderini—a man "who never knew how to be a good or a bad ruler"—became increasingly strained by the fluctuations of Italian politics.[8]

It was in the service of so weak a state, amidst such difficulties and dangers, that Machiavelli spent more than fourteen busy years. His very first mission—though trifling in itself—had a more general significance. It was to Jacopo d'Appiano, Lord of Piombino—one of several petty captains, hired by Florence to do her fighting for her—who threatened to slide out of his obligations in the hope of squeezing more cash from his employers. In March 1498 Machiavelli was dispatched to persuade him to see reason:

and thus you will offer to his Lordship for another time all that is due to his valour and good conduct, and to the love we bear him; keeping however in your language always within the limits of friendly expressions, from which he may know our good feelings towards him and may hope to realise them. But above all you must have patience if he should threaten a rupture, and let him run on, and then reply and use your best efforts to induce him also to have patience.[9]

This was Machiavelli's introductory lesson in the ambiguous and dissimulatory language of diplomacy. His next came four months later when he had to deal with the tricky Caterina Sforza of Forlì. Her son, Ottaviano, had been hired by Florence to help in a renewed effort against Pisa, and, like his condottiere brethren, he was more concerned with payment than with professional duties and refused to engage himself to Florence for a second year. The republic decided to let the negotiations drop, but was subsequently approached by Caterina who was frightened by an impending attack from Cesare Borgia, bastard son of the ambitious Pope Alexander VI. Machiavelli was sent by the Signory to negotiate for the *condotta* at a cheaper rate, and was given so difficult a time by the Countess that he felt constrained to write back to Florence that mere words and arguments would not go far towards satisfying her "unless supported in part at least by acts". And then, just when he thought that agreement had been reached, she changed her mind, saying that he should not be astonished at this, "for the more matters of that kind were examined, the better were they understood".[10] Poor Machiavelli was so disappointed that he manifested his feelings "both by words and gestures"; but was fain to return to Florence with his mission still incomplete. He would learn more self-control afterwards, and a good deal more about duplicity: though his political education was to remain, basically, a study of the fickleness and futility of the petty city-states; the worthlessness of Italian mercenary soldiers; and the debility even of major Italian polities in the face of European powers. And Machiavelli became increasingly adept as the lessons grew harder.

It was in 1500 that his political experience broadened significantly. He was present at the disastrous attempt against Pisa early in July; when the Gascon troops hired by Florence deserted; and the Swiss, unjustly mutinous over their pay, held the Florentine Commissioner to ransom. This failure was regarded as a blot upon the French escutcheon, and Louis XII was only too ready to lay the blame upon the feeble shoulders of the Florentines who, on 8 July, selected two mandatories to explain to him the true state of affairs. Francesco della Casa, seconded by Niccolò Machiavelli, accordingly set out for France; and, for the best part of six months, they did their best to exculpate Florence; but neither the king nor his principal adviser, the Cardinal d'Amboise, was prepared to listen. The Florentines wanted further French aid, and at the same time wished to avoid reimbursing Louis for the money he had already expended on the Swiss troops at Pisa. The French, on the other hand, demanded both repayment for the Swiss, and that their army in Italy should be maintained at Florentine expense. The situation was thus deadlocked; though subsequently Florence had to go some way towards meeting French demands. And in the meantime della Casa and Machiavelli, lacking even the status of official ambassadors, and constantly

short of money, had a difficult and embarrassing time of it till
they were eventually relieved by the appointment of an embassy
at the end of the year.

Throughout the following year Machiavelli was busy running
various errands for the Signory, principally to the subject city
of Pistoia which was in civil confusion. But more serious was the
developing threat of Cesare Borgia, Duke of Valentino, whose
power in the Romagna was increasing and who, in May 1501,
contemptuously wrung a *condotta* from the unwilling Florentines.
Borgia, like all enemies of Florence, talked much about a Medici
restoration; and, though prevented from full-scale hostilities by
Louis's wish to keep the republic on its feet, he was clearly a
menace. In 1502 the activities of his generals assumed more
serious proportions as Vitellozzo Vitelli fomented a revolt
against Florence in Arezzo, and then overran the whole of the
Val di Chiana—the southernmost limb of Florentine power.
On 21 June Cesare himself captured Urbino by a brilliant stratagem: but, on this occasion, he had over-reached himself. His
colleagues, seeing the treatment accorded to the Duke of Urbino
who, though an ally, had been duped by Cesare, began to wonder
about their own future. Louis XII, too, was able to see that
Borgia ambitions were becoming too vast even for his own
comfort: a single powerful state across North Italy, under Papal
domination, was a good deal less to his liking than the conventional scattering of feuding fragments. French aid was sent to
Florence, and the situation was, for the moment, saved. Francesco Soderini, Bishop of Volterra, seconded at the beginning of
his mission by Machiavelli, was sent to Cesare who demanded
that, since Florence was consistently hindering his projects, the
city's government should be changed: "if you do not wish me a
friend", he said, "you shall know me as an enemy."[11] Machiavelli, though having to return to Florence after a couple of days,
had been greatly impressed by this first sight of Florence's bogy-
man; and he was to have further opportunity for observing the
monster in action later in the year. Cesare's captains at last decided
to take the plunge, and mounted a campaign against their former
leader. Both sides demanded Florentine aid, and Machiavelli

was sent to Cesare to play for time, learn what he could, and obtain a safe conduct for Florentine merchants to and from the Levant. Machiavelli was with Cesare, first at Imola from 7 October to 10 December, and subsequently at various minor townships as the Duke hurried about accomplishing his fell deeds.

All this—Cesare's initial reverses, his patient reorganisation of resources, plotting, and ultimate triumph—were studied with scrupulous care by the fascinated Florentine Secretary who wrote long and detailed dispatches to the Signory, analysing events, and even trying to predict their outcome. But he was not deluded by Borgian successes. Cesare's ability was considerable: but he would have been nothing without a Pope for father and France as his military security. With the death of Alexander VI and the election of Giuliano della Rovere, as Pope Julius II, Cesare's little empire collapsed even more rapidly than it had been created: and Machiavelli, visiting Rome after the death of the stop-gap Pope, Pius III, was on the spot, from 27 October to 18 December 1503, to witness both the total humiliation of the former terror of North Italy and the earliest hints of Julius's dangerous temperament and ambitions.

The general situation in Italy now provided Florence with a welcome respite: though not before she suffered a nasty shock. The French army had been thrashed by the Spaniards, first at Cerignola in the spring of 1503, and again at the very end of December on the Garigliano where Piero, head of the House of Medici, was drowned. Florence was in desperate straits as the great Spanish general, Gonsalvo de Cordova, having swept all before him in Naples, was thought to be turning his attention northwards, while the Venetians were active in the Romagna. As usual Florence turned helplessly to France whither Machiavelli was sent, in January 1504, as special envoy to help the resident ambassador, Niccolò Valori. The mission was, like the greater part of Florentine diplomacy, irrelevant to the decisions of the major powers. France and Spain came to terms at Lyons on 11 February 1504, and agreed to a three-year truce. Florence was included, and the greatly relieved Signory immediately turned their incompetent attention to the perennial problem of Pisa which, thenceforth, also became Machiavelli's personal headache.

In the course of 1504, Machiavelli was busy with minor missions in connection with the Pisan war, and was also involved in an over-ambitious scheme to divert the course of the river Arno in order that Pisa might be deprived of access to the sea. The plan ended in disaster, and Machiavelli found literary consolation in writing his first extant historical work. This was the verse chronicle, the *Decennale Primo*, which, having gloomily narrated the failures of the preceding ten years, even more gloomily ends with a prognostication of worse to come: the Italian wars have not ended; the Pope, the Emperor, the Kings of France and Spain, and the Venetians, are all preparing for further hostilities; and even Florence is greedy for possession of Pisa. Machiavelli confesses that his spirit is consumed by fear: though he feels that, were Florence but to "reopen the temple of Mars", her future would be prosperous.[12] This kind of general assessment of present ills, followed by an impassioned call to arms embodying the only hope for future remedy, was to remain typical of Machiavelli's literary compositions, till the extinguishing of his own hopes was reflected in the remorseless pages of the *Florentine History*.

The call to arms was, more specifically, indicative of what had already become Machiavelli's panacea for political ills. He had seen enough of the inefficiency of mercenary forces in the Italian wars, particularly in Florence's long and disgraceful struggle with tiny Pisa. The answer, which had been given countless times by Italian military and political thinkers throughout the fifteenth century, was to abandon this costly and unprofitable mercenary system, and to replace it with a national militia.[13] This idea was now strengthened by the events of 1505, when a captain formerly in the service of Gonsalvo, one Bartolommeo d'Alviano, was thought to be planning some kind of coup, supported by numerous old enemies of Florence. Indeed, even Giovampagolo Baglioni, who was still officially in Florentine service, and had been paid for it, was rumoured to be in league with him. Therefore, Machiavelli was sent first to Baglioni, then to the Marquis of

Mantua, whom the Signory hoped to enlist to their service, and finally to Pandolfo Petrucci, the tyrant of Siena, who was making extraordinary overtures to Florence, and offering aid against Pisa. The missions were all instructive both of the untrustworthiness of mercenaries and the lack of scruples on the part of practising politicians: but they yielded no positive results. In the event, Florence did manage to scratch an army together and, surprisingly, defeated d'Alviano on 17 August at San Vicenzo. Unfortunately, the victory led to an unwarranted surge of confidence in Florence. A fresh assault was launched against Pisa; but again failed through the pusillanimity of the mercenary troops, the determined resistance of the Pisan citizenry, and the timely appearance of three hundred Spanish infantry to succour the besieged.

Other people in Florence, apart from Machiavelli, were wearied by the years of humiliation before the walls of Pisa, and were becoming interested in the project of military reform. Antonio Giacomini, disgraced by the latest abortive attempt against Pisa, now poured the vials of his wrath upon the condottieri system; and Piero Soderini, more reluctantly, was coming round to the view that a national militia might improve Florentine fortunes in the field. The matter was a difficult one, for the city was sensitive to anything which might give one citizen a commanding position within the state. It was argued that the founding of a militia would open the way to military dictatorship; or, alternatively, that recent experiences of part-time troops had been such as to discourage further attempts. These were the classic objections to the founding of a militia; and Machiavelli himself took pains to refute them, years later, in the *Art of War*.[14] But Florence had been deeply hurt by the most recent fiasco, and there was a sufficient body of favourable opinion within the city to make some kind of military experiment feasible. Soderini, therefore, hit upon an expedient enabling him to avoid, for the moment, both a full-scale militia ordinance—which would have to be passed by a probably hostile Great Council—and personal responsibility for any possible failure. Machiavelli was empowered by the Signory to produce a model army on a small scale, to demonstrate the viability of the project. The Secretary, increasingly involved in organising the scheme so dear to his heart, dashed about energetically, enrolling men and arranging for their training: though he found the work terribly difficult owing to local feuds which often made men from one area unwilling to serve with those of another. He wrote somewhat sharply to the Signory that he was proceeding as quickly as possible: "and if anyone thinks differently, let him try, and he will find out what it is to bring together a lot of peasants, and of this sort". The authorities were impressed, and wrote back saying that they knew Machiavelli was doing his best, and that the labour of getting the men together was more difficult than had at first seemed likely. Nevertheless, they added sententiously, he must keep up the good work; and that "he who does well acts quickly".[15]

Machiavelli worked hard, and by 15 February 1506 the militia were in a fit state to parade in Florence where they made a good impression. The diarist, Landucci, remarked that it was "thought the finest thing that had ever been arranged for Florence"; and further parades enhanced their reputation.[16] In the autumn Machiavelli, who had seen the papal forces reviewed at Cesena, told the Signory, with patriotic pride: "I cannot refrain from telling your Lordships that if you were to see the troops of the Duke of Urbino and those of Morattini, your Lordships would not feel ashamed of your own troops, nor esteem them lightly."[17] By the end of the year Machiavelli was able to draw up a convincing report on the experiment, his *Discourse on Florentine Military Preparation*, and the plan proceeded a stage further with a decree on 6 December 1506 for the creation of a new magistracy, the Nine of the Militia.[18] On 10 January 1507, the Magistrates were elected, and two days later Machiavelli was appointed their Chancellor.

Prior to this advancement, Machiavelli again had opportunity to study Julius II. Late in August 1506, the Pope, intent on re-establishing dominion over the Romagna, had been contemplating an attack on Perugia and Bologna, and had, accordingly, asked around for military aid—principally from France, but also from Mantua, Ferrara, Siena, and Florence. Machiavelli, under instructions to agree to the Pope's demands while delaying matters for as long as possible, was dispatched on 25 August and stayed with Julius till the end of October. He thus witnessed the Pope's triumph when Giovampagolo Baglioni humbly ceded all the fortresses of Perugia and agreed to serve with the papal forces: though he missed the flight of Giovanni Bentivoglio from Bologna, and the Pope's triumphal entry into the city.

Militia business again occupied much of Machiavelli's time in 1507; but in the course of the year the situation in Italy underwent further changes. A revolt in Genoa brought French intervention; and this, in turn, reawakened the old imperial aspirations of the Emperor Maximilian whose schemes were, as ever, shrouded in the impenetrable secrecy peculiar to those who haven't the faintest idea what they are doing. Florence decided to send a representative on a fact-finding mission, and Soderini nominated Machiavelli. The Gonfalonier's enemies had, by this time, come to regard Machiavelli as far too much of a party man, terming him Soderini's *mannerino*, or puppet: and on this occasion their opposition prevailed. On 27 June, a young aristocrat, Francesco Vettori, was dispatched to Germany; though in January of the following year Machiavelli was sent to join him.

The mission was, in many ways, an unpleasant one for both men. The Emperor disliked ambassadors, legates, mandatories, or anybody else sent to find out his intentions, and he kept them at a distance. They lived uncomfortably; found it difficult to discover worthwhile information to dispatch; and even more difficult to receive instructions from home. Even when couriers did turn up, the messages they brought were marked by characteristic Florentine ambiguity, and were, perhaps, little better than the dispatches, which arrived mutilated. One such message, long concealed in the courier's boot, proved "quite illegible"; while another, written on parchment and hidden in a loaf of bread, "had first become wet and then dry", so that Vettori could only get it out in pieces, and was able to read not more than a quarter of it, "and that in disconnected sentences".[19] To make matters worse, first Vettori and then Machiavelli fell ill: and yet the mission, though diplomatically unprofitable, was important for

Machiavelli. In the first place he made a life-long friend in Vettori, a younger man, but one of a congenially analytical cast of mind. Secondly, the five months spent by Machiavelli in Germany made a lasting impression, which was to play a great part in the later development of his political ideas.

Maximilian's plans, as was their wont, came to nothing. His projected invasion of Italy petered out in the summer of 1508; though, in December, he was involved in the next important political move in the Peninsula, when the Pope, anxious to destroy Venetian power, promoted a confederation—the so-called League of Cambrai. The Emperor, Louis XII, and Ferdinand of Aragon, together with Julius and several other Italian powers, agreed to make a combined assault over the entire extent of Venetian territory which was to be divided between them. The unequal contest did not endure for long, and on 14 May 1509, at the Battle of Agnadello, the Venetian army was vanquished. Florence rejoiced and hastened on with its own contemptible little war. The major powers were all concerned in the struggle between the League and Venice, and Pisa was left, at last, without an external protector. Louis was, however, still able to make capital out of Florence's ambitions by refusing to countenance the Pisan war till very substantial cash payments had been promised to himself, Ferdinand of Aragon, and d'Amboise. As Guicciardini bitterly remarked, Louis forced the Florentines "to buy from him the authority to recover justly her own possessions".[20] However, as soon as Florence was given this permission in March 1509, preparations were speedily set afoot for the subjugation of Pisa which was now strangled by a resolute blockade. On 8 June the town surrendered unconditionally. Florence, already hysterical with joy over rumours of the impending victory, now celebrated with a public holiday, bonfires, fireworks, and great festivity.[21] The part played by the militia in these final operations against Pisa had been restricted to blocking roads and all possible means of entrance to the city. There had been no feats of arms. The citizen soldiery had not fought anyone. But, for the moment, Machiavelli, as the architect of the militia, was also regarded as having been largely responsible for the victory—which, in a sense, he was. His career was at its zenith: but he was more than ever marked out by Soderini's enemies who were ready to seize the first opportunity to bring him down. And that opportunity was not too long delayed.

Affairs in Italy now underwent another *volte-face*. The League of Cambrai, after its initial success, began to disintegrate. Louis, for the time being satisfied with his gains, returned to France; Maximilian, having entered Italy, was as vacillating and as ineffectual as ever; and, within two months of Agnadello, the Venetians were once again on the offensive. Padua, only just lost to the Imperial forces, was recaptured and successfully defended against a vast and elaborate siege by Maximilian who decided to cut his losses or, at least, to take money where he had failed to gain glory. And, as usual, Florence had to buy off the barbarians. One instalment of this payment was escorted to the Imperial agent at Mantua by Machiavelli who was also instructed to report on the progress of military operations—now favouring the Venetians. Writing from Verona on 7 December 1509, Machiavelli remarked: "that in all the places of which the Venetians make themselves masters, they cause the image of St. Mark to be painted, but with a sword in hand instead of a book; from which it would seem that they have learned to their cost that books and study do not suffice for the preservation of states".[22] Moreover, the attitudes of the members of the League towards Venice were becoming widely divergent. With the revival of Venetian fortunes, Louis again wished to carry on the war. But Julius, gratified by his own gains in the Romagna, and by the humble submission of the Venetians, was becoming increasingly antagonistic towards the French. The upshot of all this was a political realignment which could only be viewed with dismay by the Florentine administration whose traditional allies, France and the Papacy, were rapidly moving into an intransigent hostility.

Neutrality was unlikely to remain possible, and Florentine diplomacy—at the best of times geared only to sitting on the fence—was being forced to choose between France, whose strength had often sheltered the Republic from the wrath of her enemies, and the Papacy which, under a militant pontiff, was in arms and near at hand to inflict chastisement upon its adversaries. Procrastination was, therefore, the policy of the day, and Machiavelli—by now an expert in such missions—was sent, for the third time, to France. His instructions were, typically, not to commit Florence to any decisive course of action; to persuade the French, if at all possible, not to break with the Pope; and, above all, to prevent Julius from enlisting the aid of the dreaded Swiss: "for if the Pope adds the support of the Swiss to the advantages which his money gives him and to his own personal character, it would make him too strong and audacious, and might lead to disastrous results".[23]

Machiavelli remained in France from July till October 1510, endeavouring to make the King and his Council see that the best military aid they could expect from Florence would be simply for the Republic to defend herself. The rupture between France and the Papacy seemed inevitable: the King was mortified by the Pope's attacks, and was bent on destroying both his spiritual and temporal power. The question of the Swiss was, admittedly, worrying the French though, as Louis remarked to Machiavelli, their troops were so difficult to control that he was in two minds "whether it would be better that the Pope should be unarmed, or that he should have armour on his back that would hurt him". Later, however, Machiavelli discerned that France feared the Swiss, and he thought that if the Cantons were to declare themselves in favour of the French they "would care little for all the other powers".[24]

In many ways Machiavelli was unimpressed by what he now saw at the French Court. Georges d'Amboise was dead, and there was nobody of equal calibre to take his place as the king's adviser. Yet Louis needed somebody; for, Machiavelli pointed out, he was unaccustomed to dealing with the detail of affairs and neglected them while those whose duty it was to attend to such things neither took the requisite authority nor reminded the king himself: "so whilst the physician gives no thought to the sick man, and the servant forgets him, the patient dies". Despite this, Machiavelli was still inclined towards the French and said as much in his letters, stressing the considerable gains which would accrue to Florence were she to support France and were French arms to prove successful: "and if in this affair you run some risks, your Lordships are too intelligent not to know that great results are not achieved without some danger".[25] But the Signory would not commit themselves, and when Machiavelli returned to Florence no decision had been taken, other than to strengthen internal security. The secretary was now asked to organise some experimental cavalry units to supplement the militia infantry; and this task occupied his attention during the early months of 1511, together with numerous other military duties—notably the inspection of fortifications at Pisa, Arezzo, and Poggio Imperiale.

Things looked increasingly gloomy for the tottering Soderini régime in Florence. A plot against the Gonfalonier's life, uncovered in December 1510, was merely symptomatic of widespread discontent within the city. The Medici party were gaining confidence: in part through the administration's vacillation, and in part through the winning personality of the head of the family, Cardinal Giovanni, second of Lorenzo the Magnificent's three sons. Above all, the increasing antipathy between Julius and Louis was making it impossible for Florence to maintain her dangerous equilibrium on the fence.

The Pope had opened his campaign vigorously enough, but was soon on the retreat after the French army, under its new commanders Trivulzio and Gaston de Foix, routed his forces near Imola in February 1511. By the end of May Julius was back in Rome, having lost all that he had recently gained, and having had the news that a general Council of the Church was summoned by the French to meet at Pisa on 1 September. This plan to hold a Council had already been afoot the previous autumn when Machiavelli had written from the Court of France listing the topics intended for discussion: whether it was lawful for the Pope to make war against a Christian prince without first summoning and hearing him; whether he could make war upon the king of France under any circumstances; "whether a Pope who had obtained the Papacy by bribery, and sold the benefices of the Church ought to be recognised as the Pope"; and whether a Pope who had been proved guilty of numberless disgraceful acts ought similarly to be recognised.[26] Now the plan had matured, and the Council was called. Julius's immediate response was to summon a Council of his own at Rome, thereby invalidating the schemes of his enemy.

The Florentines were in a dreadful position. Here was a supposititious general Council summoned within their own territory. If they accepted it, the breach with Julius would be irreparable. If they refused it, Louis's enmity would be assured. Their solution was a characteristic one: they submitted to Louis's demand, but attempted to keep the matter secret in order not to offend the Pope. Only four Cardinals, in fact, answered the French summons: but they were more than enough to incur Julius's odium. And on 10 September Machiavelli was sent on a three-part mission. First he was to intercept the Cardinals on their way to Pisa in an attempt to divert them; secondly he was to persuade Gaston de Foix, the French viceroy at Milan, similarly to alter the meeting place of the Council; and thirdly he was to travel on to France to pursue the same policy, or at least to have the Council delayed. In the end only this last concession was granted; though far too late to prevent Pisa and Florence from being placed under the Papal interdict.

Once again the city, dragged along by its coat tails, was committed to the French cause, as the situation in Italy rapidly deteriorated. In October, Ferdinand of Aragon, who had been watching French successes with some concern, was easily persuaded to join the Pope and Venice in the Holy League which opened its campaign in January of the following year. The French were at first successful; but the sanguinary battle of Ravenna on 11 April 1512 marked the turning point of their fortunes. They won an exceptionally hard-fought field, but lost their brilliant leader Gaston de Foix. A few weeks later the Swiss marched into Italy to serve with the Pope; and within a couple of months almost nothing remained of French power south of the Alps. Florence was left alone to face the Pope who demanded Soderini's deposition, and the participation of the city in the league against France. These demands being refused, the Spanish army advanced for the kill. Now was the testing time for the much-vaunted militia—so

stirring on the parade ground, and so triumphant when it came
to blockading a wretched and starving city. Four thousand of
these troops were garrisoned in Prato, a stronghold guarding the
principal access open to the Spanish army in their advance towards Florence.

Cardona, the Spanish general, was not greatly bothered. His
first assault on Prato failed, and he offered to negotiate with
Florence if she would receive back the Medici, pay him tribute,
and feed his troops. The republic was more divided than ever,
but in the end Soderini let the opportunity pass: and there wasn't
a second. Years later Machiavelli was to cite the incident as an
illustration of the failure of a government to recognise its own
advantage, and how greed leads to total disaster.[27] Certainly
Soderini might have done better for himself. On 29 August the
Spaniards, with only two guns in their siege train, quickly effected
an opening in the walls—"more like a window than a breach"—
and the garrison promptly turned tail, abandoning the city to a
brutal sack. The Soderini régime was thoroughly discredited;
the Medici party demanded the Gonfalonier's resignation;
Soderini, frightened for his life, took flight; a new Gonfalonier
was chosen; and the Medici returned to Florence as private
citizens. But even this was not enough. A carefully-engineered
riot resulted in a *Parlamento* which agreed that a committee of
forty citizens, hand-picked by the Medici, should revise the
constitution—which it did, most thoroughly. The Nine of the
Militia were abolished along with the Great Council, while the
Gonfalonier, as in the pre-Soderini constitution, was to hold
office for only two months. The republic was at an end, and, as
Francesco Vettori, himself a Medici sympathiser, observed:
"the city was reduced to the point of doing nothing save by the
will of the Cardinal de' Medici; and this method was the method
of perfect tyranny".[28]

Machiavelli had remained as Secretary to the Second Chancery
after the fall of Soderini: but on 7 November—amidst the inevitable spate of dismissals, reshufflings, and replacements—his
reputation as the ex-Gonfalonier's *mannerino* caught up with him,
and he was deprived of all office. And this was but the beginning

of his misfortunes. Three days later he was banished from Florence itself, but compelled, under a surety of a thousand gold florins, to remain within Florentine territory. On the 17th another decree forbade him entry to the Palace of the Signory for a year; though this was, from time to time, rescinded so that he could render up the accounts of his administration. Machiavelli's political career was in ruins, though, in view of the general leniency with which the change of government had been effected, it was not impossible that, within a couple of years, Machiavelli might have found his way back into public employment. Piero Soderini himself was able to come to terms with the Medici. His *mannerino* might have been able to do the same.

Unfortunately even this hope was dashed, when, in February 1513, a stupid pair of young anti-Medici conspirators compiled a list of likely supporters and then left it lying about. The list was found, and a plot suspected. Boscoli and Capponi, the two inept idealists, were arrested and under torture confessed to plotting a Medici assassination. Machiavelli's name was on the list and he, too, was arrested and given a taste of the *strappado*. He confessed nothing because he knew nothing; and, when the matter came to trial, his sentence was no worse than a fine. But the suspicion of the plot now hung over him, and the favour of the Medici was likely to be a good deal harder to win. In fact, it took more than seven years before he was again granted the privilege of undertaking an official transaction—albeit a trifling one—on behalf of the city.

The present book is mainly concerned with the products of Machiavelli's enforced retirement—the political, military, and historical writings upon which his fame, or notoriety, principally rest. It is, however, worthwhile, before proceeding to an examination of these works, to look a little more closely into the nature of Machiavelli's previous experience in practical affairs. He was always, in his later works, much concerned to write something "useful": and, indeed, the value of his observations on political activity derives very largely from the fact that he had been involved at first hand in a wide variety of political situations.

It is, therefore, to the point to examine these experiences, and to see how far Machiavelli's responses to them prepared the way for the works written when he had the leisure to ponder upon them.

Within the limits of his position, Machiavelli had been a very successful diplomat and administrator. As early as December 1503 the Cardinal of Volterra wrote to the Signory regretting Machiavelli's recall from Rome, and urging them to "hold him very dear, for his fidelity, zeal, and prudence leave nothing to wish for in him". And in January 1504, on Machiavelli's second visit to France, Valori, his chief, wrote back commending his "wonted sagacity and adroitness" in turning a difficult conversation, with the formidable d'Amboise, away from Florentine transgressions. Four years later in Germany, Vettori—like Valori the official head of the Florentine mission—wrote to the Signory expressing the hope that Machiavelli would not be recalled since he found the Secretary's presence necessary: though, if he were recalled, Vettori was sure that "his love of country would make him brave all possible danger and fatigue". Similar sentiments were expressed by Antonio de Filicaia, one of the commissioners before Pisa, who wrote in April 1509 that, though Machiavelli had gone off to inspect the infantry at the other camps, he had charged him to return afterwards in accordance with the Signory's instructions: "indeed nothing could be more agreeable to me than to have him here with me". And Machiavelli was still eliciting admiration during those final desperate preparations in June 1512 when the Podesta of Montepulciano informed the Signory that Machiavelli had visited the place as commissioner and that his coming was most opportune since he could harangue the city dignitaries: "as you may well imagine, Machiavelli exhorted them with great wisdom, and assured them with most excellent and efficient reasons, that they had nothing to fear, either on this occasion or under more difficult circumstances, in as much as your Lordships had such an affection for them that you would never abandon them; to which he added other good words".[29]

Machiavelli's qualities of loyalty to his state, coupled with clear thinking and lucid exposition, were well appreciated by those who saw him in action. Interesting testimony to this effect comes from the instructions given, towards the end of his life, when he was sent on a mission to seek reparation for Florentine merchants who had suffered losses in Venetian territory. The Consuls of the Wool Guild told him: "we use but few words with you, because we know your prudence and the great experience you have so often shown in affairs of much greater difficulty than the present."[30] Even this praise seems something of an understatement when one remembers the situations in which Machiavelli had been sent to represent Florentine interests with no clear guidance as to what those interests might be, and when one remembers the people with whom he had to deal.

Machiavelli had met several of the most striking personalities in Italian political affairs, and from each of them he had learned something worth speculating upon. Indeed, he had been taught valuable lessons by some of the lesser politicians, too. One of his earliest diplomatic encounters, as we have seen, with Caterina Sforza, enabled him to estimate the scant value to be attached to political promises; while his dealings with petty tyrants and condottiere captains made their worthlessness and lack of scruple equally apparent. Even the treacherous, though too transparent, Giovampagolo Baglioni had repaid study. Machiavelli had upbraided him for ingratitude and bad faith, telling him that he would henceforth be regarded as a "stumbling horse which nobody would ride for fear of getting his neck broken; that matters of this kind were not to be judged by learned doctors, but by gentlemen; and that whoever attached any value to wearing armour, and desired to win honour by his arms, could lose nothing that was prized so much as the reputation for good faith, and that it seemed to me that in this case he staked his very lightly". Giovampagolo "changed countenance" several times during Machiavelli's highly moral harangue, but he still could not be persuaded to keep his bargain with Florence. Good faith and honour were too much to demand of a condottiere.[31]

Pandolfo Petrucci—deemed, by Cesare Borgia, one of the "masters of treachery"—was infinitely more wily than Giovampagolo. And in 1505 Machiavelli, investigating the d'Alviano

business, got little change from the tyrant of Siena who had once
fled before the Borgian wrath; but had regained power, and
retained it long after Cesare had passed from the Italian scene.
The Secretary's wits must have been sharpened by the bout of
verbal fencing with Pandolfo; and Machiavelli recorded the
tyrant's ready-made apothegms, such as not wanting to make an
enemy for himself "without at the same time gaining a friend";
and his comment that, though d'Alviano might be counselled by
reason not to advance in opposition to Gonsalvo's will, yet
desperation could cause him to do so; and, though desperation
would lead to disaster three times out of four, the result could
still be uncertain. Especially, Machiavelli would have been
impressed by the tyrant's classic reply to the charge of inconsistency: "I will answer you as King Frederick answered a similar
question asked by one of my envoys; namely, that to avoid
falling into error we must shape our course according to events
from day to day, and must judge of things from one hour to
another, for time and circumstances are more powerful than
human intelligence".[32]

Pandolfo was a slippery rogue, ruthless, faithless, and adept at
small-scale stratagems: but he had no great political conceptions.
Cesare Borgia, Duke of Valentino, was a very different proposition. For a time the whole of North Italy trembled before him,
and even the King of France was disturbed by the magnitude of
his schemes and the extent of his successes. Machiavelli was tre-
mendously impressed by his first sight of Cesare: and, when he
had greater opportunity to study the Duke's methods during the
conspiracy of Vitellozzo Vitelli and other lieutenants, Machiavelli remained fascinated though more critical. The letters he
wrote during his second mission to Cesare—between October
1502 and January 1503—are the most elaborate of his diplomatic
career, as he set down detail upon detail, reported every conversation, tried to analyse the Duke's movements, and commented upon the lessons to be learnt from this master of thuggery.

Machiavelli's very first interview with Cesare, showed the
Secretary that he was going to have his work cut out; for, try as
he might, he could not get at the Duke's "real thoughts". And

subsequently Machiavelli wrote complaining that he had been given fair words, but without result; and he could not understand what was going on. This feeling was to stay with Machiavelli throughout this visit: though he soon came to recognise that, whatever the Duke did or did not say, it was unsafe to trust him in anything. The secrecy with which he shrouded his schemes initially earned Machiavelli's approval: "there is an admirable secrecy observed at this Court, and no one speaks of things respecting which silence is to be observed". But later the Secretary grew frustrated and, feeling that his letters were not giving the information required by the Signory, he begged to be excused because matters could not be guessed at: "and you must understand that we have to do here with a prince who governs by himself". Machiavelli does not wish to write "mere fancies and reveries", and it takes time to study matters well.[33]

Machiavelli was not helped by his own government's indecision. The Duke wanted a military engagement, and Machiavelli had neither the authority to contract this with him nor any other instruction but to procrastinate; and at one time he felt it pointless to seek audience with Cesare who would not grant an interview to anyone with "nothing but words to offer", and who lived "only to advance his own interests, or what seem to him such, and without placing confidence in anyone else". The rebellious lieutenants were, in the meantime, making overtures of peace, and Machiavelli again remarked that the Duke seemed to accept them, but that "no one knows what course he is going to take, for it is difficult to penetrate his designs and to know him". However, Machiavelli felt clear in his own mind that the future augured ill for the rebels; though even as late as 26 December he had to report:

the Duke is so secret in all he does that he never communicates his designs to anyone. His first secretaries have repeatedly assured me that he never makes his plans until the moment of his giving orders for their execution, and he gives these orders only when forced by necessity, and on the spur of the moment, and never otherwise. I beg your Lordships therefore to excuse me, and not to impute it to negligence on my part, if my information is not satisfactory to you, for I'm not satisfied with it myself.[34]

Borgia was not quite the most secretive politician Machiavelli was to meet. This distinction fell to the Emperor Maximilian. But there was a vital difference. Maximilian was secretive because he never knew what he intended to do: Cesare was secretive because he did know—and his intentions were always so dire that they could only succeed if kept locked within his own skull till the moment of execution. This was another quality which Machiavelli admired: the more so since, even at this stage in his career, he had already suffered, and seen his city suffer, from vacillating diplomacy and indecisive military operations. There was something awesome about the Duke who, without warning, seized Ramiro d'Orco, who had served him too well in suppressing the Romagna, and left him in the public square of Cesena "cut into two pieces" for no other apparent reason than because it was "the pleasure of his Excellency thus to show that he had the power to make and un-make men at his will, according to their merits". This extraordinary sacrifice of a faithful servant, in order to impress the populace, not surprisingly made a considerable impact on Machiavelli, who later referred to the incident in *The Prince*.[35]

This was how Cesare treated his friends. To his enemies he was no less considerate; and Machiavelli had the privilege of watching the whole process whereby the Duke ensnared his erstwhile colleagues, talking on the one hand of a treaty of amity, and, on the other, making preparations for war; till the conspirators met him for a general reconciliation at Sinigaglia on 31 December 1502. Two of them, Vitellozzo Vitelli and Oliverotto da Fermo, did not live to see the New Year in; and two others, the Duke of Gravina and Paolo Orsini, survived only until 18 January. Cesare enjoyed himself hugely, and summoned Machiavelli in the small hours, proclaiming his delight at the successful ruse "with the most serene air in the world", and astonishing the Secretary with extravagant expressions of friendship for Florence,

which, he said, should share his joy at removing the chief enemies
of the Republic, himself, and the King of France. Cesare was
remarkably effusive: but Machiavelli had learnt enough of his
methods not to be deceived and wrote that "if one could believe
him to be sincere, we might rest assured without any uneasiness;
but the experience of others makes one fear for oneself; and the
manner in which he acted towards your Lordships when there
was a question of an arrangement with you deserves serious
consideration".[36] The immensity of Cesare's treachery was such
that, once witnessed, it rendered its perpetrator for ever suspect:
a point which Machiavelli later overlooked when, in The Prince,
he took the Duke as his model new ruler, and simultaneously
argued the political efficacy of dissimulation. The real wonder of
the whole affair was less the extent of Cesare's guile, than the
stupidity of those who gave themselves into his hands.

This incident, too, found its way into The Prince, and was also
described at length in a strange narrative, the Description of the
Manner employed by Duke Valentine in killing Vitellozzo Vitelli,
Oliverotto da Fermo, the Lord Pagolo, and the Duke of Gravina Orsini.
This has generally been regarded as an early work written,
perhaps, shortly after the event it describes. But it seems much
more likely to have been written late in Machiavelli's life: for its
literary tone, its isolation, and its discrepancies with what Machiavelli knew had actually happened at Sinigaglia, all argue composition for some unfulfilled section of the Florentine History.[37]

Years later, Cesare Borgia became, for Machiavelli, a personification of those composite positive qualities requisite for political
success, which he chose to label virtù. But in 1502, Machiavelli
had been rather more struck by Cesare's remarkable fortune.
Indeed, this good luck appears to have excited widespread
astonishment; and in Machiavelli's first week at the Court,
Agapito, the Duke's Secretary, spoke a great deal on this subject—
remarking that the efforts of his enemies had merely resulted in
fresh overtures for his friendship from Florence, Venice, and the
King of France himself—adding that some account must needs be
taken of such good fortune. A few days later Machiavelli himself
ventured an opinion as to the Duke's position: "so long as the

present Pope lives, and so long as the Duke preserves the friendship of the King of France, he will not be abandoned by that good
fortune which until now has steadily increased: for those who
have given indications of being hostile to him are too late to do
him much harm, and will be still more unable tomorrow than
they are today". In the following week Machiavelli repeated his
view that, ever since he had been with the Court, the Duke's
government had been maintained "exclusively by his good
fortune founded upon the confident opinion that the King of
France will furnish him with troops, and that the Pope will
supply him with money". Cesare, said Machiavelli, was a "daring
and fortunate man, favoured by the Pope and a King". But, as
the Secretary gained confidence—despite the Duke's insistence
that Florence should enter into a firm agreement—he felt able to
issue a warning that times vary, and that evil and good fortune do
not always remain on one side: a prophetic remark when one
remembers Cesare's degradation exactly one year later.[38]

Early in December, Machiavelli wrote to the Signory informing them that he discerned signs that the Duke was perhaps less
disposed to follow his own caprices, and recognised that not
everything would "yield to his good fortune". However, after
Sinigaglia, the Duke was again full of confidence; and Machiavelli,
pondering the outcome of his impending contest with Pandolfo
Petrucci, confessed that the matter could not be foretold. Pandolfo was certainly head of a state of great reputation which he
ruled with sagacity; and he had, moreover, hope of military
support. But the Duke was remarkable, "with his unheard-of
good fortune, with a courage and confidence almost super-
human, and believing himself capable of accomplishing whatever
he undertakes".[39] In the event, Pandolfo fled before Cesare's
wrath: though within a couple of months he had been restored
through the intervention of Louis XII who, doubtless, considered
that the Borgias were getting too big for their boots.

Nevertheless, apart from the Duke's extraordinary luck there
were other more positive factors contributing to his success. We
have already noted his secrecy and decisiveness: and another
feature of his government, which Machiavelli could not forbear

remarking on, was his readiness to disburse vast sums of money to further his objects. "He has spent," wrote Machiavelli, less than two weeks after he had first arrived at Court, "since I have been here, as much money for couriers and special messengers as anyone else would have spent in two years." The criticism was left implicit, but Machiavelli must certainly have been thinking bitterly of the niggardliness of his own government when he had been struggling on a pittance in France, and relying upon the good offices of private merchants in order to get his letters through to Florence. Machiavelli was also impressed by the military organisation favoured by Cesare who had learnt, from the subversive activities of the Vitelli and the Orsini, that the best way to hold a state was "to be armed with troops of his own, to treat his subjects kindly, and to make his neighbours his friends". Moreover, Machiavelli added, "the party that knows best how to impose upon others will carry the day; and he will best impose upon the others who is strongest in troops and allies".[40]

There is one other political point, taken by Machiavelli, worth mentioning here. As the representative of a régime universally regarded as feeble, dilatory, and deliberately evasive, Machiavelli was especially conscious of the difference between negotiating from a position of strength and from one of weakness. He had found a "friend" at the Duke's Court with whom he had long political conversations; and, during one of these, this "friend" gave him a piece of advice for the Florentine Signory.

Remind them also of another thing, namely that it might easily happen that the King of France should direct your Signory to maintain the engagement of the Duke, and to place their troops at his service, which they would in that case be obliged to do without receiving any credit for it. And therefore you should remind your Signory that, when a service has to be rendered, it is better to perform it of one's own free-will, and so as to have it appreciated, rather than otherwise.

Years later, in May 1521, on the first mission entrusted to him since his fall from office, Machiavelli "dexterously" told the

Minorite Friars at Carpi "that it was wisdom on the part of men to know how to give that which they can neither sell nor keep".[41] It is as imperative for the weak as for the strong to be realistic in their assessment of a political situation.

By no means all Cesare's political manœuvres, during the winter of 1502/3, were new to Machiavelli. But rarely could they have been more effectively demonstrated. It is an axiom of good teaching that the pupil learns best when he himself participates in the lesson. Machiavelli had been present at the culmination of the Duke's plot against his enemies; and it was the first time that the Secretary had been close to such carefully-contrived violence. It is scarcely to be wondered at that he could never forget Cesare Borgia in the moment of fiendish triumph. Machiavelli, however, was also on the spot to witness Cesare's eclipse in Rome after the accession of Julius II; and he recorded this just as meticulously as the successes of the previous year. The experience was particularly valuable for, on this occasion, Machiavelli found himself in a stronger position than the Duke, and was able to employ his diplomatic skill to great effect, and with ever-diminishing fear of retaliation. He could also watch the Pope taking his first tentative steps towards temporal power: and Machiavelli was as fascinated by this as he had been by the plot at Sinigaglia.

Initially Cesare had entertained hopes of the new pontiff; and Machiavelli reported, with a great air of judiciousness, the various opinions then circulating in Rome concerning the likely relationship between the two politicians. Some, said Machiavelli, thought that the Duke would go to Genoa; others that he would stay in Rome to be made Gonfalonier of the Church.

Others again, who are no less sagacious, think that, inasmuch as the Pontiff had need of the Duke in his election, and having made him great promises therefor, he finds it advisable now to feed the Duke on hope; and they fear that, if the latter should not decide upon any other course than to remain in Rome, he may be kept there longer than may be agreeable to him; for the Pope's innate hatred of him is notorious. And it is not

to be supposed that Julius II will so quickly have forgotten
the ten years of exile which he had to endure under Pope
Alexander VI.

Machiavelli concluded by remarking that the Duke allowed
himself to be carried away by sanguine confidence, "believing
that the word of others is more to be relied upon than his own"—
a knife-thrust observation which he was to develop a few months
later in the *Decennale Primo*, where he remarked that Julius fed
Cesare with hopes while the Duke "believed that he would find
in another that pity which he never knew".[42]

While affairs were yet in a state of uncertainty Machiavelli
spoke with the Duke to see "whether there was anything to fear
or to hope from him". The encounter seemed to last "a thousand
years" while Machiavelli listened to a vehement and hysterical
outburst against Florence. "I lacked", said the confident Secretary, "neither matter nor words to answer him, and yet I thought
it best to soothe him, and managed as adroitly as I could to break
off the interview." Machiavelli was well on top of the situation,
and wrote back to the Signory asking how he should behave
towards the Duke and whether he should "keep him in hopes,
and how".[43] As usual, the inept administration at home sent no
adequate instructions, and Machiavelli was left uncertain whether
they wished him to encourage the Duke or not. However, he
assiduously reported affairs in Rome, noting that others had
sensed a deterioration in Cesare's powers. The Cardinal of
Volterra thought him irresolute, suspicious, and unstable; while
the Cardinal of Herina had said that the Duke "seemed to have
lost his wits, for he appears not to know himself what he wanted,
and that he was confused and irresolute". Machiavelli ventured
his own opinion that the deterioration may have come about as a
result of "his natural character, or because the blows of fortune
which he is not accustomed to bear, have stunned and con-
founded him".[44]

The once powerful Borgia had become a mere dupe, as the
Pope plotted to encompass his downfall by indirect means. And
even Machiavelli spoke soothing words to his face, while secretly

advising the Signory to ignore the Duke's envoy. Even Cesare's old officers remained in Rome—after their master had departed for Ostia, to salvage his military forces—since they were unwilling to share the Duke's ill-fortune. Machiavelli, gaining confidence in his own judgement, advised the Signory that, if there were new reasons for favouring the Duke then they should do so, "although the Pope would rather that you gave him a kick": and he made it clear that the military aid pledged to the Duke was so hypothetical and unlikely that "everybody here laughs at him".[45]

Cesare apparently made one last gesture of defiance. He refused to hand over his remaining fortresses in the Romagna to the Pope, and was promptly taken prisoner. In Machiavelli's view "the Duke has finished his role here for ever". Various rumours were circulating in Rome, including the news that the Duke had been thrown into the Tiber by order of the Pope. Machiavelli wrote,

> I can neither confirm nor deny this statement, but I believe that, even if it be not true now, it certainly will be ere long. And we now see how honourably this Pope begins to pay his debts, and how he wipes them out as with a sponge. Nevertheless everybody blesses his hands, and will do so still more the more decidedly he goes ahead. But since the Duke is taken, whether dead or alive, we can now act regardless of him.

Thenceforth, Machiavelli mentioned Cesare only briefly: saying that his sins had brought him little by little to expiation; that his affairs had recently undergone a thousand changes, "though in truth these have always been downward"; that many conjectured that his end would be a bad one; and, finally, that the Duke was "little by little slipping into his grave".[46]

The Borgia menace was at an end. It had been virtually so since the accession of Julius; and Machiavelli had been quick to grasp the point. Both his rather contemptuous references to the Duke in his letters, and—even more significantly—his confident handling of the trapped monster, make it abundantly clear that

Machiavelli recognised Cesare for what he was. In fact it is hard
to discern, even in the letters of the previous year, when Cesare
was at his most dynamic and dangerous, the admiration which
critics always claim Machiavelli felt at that time. Rather, the
reverse is true. Machiavelli certainly admired facets of the Duke's
political personality—the ruthlessness, dynamism, adroitness,
fixity of purpose, and determination to create first an army and
then a new state. But he recognised, from the outset, that Borgian
successes were based primarily upon a fortunate concatenation of
circumstances. When, in later years, Machiavelli was thinking
about politics in a more theoretical manner, he came to emphasise
Cesare's positive qualities, and to ignore the element that luck
had played in his career. The former suggested themselves as
particularly appropriate to the purposes of *The Prince*: while the
negative ending—when Cesare lost his grip on affairs—was,
dramatically speaking, irrelevant. And Machiavelli, as we shall
see, again and again, was more concerned with literary effects
and rhetorical conviction than with strict historical accuracy.

Machiavelli was no more under any illusions about Cesare
Borgia in 1513, when he wrote *The Prince*, than in 1503 when he
chronicled the Duke's folly in trusting Pope Julius. Nor, as is
often said, did he idealise Borgia. He merely recognised that,
politically, much of Cesare's work had been effective. There was
no reason why another leader of sufficient energy and spirit,
taking Cesare as an exemplar, should not improve upon his
achievements. The idealisation was simply of a method, not of a
man. Nevertheless, in ignoring the factors which he himself
knew to be true and had commented upon so acutely in his
letters, Machiavelli—while enhancing the impact of his writing—
seriously weakened the fabric of his argument.

The only other great Italian figure with whom Machiavelli
made personal contact as a diplomat, and who made a lasting
impression, was the instrument of Cesare's downfall—Pope
Julius II. Machiavelli had two close looks at this belligerent pontiff,
the first being the mission of 1503, when the Secretary had been
sent to Rome to report on the papal election after the death of
Pius III. Machiavelli exercised all his wit to describe the situation

accurately, noting that the new Pope had made so many contradictory promises in order to gain the election that somebody was bound to be disappointed: and that Cesare, whom the Pope despised, was going to be one of the unlucky ones, despite Julius's reputation as a man of "entire good faith".[47]

More important, politically, was the Pope's attitude towards the Venetians, whose aggression in the Romagna was a source of anxiety for the nervy Florentine administration. Machiavelli, writing that no efforts were spared in stirring Julius to action, pointed out that the situation was difficult because:

> having as yet neither troops nor money, and being under obligations to everybody for his election and for the general support he has received, he cannot as yet take a decided part in anything; and therefore he is obliged rather to pretend neutrality until the changes of time and things oblige him to declare himself, or until he is so firm in his seat that he may favour one or the other party, and engage in any enterprise he may please.

It did not take Machiavelli long to size up the Pope's personality. As a matter of fact, Julius himself made this abundantly clear, complaining that he was very displeased with the Venetians, but could not be more active in these early stages of his Pontificate since, having neither troops nor money, he was "constrained by necessity to act contrary to his nature". Machiavelli could, for the time being, elicit nothing more promising; but he did write to the Signory expressing his opinion that hopes might yet be founded upon the Pope's "choleric temper and honourable character"; for while the former would inflame him, the latter would impel him to act against those who might injure the honour of the Church under his Pontificate.[48]

At one point, towards the end of November, both Machiavelli and the Cardinal of Volterra did begin to wonder whether Julius was being rather more devious than they had, at first, thought. The Cardinal asked d'Amboise whether the Pope was, despite all his protests, conniving at Venetian aggression in the Romagna;

but they concluded that he was not "a man of double-dealing, but rather abrupt and impetuous". Time was to show that he could be both; and Machiavelli, studying his dealings with Borgia, already considered Julius as an unscrupulous and potentially dangerous personality, noting with approval his reactions to the capture of the dreaded strangler, Don Michele Coriglia, Cesare's diabolic henchman. Julius was delighted because it seemed that now all the crimes committed in Rome during the last eleven years would be revealed. Moreover, the Pope said that he wanted to talk with Don Michele "to learn some tricks from him, so as to enable him the better to govern the Church"; and he hoped that the captured ruffian would arrive at Rome in good time "so that he might make use of him in the triumphal procession". And almost the last thing Machiavelli wrote on this first embassy to Rome was a sarcastic gibe at Julius's anxiety to receive the French envoys whose arrival had been delayed by snow: "he bears it patiently, however, as the cause of it is a power higher than himself".[49]

It took Julius some time before he could give full rein to his "choleric temper", but keen politicians were watching him warily; and, in the summer of 1505, Machiavelli carefully noted down a conversation with Pandolfo Petrucci in which the tyrant of Siena expressed his fear that the Pope might one day become "another Alexander VI". Within a year this prophecy was being fulfilled; and Machiavelli was again present during Julius's initial move against the Romagna, noting with amazement the temerity of the Pope and the pusillanimity of Giovampagolo Baglioni who, he thought, had the Pontiff at his mercy. Julius's monumental daring and his success despite seemingly impossible odds were later repeatedly cited by Machiavelli as an instance of the achievements possible for a man whose actions are in conformity with his fortune.[50]

Julius was a ruler well worth studying. When, for example, he moved on from Perugia to Bologna, ambassadors from the latter city came to remind him of treaties made by his predecessors, which he had himself confirmed. Julius promptly crushed them:

if the people of Bologna were devoted to the Church, it was no more than their duty, for they were under obligations to the Church, which was as good a mistress to them as they were good servants to her; that he had come in person to liberate the city from her tyrants; and that as to the treaties he cared neither for those made by other Popes, nor for that made by himself, for neither his predecessors nor himself could have done otherwise, and that it was necessity and not his freewill that had made him confirm the treaty; but that the time had now arrived for correcting these things, and it seemed to him that if he did not do so he would have no excuse to offer to the Almighty.[51]

The Pope concluded that if the government of Bologna pleased him he would confirm it, otherwise he would change it, if necessary by force of arms—for which purpose he had provided himself with an army which would make "all Italy tremble, let alone Bologna". There was not much that one could reply to this kind of thing, and the ambassadors staggered away, numbed by this forthright repudiation of solemn promises. The lesson was not a new one for Machiavelli who had already seen more promises broken than he was ever to see faithfully observed. But Julius's faithlessness was proclaimed with irresistible brutality; and Machiavelli, realising more than ever the formidable and unstable nature of this Pontiff, reported that everybody was of the opinion that, if the Pope were to succeed against Bologna, he would immediately embark upon more important enterprises, and that Italy would "now or never . . . be relieved of those who have plotted to devour her".[52] The sequel was less stirring: for though Julius crippled Venice, and contrived to have the French temporarily driven from Italy, he was likewise instrumental in increasing Spanish interference in the Peninsula, in bringing about the downfall of the Florentine republic and the restoration of the Medici, and, in general, for making Italy more than ever a prey to the barbarians. This, said Machiavelli, was the debt Italy finally owed to Pope Julius.[53]

Perhaps Machiavelli recalled a detail of his first mission to Rome when the Venetian ambassador had blamed the Popes for the ruin of the Romagna for two hundred years, through their ambitions "to establish first one then another as master of that province".[54] Already, by 1510, Machiavelli was seeing in the ambitions of Julius not merely the ruin of the Romagna, but possibly that of all Italy—and certainly of Florence. And he wrote that Louis, in his determination to depose the Pope, was trying to raise so vast an army that its progress would not be war, "but simply a promenade to Rome"; adding that, if only Florence were situated elsewhere, "all this would be very desirable, so that our priests might also taste a little of the bitterness of this world".[55] Machiavelli grew to despise Julius and the temporal power of the Church which this Pontiff so strikingly represented; and his hatred was most dramatically expressed in the *Discourses*, when he bitterly castigated Giovampagolo Baglioni for that missed opportunity at Perugia in 1506. As a matter of fact, Giovampagolo did better for himself by submitting to the Pope: but Machiavelli, thinking in broader terms, could only regret that extreme action might have shown ecclesiastics "how little men are respected who live and rule as they do".[56]

Of all the soldiers, prelates, and rulers whom Machiavelli encountered in the course of his career, Cesare Borgia and Julius II impressed him most: and this despite the fact that he had also met two reigning monarchs, Louis XII and the Emperor Maximilian. Neither of these made any great impression on the Secretary; though the power wielded by the former, and dissipated by the latter, did provide him with much food for thought. France and Germany were important to Machiavelli for reasons other than the personalities of their rulers.

Machiavelli was four times in France, but his first mission in 1500 was his only lengthy stay in that country. It was Machiavelli's first experience of precisely how contemptible his beloved Florence seemed to the Ultramontanes, and, indeed, just how dilatory, stingy, and mean spirited the administration he represented really was. The French wanted to be paid despite the failure of the Pisan venture, and until this were done they would not lift a finger to help Florence. Machiavelli had to listen to a num-

ber of home truths from the King and his ministers. The truths
were always the same: that "the real cause of all the difficulties
was the want of unity in Florence, where one party wanted Pisa
and the other party did not want it"; and that Florence lost Pisa
through miserliness, for in such affairs "you must keep your
money bags open; for in that way you spend but once, while
otherwise you spend six times".[57]

Machiavelli quickly learned another important lesson at the
French Court which was swarming with Florence's enemies who
were well received because they know "how to acquire *amicos de
mammona iniquitatis*, whilst your Lordships believe that you need
no other help but justice and reason". Justice and reason: two
priceless commodities in normal circumstances, but seemingly
worthless in France. Arguments, said Machiavelli, were useless:

> for they hold a very different language about all these things
> from what you do, and view them with another eye alto-
> gether from that of persons who are not of this Court; for they
> are blinded by their power and their immediate advantage,
> and have consideration only for those who are either well
> armed, or who are prepared to pay. It is this that does your
> Lordships so much harm, for they imagine you lacking both
> these qualifications. As regards the first point of being well
> armed, they see that ordinarily you are without troops. And as
> to the second, namely, the question of their own advantage, they
> have given up all hope, for they believe that you consider
> yourselves as having been badly served by them, and that you
> have lost all confidence in them in consequence of their con-
> duct in the late affair of Pisa. They call you *Ser Nihilo* (Signor
> Nothing), and baptise your inability discord amongst your-
> selves; and the ill conduct of their troops they ascribe to your
> bad government.[58]

Machiavelli and della Casa—feeling increasingly inadequate—
wrote that new ambassadors of rank and quality should be sent,
and that they had better come with instructions to pay the Swiss
and "with means enough to make friends". Everybody was

looking out for his own interests, and whoever did not resort to bribery was in the position of one who believed that he could win a law suit "without paying for an attorney". The entire mission passed in this way; with Machiavelli and della Casa living in near penury through lack of adequate remuneration; having every day to endure the insults of the French who made no secret of their contempt; and trying to evade the increasingly importunate demands for money, by referring to a full embassy which was supposed to be on its way from Florence. "So you have said, it is true," d'Amboise remarked one day, "but we shall be dead before the ambassadors come." And he added darkly, to the Florentine's discomfort, "but we shall make efforts that others may die first". Eventually the embassy was dispatched, and Machiavelli was able to escape back to Florence, still smarting from the humiliations which, as the republic's proxy, he had endured, and with one miserable truth imprinted on his memory: "preserve the friendship of the King, and then you will not need his assistance; but if you lose his good graces, all the help will not suffice you".[59] Florence had been well and truly cut down to size, and, in Machiavelli's subsequent visits, the situation remained very much the same—however much the Secretary sweetened the pill of his government's low repute. As he wrote in August 1510: "the character of the French is naturally suspicious, and they suspect your Lordships the more, because they know you to be prudent, and therefore not apt to expose your interests to great risks".[60] This was merely a nice way of saying that the French despised Florence's cowardliness, tardiness, and meanness.

Some time late in Machiavelli's diplomatic career—after the battle of Ravenna on 11 April 1512, and almost certainly before his dismissal in November of the same year—he wrote a *Description of the Affairs of France* in which he set forth the strength and the weaknesses of that kingdom.[61] The former was primarily the result of unity and centralisation, for recent times had seen an end of the powerful duchies which had been a constant source of trouble in themselves, and an open invitation to external foes such as England. Now the crown of France virtually controlled them all, and had at its command vast resources of man-power; though a great part of the nation's wealth found its way into clerical pockets. From the military point of view, however, Machiavelli was not greatly impressed. Men-at-arms were clearly the national forte; but French infantry was poor, because the townsfolk were unused to war and, moreover, so cowed by the nobles as to be "pusillanimous and base". The only native infantry were the Gascons who might have imbibed something of the spirit of their Spanish neighbours.

But for some years since they have shown themselves better thieves than soldiers; nevertheless, in defending and assaulting of towns they do well enough, but in the field they are but indifferent, quite contrary to the Germans and Swiss, who are not to be dealt with in the field, but in storming or defending a town they are good for nothing; and I suppose it proceeds from hence that they cannot in both cases keep the same order which they observe in the field. Wherefore the King of France makes use of Swiss and lance-knights, because his men-at-arms dare not rely upon his Gascoigns in time of service. And if his foot were as good as his men-at-arms, no doubt but the king of France would be able to defend himself against all the princes in Europe. The French are naturally more fierce and hot than dexterous and strong, and if resisted handsomely in their first charge they slacken and cool, and grow as timorous as women. They are likewise impatient of distress or incommodity, and grow so careless by degrees that it is no hard matter, finding them in disorder, to master and overcome them.

The Spaniards, the Swiss, and the English all inspired the French with fear: the last because of their ancient reputation; the two former because they were, in fact, superior in warfare. But, as Machiavelli pointed out, geographically France had little cause for concern: the Spaniards were put at a disadvantage by the Pyrenees; and the Swiss, though able to defeat the French in the field, were not adept at storming strongholds, and were therefore loath to advance far into the country, leaving well-fortified border towns in their rear. As for Italy—France had nothing at all to worry about from that quarter. Not only was the foot of the Appenines well fortified with strongholds; but "there is not a prince in Italy able to undertake him, nor are the Italians now in such unity as in the days of the Romans".

Machiavelli, like all his countrymen, hated the French: and with good reason. He found in them neither true military valour nor genuine political wisdom. He gave vent to his spleen in his *Of the Nature of the French*, a short collection of acid aphorisms including the following:

> They think so much of the present advantage or disadvantage, that they remember but slightly past injuries or benefits, and take little heed of the future, good or evil. They are cavillers rather than prudent; and care little what is said or written of them. They are more eager for money than for blood and are liberal only in fine speeches.
>
> Whoever wishes to carry a point at Court must have plenty of money, great activity, and good fortune. If they are asked to do a favour, their first thought is, not whether they can render the favour, but what advantage they can derive from it for themselves. If they cannot be useful to you, they make you fine promises; but if they can serve you, they do it with difficulty or never.
>
> In adversity they are abject, and in prosperity they are insolent.
>
> They are fickle and light-minded, and have faith only in success.
>
> They are enemies of the language of the Romans, and of their fame.[62]

Yes, the French were a contemptible crew. And this made it all the more galling to remember that they had been able to turn the Peninsula upside down, like a whirlwind; to take Italy "with chalk"; and to voice openly their own disdain for Florence, and for the other Italian "Powers", who came cringing and begging for aid at every difficulty. Political power, it seemed, had little to do with just deserts. It depended solely on the ability to

put a huge army into the field, and keep it there longer than anyone else. This was the main lesson to be learned from France.

With Germany the story was rather different. Machiavelli's
single visit impressed him enormously—even though he had only
seen a few parts of the Tyrol, and had merely passed through
Switzerland—and he composed three accounts of the nation.
The first of these, the *Report on the Affairs of Germany*, was written
on 27 June 1508, the day after his return from his mission to the
Emperor. The *Discourse upon the Affairs of Germany and upon the
Emperor* was a very brief note prepared for the ambassadors going
to Germany in the following year. And finally, the *Description
of the Affairs of Germany*—possibly written at about the same time
as the *Description* of France—was a more literary re-working of
the *Report*, omitting the description of Maximilian which had
been prominent in the earlier version.[63]

For Machiavelli, Germany was to remain the paragon of all
civic virtues. It was true that there were such mutual divisions
between the cities, the princes, and the Emperor himself, that
Germany was incapable of united action; and that the Emperor,
despite his vast potential power, was impotent. But this was no
matter, in Machiavelli's view, compared with the strength of the
free cities, where the people lived a frugal but sufficient existence,
only troubling themselves about absolute necessities, and "by
that means their necessities are much fewer than ours". Machiavelli was to erect Germany and Switzerland on increasingly lofty
pedestals: in *The Prince*, the *Discourses*, *L'Asino*, the *Art of War*,
and in the *Florentine History*. His view of these cities was alarm-
ingly naïve, with the Germans going about their business, un-
assuming, valorous, devout, scrupulously honest, and enemies
to vice. Who fed the Secretary with all this curious information
it is impossible to say: but why he should have been so carried
away is not difficult to determine. Machiavelli's was essentially
a city-state mentality. Great kingdoms such as France or Spain
were beyond his grasp, and the facts and figures scattered about
the *Description of the Affairs of France* carry little conviction.
Nor could he satisfactorily compare such vast centralised nation
states with the Italian polities of his experience. The German

cities, however, were another matter. These could be contrasted with Italy: and the results were dramatic. In Italy the states were at the mercy of foreign invaders; they could only wage war for their own defence—or to recover their own possessions—under the aegis of barbarians, and by employing unsatisfactory mercenary troops. Yet there were the German cities, without the ambitions of their Italian counterparts, seemingly free to fashion their own destiny and, above all,

> their soldiers are but little expense to them, for they are always well armed and well exercised; and on their festival days, instead of the common recreations, one takes his musket, another his pike, one one sort of arms, another another, and, practising among themselves, they grow very ready and dexterous; and after they are arrived at some degree of perfection, they have certain honours and salaries conferred upon them, which is the greatest part of their charge. So that in every free town the public treasury is rich.

This was the answer, of course. The German cities were peopled by armed citizens. They could defend themselves, and did not have to waste their wealth on treacherous proxy fighters. For years before his visit to Germany, Machiavelli had been obsessed by the ideal of a citizen army; and, since 1506, he had been striving to create a militia for Florence. In Germany he saw striking evidence to substantiate his dream, and he wrote about it with enthusiasm.

Nevertheless, though the civic spirit of the Germans could not be too highly praised, Machiavelli discerned the weaknesses as well as the strength of their armed forces; and he concluded his *Description* with a brief account of German soldiery, which he distinguished from the Swiss whom he deemed superior. The cavalry, he wrote, was technically weak due to the poor design of their horse accoutrements. The infantry, on the other hand, though ineffective in siege work and in conditions where they could not maintain their battle array, were very successful in the open field. And Machiavelli cited their performance at Ravenna where "if it had not been for their lance-knights, the French had been beaten"; and again in the Spanish attack on Guyenne when "the Spaniards were more fearful of a body of ten thousand German foot, which the King of France had in his service, than all the rest of his army, therefore they declined coming to battle with all the art they could use".

The *Description of the Affairs of Germany* was probably among the very last things Machiavelli wrote before his dismissal. And it is fitting that, like the *Description of the Affairs of France*, it should largely be taken up with observations on military matters, and that it should conclude with a technical analysis of German arms. Warfare had been Machiavelli's concern since he entered public service nearly fifteen years previously: his very first official report had been a summary of the Pisan war; and his highest political office, and his greatest assumption of responsibility, had been as Secretary to the Nine of the Militia. For Machiavelli, as we shall see, good arms meant good laws. This was why the German cities were vigorous and independent, and why the Italian states were corrupt and servile. Military strength was to remain for Machiavelli the basis of healthy political life; and Germany and Switzerland were to remain his prime examples of modern political virtue.

The relevance of these political experiences to Machiavelli's later political and historical writing is obvious enough. He himself frequently alluded to them in detail, or cited them as the basis of his general political theorems. But when one endeavours to find—in the *ad hoc* writings of this early, active part of Machiavelli's life—more specific affinities to his later theories, the way becomes difficult and dangerous. It is true, beyond all doubt, that he did, from time to time, adumbrate ideas in his legations which he was subsequently to develop more fully; and that he penned phrases which were later echoed in more famous literary passages. But one cannot go further than this without unduly distorting the evidence and without tearing Machiavelli's diplomatic and administrative career from its context. Machiavelli learned his lessons in a hard school, and there were many other gifted pupils—though few who achieved his literary maturity.

The language and the sentiments of Machiavelli's legations were the language and sentiments of Italian Renaissance diplomacy. It is no difficult matter to find choice *bons mots*, acute observations, and pithy characterisations scattered about Machiavelli's letters: such things as telling the Signory that it was not "present fear" which would make Pandolfo Petrucci act, "but that of the future"; that though an informant against Pandolfo had good manners and seemed very intelligent, he had shown himself "so violent against he who governs here that it destroys my faith in him"; and that it was difficult to believe d'Alviano's movements were of such importance and at the same time also believe that Pandolfo could stop them at his pleasure.[64] We can find numerous instances of Machiavelli's own pragmatic wisdom and political expertise: as, for example, when he wrote that it was difficult to judge reports concerning Gonsalvo and the King of Naples, "as are all other things that depend upon the arbitrary will and pleasure of men"; that the Signory should take a prompt decision for, or against, France, "as opportunity is anyhow but short lived"; and that Louis XII should prevent the destruction of his friends by those who seek only their own aggrandisement, "by adopting the practice of sovereigns who wished to establish their power in a foreign province; namely, to weaken the powerful, conciliate the subjected, sustain their friends, and to beware of associates, that is to say, of such as want to exercise an equal share of power with them in that province".[65]

We can even find Machiavelli practising subtle deceits on his own behalf: advising the Florentine Signory to raise themselves in Borgia's estimation by fulfilling some of his demands for troops and "representing the number double what they really are, for the Duke will not be able to get reliable information"; and sending a letter to Florence, carried by Cesare's own envoy, with a passage in code advising the Signory to ignore his demands which were unwelcome in Rome.[66] On one occasion during his mission to Rome in 1506, Machiavelli was approached by Baglioni enemies and supporters, and not knowing the best course of action for Florence, he wrote "I listen to them all, but do not commit myself, and say to each that he is right."[67]

Machiavelli was, clearly, a very efficient diplomat: but, in this, he was by no means unique. A glance at the brilliant reports of some of his Venetian counterparts—especially Antonio Giustinian—will demonstrate that the combination of description, cool analysis, and pungent aphorism, was widely favoured in diplomatic circles. The very instructions given to ambassadors or legates show the same spirit. Machiavelli, on his first mission to France, was advised not to blame Beaumont, the French commander, till a favourable opportunity should present itself, and then he was to do so "energetically", charging Beaumont with "cowardice and corruption". Until the time were suitable Machiavelli was to speak of the commander in an honourable manner, throwing all the blame upon others, and avoiding saying anything against him in the presence of the Cardinal d'Amboise: "for we do not wish to lose his good will, unless we can thereby gain a corresponding advantage in another direction". Lenzi, the returning ambassador, similarly advised Machiavelli and della Casa not to stress Beaumont's culpability, because it was necessary to preserve the good will of the Cardinal "for objects of greater magnitude, or when we may need him to relieve us from even heavier charges". And Lenzi added that it was necessary to demonstrate the wrongs done to Florence by Lucca, "making it appear as bad as you can, without, however, manifesting any passion."[68] When the Signory sent Machiavelli to Rome in 1503, they instructed him to present himself to those cardinals "whose good will it is most important to conciliate", and told him to regulate his language as he might deem best "to suit each of these cardinals".[69] Again, on his mission to Baglioni in 1505, Machiavelli was told to emphasise the Signory's grief that the Condottiere would not meet his commitments: "you will shape your remarks to him in such wise as to make it appear that this is the only object of your mission, and that we do not see in his determination not to fulfil his engagement anything more than what he himself would have us believe".[70] Similarly, Antonio Giacomini, commissioner at the camp before Pisa, was advised to employ "force and stratagem" in his operations; to find out, by creating a disturbance, whether "chance may have prepared some advantage for us without our being obliged to make greater efforts"; to ravage Lucchese territory so that the Lucchese "having to care for their own wounds, may not attempt to heal those of others" and might know "the fruits of war, after having rejected those of peace"; and, finally, that he should act promptly before Florentine troops should have forgotten how to conquer, and before their enemies should have forgotten how to be beaten.[71] These terse, realistic aphorisms could well have been written by Machiavelli: but they were, in fact, contained in the Signory's letter of instruction to their commander.

This was the way in which politicians, diplomats, and administrators chose to express themselves. Examples could be multiplied almost endlessly: Valori, writing from France in 1504, that "if powerful princes use words without arms to enforce them, it only serves to compromise their dignity"; Vettori writing from Germany, concerning the King of France and the Emperor, that "it is supposed that the two sovereigns would prefer peace at the expense of others, to war at their own cost, even with the hope of some gain"; and Antonio Giustinian impaling Alexander VI's protestations of sincerity with a phrase—that it was almost as though the Pope's words "came from his heart instead of his mouth".[72]

Such cynical and telling aphorisms were the currency of Italian diplomacy. Machiavelli was a brilliant practitioner of the art: his letters are, perhaps, better than those of most, though by no means all, of his contemporaries; and his political analyses are, perhaps, more acute than those of many others. My point, however, is neither that Machiavelli was outstandingly brilliant, nor, on the other hand, that he was merely typical. It is rather to suggest that his political experience had provided him both with material for speculation, and with a useful manner of expression: but that he is not to be regarded as necessarily unique in this. The difference between Machiavelli and the great majority of his colleagues, is that he advanced from these *ad hoc* observations to attempt a more general theoretical examination of the underlying realities of political action. It is, of course, impossible to speculate about historical might-have-beens: but it is at least likely that, had Machiavelli remained active in Florentine affairs throughout his life, we might well have lacked *The Prince*, the *Discourses*, and probably the *Florentine History* in its present form—if not the *Art of War*. His reading public would now be limited entirely to professional historians who would recognise him as merely a very acute and highly literate Florentine civil servant.

Machiavelli's dismissal in 1512, and his even deeper disgrace after the Boscoli plot, was his personal tragedy. Posterity, however, has good reason to be grateful to the revolution which provided Machiavelli with the enforced leisure in which to ponder the reasons for political success and failure.

2

The Evolution of The Prince

ON 11 MARCH 1513 Cardinal Giovanni de' Medici was elected as Pope Leo X. Florence celebrated in a frenzy of high spirits, prisoners were set at liberty, and, among the rest, Niccolò Machiavelli staggered from his cell—free but unemployed. He immediately wrote to his only powerful friend, Francesco Vettori—Florentine ambassador at the Court of the previous Pontiff, Julius II—saying that he would not go over the long story of his misfortune, but hoped that he would not run into such trouble again, "both because I shall be more careful and because the times are more liberal and not so suspicious". This was clearly wishful thinking on Machiavelli's part, and the direction of his dreams is immediately revealed: "Keep me, if it is possible, in our Lord's memory, so that, if it is possible, he or his family may employ me in something or other, because I believe I would bring honour to you and profit to myself."[1]

A job was what Machiavelli desired, and he was not very particular as to what it might be. Vettori could do little, but wrote back encouragingly in general terms which cost him nothing but seemed to cheer the fallen Secretary. Machiavelli replied that he had borne his recent tribulations so bravely that he loved himself for it, that he felt himself stronger than Vettori had thought, and that, "if these masters of mine decide not to let me lie on the ground, I shall be glad of it, and believe I shall conduct myself in such a way that they too will have reason to approve. If they decide differently, I'll get on as when I came here, for I was born poor and I learned earlier to stint myself than to prosper."[2]

It was just as well that Machiavelli should prepare himself for the worst—though he was naïvely expecting something a good deal better—for Vettori soon reported that his case did not stand at all well with the new Pope. Machiavelli was badly shaken by this news. Politics, he knew, were unpleasant and unpredictable, yet he could not keep his mind from the world of affairs:

If you are sick of discussing affairs, as the result of many times seeing things turn out contrary to the notions and concepts you form, you are right, because the like has happened to me. Yet if I could speak to you, I couldn't keep from filling your head with castles in Spain, because Fortune has determined that since I don't know how to talk about the silk or the wool business, or about profits and losses, I have to talk about the government, and I must either make a vow of silence or discuss that.[3]

Those now in authority were not likely to be interested in Machiavelli's views on politics or anything else; but he still entertained hopes of employment. Perhaps when Giuliano de' Medici, or Cardinal Soderini, visited Rome there would be opportunity for Vettori to do Machiavelli some good for, he wrote, "I cannot believe that if my affair is handled with some skill, I won't succeed in being employed at something, if not in behalf of Florence, at least in behalf of Rome and the Papacy, in respect to which I ought to be less suspected."[4] So Machiavelli was prepared to accept anything provided that it were some kind of political service. This was his life. Nothing else mattered. But the hoped-for preferment did not come; and Vettori, unable or unwilling to do anything for his friend, sought to divert his attention by posing political conundrums concerning current affairs—absorbing enough for Machiavelli, but unremunerative, and too theoretical and sporadic to make him forget his plight.

The spring passed and the summer came, and on 26 June Machiavelli wrote to his nephew, Giovanni di Francesco Vernaccia, that it was a miracle that he was still in the land of the living: "because my office has been taken from me and I have been on the point of losing my life, which God and my innocence have saved for me". Despite all the evils he had endured, he was alive and well, but had nothing else that was good. Then, a month later, he again complained to his nephew that he was well in body but "in everything else ill".[5] How could Machiavelli be well, away from the world of affairs? For nearly fifteen years he had been engaged non-stop in exciting, dangerous, and complex political activity. He had galloped at top speed all over North Italy, to France, and even to Germany; he had conversed not only with princes, but with a King and an Emperor; he had been entrusted with a military administration to fashion a fighting force from nothing; he had taken part in campaigns; and he had been a public figure. Now he was a nobody, living mainly away from Florence at his farm in San Casciano, trapping birds, reading poetry, chatting with the natives at the local inn, playing *cricca* and trich-trach, his mind taken up with trifles. He longed desperately to return, in however humble a capacity, to active political life. But how? His erstwhile friends could avail him nothing. What could he do to help himself? A gift of thrushes to Giuliano de' Medici, with an accompanying sonnet, if ever delivered, evoked no response.[6] But Machiavelli was a politician and writer not a bird-catcher; and the idea of a far more apposite and effective gift now occurred to him. He would write a book of such manifest importance and intellectual power that the Medici, impressed by its author's political sagacity, would hasten to offer him a post forthwith. The book—provisionally entitled *De principatibus*, and known to posterity as *The Prince*—was quickly written; and it certainly caused something of a stir.[7]

The idea for this work did not, however, come suddenly to Machiavelli. His years of diplomatic activity, his close observation of power politics, his involvement in military organisation, and the final overthrow of the government he had served so unflaggingly, all went into the making of this book. But, more specifically, its major themes had been in Machiavelli's mind since his loss of office. This is made abundantly clear in the draft of a letter prepared in January 1513—before Machiavelli was imprisoned—ostensibly as a reply to a note from the ex-Gonfalonier, Piero Soderini. The text of these *Ghiribizzi*

(Fantasies) is very sketchy and full of ideas merely hinted at in a few words; and indeed it reads less like a letter to a fallen politician than like rough notes for *The Prince*.[8]

Machiavelli writes that the strange events of recent months have not evoked wonder in him—if they had then he would be obliged to confess that he had not "comprehended while reading and experiencing the actions of men and their methods of procedure". Unlike Soderini, Machiavelli sees events as do the multitude who judge by results and not by the means employed to achieve them. People behave in a variety of ways, and similar results are frequently obtained by quite different methods: Hannibal and Scipio, in particular, each gained the highest military glory, one with "cruelty, treachery, and lack of religion", and the other with "mercy, loyalty, and piety". Modern princes, too, have held power, some by disarming their citizens, others by arming them, some by destroying fortresses, others by building them. Some politicians were successful through their careful assessment of every undertaking; yet "this Pope Julius, who hasn't a pair of scales or a yardstick in his house, gains through chance—though unarmed—what through organisation and arms he scarcely could attain".

We have seen, continues Machiavelli, and still see every day, those who gain or lose kingdoms; and a man who is praised while gaining "is reviled when he is losing". And those who, after long prosperity, suffer eclipse never blame themselves, but "accuse the heavens and the action of the Fates". Why should different procedures sometimes be equally effective or equally damaging? "I do not know," says Machiavelli, "but I should like to know." Nature has given men very varied dispositions and imaginations which, of course, affect their actions. On the other hand "times vary and affairs are of varied types", so that when a man's mode of action harmonises with the time he will be successful, and when his actions are out of harmony then he must fail. Hence two men, working differently, may yet be successful in their own spheres. Difficulties arise because people's imaginations and actions do not change, whereas times and affairs alter constantly, so that a man's career fluctuates between good fortune and bad.

And certainly anybody wise enough to understand the times and the types of affairs and to adapt himself to them would always have good fortune, or he would protect himself always from the bad, and it would come to be true that the wise man would rule the stars and the Fates. But because there never are such wise men, since men in the first place are short-sighted, and in the second cannot command their natures, it follows that Fortune varies and commands men and holds them under her yoke.

The problems posed by such fluctuations in human affairs, the role of Fortune, and the ways in which it is necessary to adapt actions to suit the times, were all to worry Machiavelli throughout the year; and eventually—incorporating ideas, and even phrases, strikingly similar both to the *Ghiribizzi* and to subsequent letters—he answered the questions more fully in *The Prince*.

The genesis of this book is described in a letter, written to Vettori on 10 December 1513, where Machiavelli, having given an account of his humdrum day-to-day existence, relates that, in the evening, he returns to his home and his study where he enters "the ancient courts of ancient men", speaks with them, and asks them the reasons for their actions: "and they in their kindness answer me: and for four hours of time I do not feel boredom, I forget every trouble, I do not dread poverty, I am not frightened by death; entirely I give myself over to them". In the course of these studies, says Machiavelli,

I have noted everything in their conversation which has profited me, and have composed a little work *On Princedoms*, where I go as deeply as I can into considerations on this subject, debating what a princedom is, of what kind they are, how they are gained, how they are kept, why they are lost. And if ever you can find any fantasy of mine [*alcuno mio ghiribizzo*] pleasing, this one should not displease you; and by a prince, and especially by a new prince, it ought to be welcomed. Hence I am dedicating it to His Magnificence Giuliano. Filippo Casavecchia has seen it; he can give you some account in part of the thing

in itself and of the discussions I have had with him, though I
am still enlarging and revising it.[9]

Really, nothing could be more explicit. In a few lines we have
the essential Machiavelli, and an unequivocal answer to many
questions constantly formulated and reformulated by commentators. Machiavelli's principal interest in life lies in political affairs
and in the underlying reasons for men's actions; he has studied
ancient history and noted every significant exemplar; one result
of this activity has been a work on Princedoms which will be of
especial value to a new prince; and the new prince who should,
most especially of all, welcome it is Giuliano de' Medici. The
reason for writing the book is apparent:

> The giving of it is forced on me by the necessity that drives me,
> because I am using up my money, and I cannot remain as I am
> a long time without becoming despised through poverty. In
> addition, there is my wish that our present Medici lords will
> make use of me, even if they begin by making me roll a stone;
> because then if I could not gain their favour, I should complain
> of myself; and through this thing, if it were read, they would
> see that for fifteen years while I have been studying the art of
> the state, I have not slept or been playing; and well may any-
> body be glad to get the services of one who at the expense of
> others has become full of experience.

Machiavelli was desperate for employment, both because he
needed the money and because he needed to be involved in
public affairs; he was willing to do anything; and he thought
that his new book, if read, would demonstrate his value to the
state and lead to an improvement in his fortunes.

But things did not improve. Machiavelli had ended this letter
of 10 December with an appeal for Vettori's opinion on how best
to act in this matter—should Machiavelli come to Rome or should
he not? Vettori did not reply until the question was repeated
nine days later, and then he merely said that he would tell Machiavelli whether or not a visit to Rome would be a good idea when

he had seen the manuscript.[10] Machiavelli promptly forwarded a few chapters, but could still elicit nothing more than vague assurances from Vettori. And so the whole year, 1514, slipped away. In February Machiavelli jestingly relates how he is even beginning to get on the nerves of his common friends.[11] In the summer he is still out of work and wondering what on earth he should do. He finds that no one even remembers his former services to the state, or thinks that he is good for anything. It is impossible, he says, to continue long in this fashion because he is using up all his money so that, if God did not help him, he would be forced to leave home "and hire out as a tutor or a secretary to a constable, since I can do nothing else, or fix myself in some desert land to teach reading to boys, and leave my family here, which could reckon that I am dead, and would get on much better without me, because I am an expense to them, being used to spending, and unable to get on without spending".[12]

The story remained the same. In December Machiavelli still bemoaned his fate, and, while thanking Vettori for his good offices, grumbled that he could never repay him for he felt unable to do good either to himself or to others. If Fortune wished that the Medici employ him either on public or private business, in Florence or abroad, he would be satisfied; and, low though his hopes had sunk, he still did not doubt his own abilities. This vestige of his self-respect yet remains. Were this to go then, indeed, might Vettori grieve for him: "but that which has to be, let it be".[13]

A job, public, or private, here, there, or anywhere—this is what Machiavelli wanted. But, despite his literary distillation of political wisdom, he was not going to be lucky. It has been said that *The Prince* was written "primarily for its own sake, not for use as a testimonial".[14] Yet the tone, and the very words, of Machiavelli's letters make it plain that the converse is true. Machiavelli desired, above all else, official recognition from the new Medici régime, and he thought that his book would enable him to get it. The Medici, with Spanish support, had regained control of Florence in September 1512; and a few months later the Cardinal Giovanni de' Medici had been elected Pope. It now seemed feasible to many observers that the Medici party would build up their power in North Italy; and already the Pope was concocting a state for Giuliano, his younger brother, by taking over Parma, Piacenza, Modena, and Reggio. The historian Nardi wrote that, "the greatness and felicity of the present Pontiff had, in men's opinion, such power at that time, that there was nothing so great and beyond measure which could not be hoped for from the exaltation of Giuliano Captain of the Holy Church, and of Lorenzo his nephew".[15] Machiavelli shared the general belief in the possibility of all this, and, prompted by recent conversations with Paolo Vettori who had visited Florence in the train of Giuliano de' Medici, he wrote to Francesco Vettori on 31 January 1515 concerning the potentialities of Giuliano's position.

It seems to me that his dominion is good and strong, and such that under any conditions he can hold it, if in the beginning it be well governed. And if he is going to govern it well, he needs to understand well the nature of the subject. These new states, taken by a new ruler, offer, if they are to be kept, countless difficulties. And if there is difficulty in keeping those that are used to being all in one body, as, for instance, the dukedom of Ferrara, much more difficulty is found in keeping those that are newly made up of different members, as will be this of Lord Giuliano, because one part of it is a member of Milan, another of Ferrara. Therefore, he who becomes prince ought to consider making them into a single body and accustoming them to recognise one ruler as soon as possible. This can be done in two ways, either by living there in person, or by setting up a deputy there who will rule them all; so that those subjects, though of different cities and divided among various opinions, may look to one only and regard him as prince. And if his Lordship, wishing to remain for the present in Rome, should put there one who knew well the nature of things and the conditions of the places, he would lay a strong foundation for his new state. But if he puts into every city its own head, and his Lordship does not live there, that state will always be disunited, without reputation for him, and without bringing the prince respect or fear. Duke Valentino, whose works I should always imitate if I were a new prince, realising this necessity, made Messer Ramiro President in Romagna; that decision made those peoples united, fearful of his authority, fond of his power, and trustful in it; and the love they felt for him, which was great, considering his newness, resulted from this decision.[16]

This is virtually an epitome of *The Prince* which is specifically concerned with new states made up of different members, ruled by new princes who are enjoined to follow the procedures of Cesare Borgia. The particular new prince whom Machiavelli has in mind is the original dedicatee of the book, Giuliano de' Medici; and the method merely hinted at in the letter—where Machiavelli says that it may easily be demonstrated "because it is true"— had already been set forth, together with its expected results, in *The Prince*.[17]

But why should the Medici take any notice of a former servant of the Republic, who had consistently opposed their interests till the very moment of their restoration? Machiavelli himself anticipates, and meets, this difficulty in a neat, though far too obvious, piece of special pleading incorporated into Chapter XX of *The Prince*. Whom, he asks, should a new prince trust? The situation varies with the individuals concerned; but, in the main, men originally hostile to the prince—provided that they be such as require assistance to support themselves—can always be won over with the greatest ease; and they will serve the prince faithfully because they need to cancel by deeds the bad opinion he has of them. Thus they will be more valuable to the prince than those who, feeling too secure, may neglect his affairs. This is strongly reminiscent of his letter of 10 December 1513, when he told Vettori that those in authority might well be glad to employ someone of his experience: "and of my honesty there should be no doubt, because having always preserved my honesty, I shall hardly now learn to break it".[18]

That Machiavelli saw himself in the guise of special adviser to the Medici—as a man who should be employed, despite having been on the wrong side of the revolution—is clear also from the dedicatory letter preceding *The Prince*. This, though addressed to Lorenzo de' Medici, Giuliano's nephew, was suitable for any member of the family who might fit into Machiavelli's schematic ambitions, both personal and political. Machiavelli depicts himself as one who, striving to win the favour of a prince, finds nothing more valuable to present than "the knowledge of the actions of great men acquired by my long experience of contemporary affairs, and a continual reading of those of the ancients" which he has digested into a little volume. This, in a brief sentence, is the famous Machiavelli "method"—such as it is. Practical experience, collated with historical study, provides a penetrating analysis of great actions. The purpose of it all, says Machiavelli, is to enable his prince to comprehend, in the shortest time, knowledge acquired by the author only after years of difficulty and danger. The matter is important—so important, indeed, that Machiavelli has not embellished his work with extrinsic literary "allurements or adornments", for he hopes that its intrinsic truth and gravity may sufficiently recommend it. It is all very consequential. The immediate point, however, is less elevated, and emerges at the end of the dedication: "Let your Magnificence then accept this little gift in the spirit in which I send it; wherein, if you diligently read it, you will recognise my extreme desire that you should attain to that greatness which Fortune and your other qualities promise. And if your Magnificence should, from the summit of your greatness, some time turn your eyes to these humbler regions, you will perceive how undeservedly I have to endure a great and unremitting malignity of Fortune."[19]

Many thinkers had written on princes and princedoms. Since ancient times, the majority of those engaged in political speculation had tried their hand at this sport. How could anyone write yet again on this hoary topic in such a way as to arrest the attention of the mighty? Machiavelli appreciated that his own attempt to give rules for princely conduct might seem presumptuous, especially since he was deliberately departing from the methods of his many predecessors medieval and modern; and in Chapter XV of *The Prince* he writes:

But since it is my object to write something useful to whoever reads it, it seems to me more profitable to follow the real truth of the matter than an imaginary view of it. For many republics and princedoms have been imagined which were never seen or known to exist in reality; because there is such a distance between how one lives and how one ought to live, that he who abandons what is done for what ought to be done sooner learns his ruin than his preservation; because a man who wishes to make a profession of good in everything, comes to ruin among so many who are not good. Wherefore it is necessary for a prince, wishing to maintain himself, to know how not to be good, and to use this—or not use this—according to necessity.[20]

Thus Machiavelli feels that his original contribution to the vast corpus of prince literature lies in his discussing political situations as they occur in actuality and not as philosophers would like them to occur. Moreover, as we can see from his statements on method, he felt that, by viewing politics realistically, and by collating his own experience with historical data, he would be able to formulate rules for political conduct useful to all those who had the responsibility of governing a state. However, in the present instance, he was more especially concerned with the new prince; that is one who acquired territories, not accustomed to his rule, which he had to weld together by his own ability and ingenuity. Again and again, throughout the work, Machiavelli is at pains to emphasise this purpose; things must always be "particularly noted" by the new prince; it is always new states which are "especially full of dangers"; examples of *virtù* are always taken, whenever possible, from those who may be categorised as new princes; and, as the work progresses, Machiavelli stresses that a new prince, observing his suggestions, could become even more secure than an hereditary ruler. The *dénouement*, when it comes in the last chapter, is no surprise. The new ruler, for whom Machiavelli's instructions have been conceived, is the prince of the Medici.

However, the taking and maintaining of a few towns scarcely

constitutes a grand conception; and Machiavelli, both as politician and man of letters, needed something more dramatic as the theme of a work designed to impress those in authority. What precisely, then, should the Medici undertake? The answer is unequivocally given in the closing chapters of *The Prince*: but to appreciate fully the ingenuity of Machiavelli's approach, as well as its more obvious dynamism, it is necessary to consider the structure of the entire work.

The Prince, though presented as a continuous sequence of chapters, falls into five clearly defined, but interdependent, sections. Between Chapters I and XI Machiavelli delimits his subject which concerns the different kinds of princedoms, how they are acquired, and how they are maintained. Thus Chapter II briefly discusses hereditary states; Chapter III deals with mixed principalities, that is those not entirely new; Chapter IV illustrates the argument with specific examples; and Chapter V sketches a method whereby such states may be governed. Machiavelli next comes to new princedoms, his main concern, which he divides—in the ensuing chapters—into those won by a prince's own arms and *virtù*; those won by fortune and the arms of others; those won by crime; and those won by the favour of fellow citizens. The longest of these chapters is the seventh, where Machiavelli enlarges upon the career of Cesare Borgia whom he considers, as in his letter of 31 January 1515, the perfect model of a new prince, and especially of a new prince who gains his initial successes with the aid of Fortune and the arms of others. The parallel is obvious: the political achievements of the Borgia with papal and French aid may be repeated and even transcended by the Medici, restored by Spanish arms and now in command of the Papacy. These implications are taken up when, having given in the tenth chapter a few rules for computing the strength of all states, Machiavelli completes his account of the types of princedoms in Chapter XI, where he deals with ecclesiastical principalities in general and the papacy in particular. These may be acquired either by *virtù* or by Fortune, and can be held without either, since the ancient ordinances of religion enable ecclesiastical princes to retain power however they behave. Machiavelli has something pertinent to say about recent pontiffs: the labours of Alexander VI and Julius II have resulted in a tremendous accession of strength to the Papacy, and he hopes that the present Medici pope, Leo X, finding the pontificate great in arms, will make it still greater and more venerated by his goodness and his "infinite other virtues".[21]

Machiavelli next proceeds to the practical problems arising from the acquisition of a state. How does the prince lay a sure and lasting foundation for his rule, and how can he defend or increase his territories? "The main foundations which all states have, new, as well as old or mixed, are good laws and good arms: and because there cannot be good laws where there are not good arms, and where there are good arms there must needs be good laws, I will omit discussion of the laws and will speak of arms." So Machiavelli introduces his consideration of military affairs, discussing, in Chapter XII, types of armies in general terms before moving on to a condemnation of mercenaries. The following chapter analyses the unreliability and dangers of auxiliaries and of armies consisting of mixed and national troops, and concludes with a forceful assertion that states without their own troops are absolutely at the mercy of Fortune. Yet, "it is easy to find the way to organise one's own arms, if one will examine the methods . . . mentioned above by me, and if one will observe how Philip, father of Alexander the Great, and many other republics and princes have armed and organised themselves: to which rules I refer myself completely".

This assertion, both of the need to learn such rules and the practicability of the task, leads naturally into the following chapter, enlarging upon the prime importance of the art of war to a prince.

A prince, therefore, should have no other object or other thought, nor take anything for his art, besides war and the orders and discipline thereof: because that is the only art proper to one who commands. And it is of such *virtù*, that not only does it maintain those who were born princes, but frequently enables men to rise from a private station to that rank;

and, on the contrary, it is seen that princes who give more thought to their pleasures than to arms have lost their state. And the primary cause which makes you lose it, is to neglect this art; and the cause which makes you acquire it, is to be proficient in this art.[22]

And the way to gain skill in this art is through constant study both in the field, in theoretical discussion, and in wide reading. Machiavelli is particularly insistent on the importance of history as a mentor in this respect—and history is depicted here specifically as the actions, victories, and defeats of great men. Indeed Machiavelli goes so far as to suggest that the prince should take as his exemplar "one who was praised and celebrated before him, and whose achievements and deeds he always kept before him: as it was said Alexander the Great imitated Achilles; Caesar, Alexander; Scipio, Cyrus". Machiavelli does not realise that his suggestion could result in a law of diminishing fleas, with his prince imitating a great man who imitated a great man, and so on. As far as this kind of simplistic belief in the value of historical exemplars is concerned Machiavelli is very much an unimaginative traditionalist; and he was subsequently criticised for this by Francesco Guicciardini.

It is in the next section of *The Prince*, from Chapters XV to XIX, that Machiavelli comes into his own as a dynamic thinker—as a revolutionary in a very literal, if somewhat superficial, sense. For centuries, political theorists had felt constrained to compile a list of the virtues necessary for the good ruler; and always this political goodness had been equated with moral goodness. It is true that such virtues were often increased in magnitude as, for example, in the case of generosity which, for princes, was manifested by munificence and even magnificence. But, essentially, public virtue was identical with private virtue, and princes, like their subjects, were exhorted to be merciful, humane, chaste, constant, mild, and devout. It was taken for granted that, with such qualities, they would win everlasting renown; while, conversely, vice would earn them eternal opprobrium.[23] In the prince literature of the Middle Ages, and on into the Renaissance, this kind of virtuous catalogue formed a constant feature; and in Chapter XV of *The Prince* Machiavelli states explicitly that he is going to deal with "the rules of conduct for a prince towards subjects and friends" in a manner never hitherto attempted. Moral virtues are all very well, but necessity frequently forces a ruler, who wishes to maintain his state, to commit deeds which are, by all conventional standards, not moral. Therefore, "putting on one side imaginary things", Machiavelli feels obliged to conclude that political morality must be different from private morality; that a prince must know how to act according to the dictates of real situations regardless of normal ethical considerations; and that, in acting in this way, "he should not even concern himself about incurring infamy for those vices without which he could, with difficulty, save the state: because, if one considers everything well, it will be found that something which seems *virtù*, being followed, will bring about his ruin; and something else, which seems vice, being followed will bring security and his well being".

Having introduced his new political morality, Machiavelli proceeds, in the following three chapters, to turn the old catalogue of virtues upside down. Thus he suggests that meanness (*miseria*) is more advantageous to a prince than liberality; that cruelty is, on the whole, politically more efficacious than clemency; that it is better to be feared than loved; and that, in many circumstances, to keep one's word is dangerous, while violating faith may be beneficial. In all this, however, Machiavelli stresses the importance of appearances. Whatever foul deeds the prince may have to perpetrate, he must always strive to retain an appearance of conventional morality—for it is essential, as Machiavelli points out in the disproportionately-long Chapter XIX, that the ruler avoid being despised or hated.[24] In a sense Machiavelli is here lapsing into an ill-considered conventionality. The contempt and hatred of subjects had always been regarded as the surest way to a ruler's ruin. Tyrants—classical, medieval, and Renaissance—always perished miserably; and later critics of Machiavelli were quick to point out that no prince, following this new and perverse morality, would be able to retain a reputation for conventional virtue, and that, once he were exposed, the contempt and hatred of his subjects and of all peoples would inevitably ensue.[25] Machiavelli, half anticipating such an objection, attempts to meet it by examining at some length the careers of a succession of Roman emperors, from Marcus to Maximinus. He establishes that all, with the exception of Marcus—whose title was, in any case, hereditary—and Severus who had a super-abundance of *virtù*, came to a bad end either through being hated, despised, or both. However, none of this demonstrates how to avoid these pitfalls; and the assertion that Severus knew "how to counterfeit the fox and the lion", gets us nowhere.[26] Machiavelli is merely saying that, in order to carry out deeds of cruelty, ruthlessness, and violence, without incurring odium or contempt, it is necessary for a prince to be very ferocious and very cunning. This—even making allowance for the impossible nature of the task Machiavelli has set himself—is pretty poor stuff.

Machiavelli is certainly not in total dialectical command of his material at any point in *The Prince*; but nowhere is his weakness more apparent than in the next section: Chapters XX and XXI are mere rag-bags of largely-unrelated precepts; while the very brief Chapters XXII and XXIII—concerned entirely with the ways in which a prince should choose his advisers and avoid flatterers—seem principally designed to elaborate the special pleading, already alluded to, in Chapter XX when Machiavelli suggests that the best servants a new prince can find are those who have faithfully served the previous government. "Good counsels," says Machiavelli, "whencesoever they come, are born of the wisdom of the prince, and not the wisdom of the prince from good counsels"; and the wise prince will recognise and choose good counsellors, avoiding those who merely flatter and fawn.[27] And the wise prince of the Medici will, surely, choose the humble ex-civil servant, Niccolò Machiavelli, as his counsellor—though, in view of the grandiose schemes projected in the closing chapters of *The Prince*, it is difficult to see how Machiavelli would have exonerated himself from the charge of flattery.

So we come to the final section of the work when, for the first time, the whole of Machiavelli's conception is made specific in time and place. The time is now. The place is Italy. Chapter XXIV opens with a brief summary of Machiavelli's main conclusions thus far, and then proceeds to relate these to the Italy of his own day. Why have the Italian princes so consistently failed to maintain their states? The first reason, common to all, is that they do not have their own arms but have always relied on others—a cardinal sin. Secondly, they either have their ordinary subjects hostile to them, or, if the people are friendly, then they do not know how to secure the nobles. "In the absence of these defects, states that have power enough to keep an army in the field cannot be lost." The princes of Italy, says Machiavelli, returning to an idea already adumbrated in the *Ghiribizzi* of January 1513, should not blame Fortune for the loss of their principalities, but rather their own indolence or cowardice. In times of peace they never made provision for a changing situation; and when times were bad they took refuge in flight hoping that the people, at length disgusted with the conquerors, would recall them. But deliverance dependent upon the strength of others is valueless, and "those modes of defence are alone good, certain, and lasting, which depend upon yourself and your own *virtù*".

The next chapter goes more deeply into the relationship between *Virtù* and Fortune. Machiavelli claims that Fortune may, to some extent, be controlled by *virtù*—a composite quality which, in this particular context, comprises the ability both to adapt to changing circumstances and to prepare, in times of peace, for sudden and violent alteration. Italy, once again, exemplifies what happens when there is no such restraint upon the caprices of Fortune. Machiavelli, adapting a metaphor previously used in one of his letters to Vettori, likens the actions of Fortune to the surging of a flood, and "if you consider Italy which has been the seat of these changes—and that which has given them their first impulse—you will see her to be a plain field without dykes and without any shelter; because had she been protected with the requisite *virtù*, like Germany, Spain, and France, either this flood would not have wrought the great changes which it has, or it would not have come here at all". At the very end of this chapter Machiavelli suggests that the prince had best be bold and venturesome in his dealings with Fortune which, he says, favours the brave. But boldness is not always the quality requisite in a given situation, and Machiavelli develops the point, made previously, that often what men think of as Fortune, uncontrolled and uncontrollable, is merely their own failure to make their actions fit the occasion. Again, as in the *Ghiribizzi*, the remarkable successes of Pope Julius II are taken as an example of the efficacy of boldness when the times were propitious—though had the times "overtaken him, rendering a cautious line of policy necessary, his ruin must have ensued, since he could never have departed from those methods to which nature inclined him". So, Machiavelli concludes, "since Fortune changes and men stand fixed in their ways, they are prosperous so long as there is congruity between them, and the reverse when there is discord".[28]

The famous final chapter of *The Prince*—often, though inexplicably, described as an afterthought largely unrelated to the rest of the work—follows directly from this discussion of Fortune, *Virtù*, and their concurrence with propitious times.

Having, then, considered all the things discussed above, and thinking to myself whether, at the present time in Italy, the times might serve to honour a new prince, and whether there is the matter here to give opportunity to a prudent and *virtuoso* man of introducing a form which would do honour to himself, and good to the generality of the people of Italy; it seems to me that so many things concur in favour of a new prince, that I do not know that there was ever a time more apt than this.

Italy is now reduced to extremities similar to those endured by the children of Israel up to the time of Moses, the Persians prior to Cyrus, and the Athenians before Theseus. So the time is ripe for a saviour to lead the people of Italy to greatness. Machiavelli's language here becomes extraordinarily mystical and fervent: "although lately some spark may have been shown by someone, which made us think that he was ordained by God for her redemption, nevertheless it has afterwards been seen in the further course of his actions that he was rejected by Fortune". This, despite its deliberate imprecision, is a clear reference to the ambitions, and ultimate failure, of Cesare Borgia. The idea that anyone could consider Cesare as God-given would have seemed as bizarre to Machiavelli's Florentine contemporaries as it does to us; but at this juncture the author is carried away by his dominant theme. Cesare Borgia had got as far as he did by a combination of his own *virtù* and a favourable Fortune—the latter, as we know from Machiavelli's diplomatic correspondence, consisting of a papal parent and French support. Italy, says Machiavelli, is ready and willing to follow a banner, if only someone would raise it. And who better than a prince of the house of the Medici with its *Virtù* and good Fortune, "favoured by God and by the church of which it is now the chief, and which can be made the head of this redemption"? Again Machiavelli presses upon his intended princely reader the need to follow the example of great men. Again he hammers home his point that "nothing honours a man, newly risen to power, more than to establish new laws and ordinances: for these when they are well founded and have a greatness in them, make him revered and admired". And again he prescribes his favourite political panacea—the prince must have his own arms:

> it is necessary, before all other things, as the true foundation of every enterprise, to be provided with one's own arms; because one can have no more faithful, true, or better soldiers. And although each of them may be good, all together they will become better, when they see themselves commanded by their prince, and honoured and maintained by him. It is necessary, therefore, to prepare oneself with these arms, to be able to defend oneself, with Italian *virtù*, against foreigners.

Machiavelli now ends his arguments with a brief, semi-technical discussion of the art of war—strongly reminiscent of his epistolary analyses of the Swiss and Spanish written during 1513—designed to emphasise that everything he has been saying is practicable. The Spanish infantry cannot resist cavalry; the Swiss infantry can defeat cavalry, but cannot cope with the close foot-fighting of the

Spaniards: it is possible, therefore, to create an army combining the virtues of both, with the defects of neither.

It can be done. Italian arms, adequately led, can triumph over all. And, with a short rhetorical flourish, Machiavelli calls his prince and the Italian people to arms:

> One must not, therefore, let this opportunity pass, so that Italy might—after so long a time—see her saviour. Nor can I express with what love he would be received in all those provinces which have suffered from these foreign floods; with what thirst for vengeance, with what resolute fidelity, with what devotion, with what tears. What doors would be closed to him? What peoples would deny him obedience? What envy would oppose him? What Italian would refuse him homage? To everyone this barbarian dominion stinks. Let your illustrious house, therefore, take up this task with that spirit and with that hope with which just enterprises are undertaken: so that, under its ensign, this land may be ennobled, and under its auspices that saying of Petrarch may prove true:

> > *Virtù contro a furore*
> > *Prenderà l'arme, e fia el combatter corto;*
> > *Chè l'antico valore*
> > *Nell'italici cor non è ancor morto.*[29]

The Prince, despite its naïveties, inconsistencies, and stylistic lapses, is a deliberately structured work; and the apex of this structure is the call to the Medici to unite Italy—or rather North Italy—and lead it from the dominion of the barbarians. The structural significance of this patriotic flourish, and the fervent tone in which it is expressed, make it appear as the prime reason for Machiavelli's putting pen to paper, and give the impression, moreover, that the author seriously believed such unity to be possible. But barbarians, of one sort or another, had been the bane of Italian politics for more than a millennium; and, frequently, that long period had been punctuated by similarly hostile references to the outsiders, and equally impassioned appeals for some saviour to unite the Italians and lead them to liberty. Scarcely ever had these outbursts been related to political reality. What of Machiavelli's?

We know that Machiavelli's original assessment of Cesare Borgia and his ambitions was far less elevated than the messianism evident in *The Prince*, and it is impossible to accept any suggestion that Machiavelli may have changed his mind through hindsight. It is true that Cesare, when destroying the petty tyrants of the Romagna, had claimed to be doing a service to Italy; but Machiavelli would hardly have forgotten that his successes were due far less to his *virtù* than to his Fortune—and more especially to the continued favour of the stinking barbarians themselves, the French.[30] The fact is that Cesare offered an example of a certain dramatic, and relevant, aspect of *virtù*; and, more important, his special advantages suggested a striking parallel with the present situation of the Medici. But a permanently effective union of Italy was another matter, and, considerable as was Machiavelli's admiration for all great men of action, it is unlikely that he had any confidence in his grandiose masterplan.

One has but to consider the letter to Francesco Vettori, dated 10 August 1513, to see Machiavelli's real assessment of Peninsula politics:

As to the union of the Italians, you make me laugh, first because there never will be union here to do anything good. Even though the leaders should unite, they are not sufficient, because there are no armies here worth a farthing, except the Spanish, who, because they are few, are not enough. Second, because the tails are not united with the heads. The people of this nation will compete in submitting to the Swiss before they will move a step to use any opportunity that arises.[31]

Two weeks later, Machiavelli, again writing to Vettori, gives a brief and brutal summary of the contemporary European states and their rulers:

we have a Pope who is wise, and therefore serious and cautious; an Emperor unstable and fickle; a King of France inclined to anger, and timid; a King of Spain stingy and avaricious; a King of England rich, fiery, eager for glory; the Swiss brutal, victorious, and arrogant; we in Italy poor, ambitious, cowardly.[32]

Vettori had suggested to Machiavelli that one day the armies of Italy would be in a state to deal with the invaders, but Machiavelli rejects this as an impossibility; first, because the armies of Italy would always have several leaders who would be disunited; and second, because "I cannot see that a leader can be found who will keep them united". Machiavelli ends this letter with a long analysis of the power of the Swiss whom he regards as the greatest modern example of political and military *virtù*. All the preoccupations of *The Prince* are already here: the stress on having one's own arms—"the best armies are those of armed peoples, and they cannot be resisted except by armies similar to themselves"; the arguments by historical example, ancient and modern; and the belief in *virtù* and the efficacy of great leaders. He doubts that the Swiss will produce an empire like the Romans, but does believe that they can become masters of Italy by reason of their nearness and through the disorders and vile condition of the Italians:

And because this frightens me, I wish to remedy it, and if France does not suffice, I see no other resource; and I am now ready to weep with you over our ruin and servitude, which, if it does not come today or tomorrow, will come in our time. And Italy will owe that to Pope Julius and to those who do not protect us, if protection can now be found.[33]

Given Machiavelli's state of mind it is impossible—even if we choose to ignore stylistic considerations—to postulate that the last chapter of *The Prince* is an afterthought. It is certainly a rhetorical flourish—but it is not *merely* that. On the contrary, it expresses Machiavelli's intense personal anguish that his Italy should represent the ultimate in political corruption, and that its divisions and weaknesses had made it a prey to other powers.

On the other hand, in view of the opinions expressed both in his letters and in his subsequent writings, and in view of his intimate knowledge of the political situation of Italy in relation to the major powers, Machiavelli could have had little hope that anything would come of his heartfelt plea. Anything, that is, except employment by the Medici.

3

The Discourses

THE PRINCE DID not earn for its author the public employment he desired; and another Florentine, Riccardo Riccardi, writing more than fifty years after Machiavelli's death, told a story of how Machiavelli had presented his treatise to Lorenzo de' Medici at the same time as another suitor was offering a pair of racing dogs—the dogs proved more acceptable, and Machiavelli "departed in anger". This tale tells us more about Lorenzo's posthumous reputation than about Machiavelli's real activities; but it is the only evidence that *The Prince* ever came, officially, into the hands of the Medici for whom it was intended.[1] In any case, had they read it, it is doubtful that they would have been much impressed by its zealous unreality. Despite *The Prince*, Machiavelli was still in the political wilderness where he was to remain for many years more: his first official recognition—and that a trifling one—did not come till after the death of Lorenzo in May 1519, when, together with other citizens, he was asked to make suggestions concerning the government of Florence.

During these continuing years of enforced retirement, Machiavelli occupied himself with a good deal of reading and writing; and the principal product of these efforts was the *Discourses upon the First Decade of Titus Livius*. This work is now commonly regarded as Machiavelli's masterpiece: and certainly on one level this is a true verdict. In the course of its three books, the reader is buoyed up with a succession of challenging aphorisms, trenchantly presented general theorems, and seemingly incisive appraisals of events both ancient and modern; the whole, withal, conveying an impassioned appeal for political regeneration from the ruins of modern degradation. However, closer acquaintance brings with it an ardent desire for less style and more penetration; for the maxims, aphorisms, and theorems seem, far too often, a surface gloss concealing a fabric of unsystematic thinking.

In fairness to Machiavelli it must be admitted that it is difficult to judge the general conception of this work from surviving texts. There is some scattered evidence that the *Discourses*—as we know them both from the manuscripts thus far located (all later than Machiavelli's lifetime), and from the earliest printed versions— are neither in the original order of composition, nor, again, in any sequence finally accepted by Machiavelli. Giunta, writing only four years after Machiavelli's death, says that some of the author's friends had suggested that Machiavelli himself was not well satisfied with the *Discourses*, and had intended to reduce the number of chapters therein, and to revise some of the material. Giunta adds that it had been further suggested that signs of such revision were evident in the author's own hand *"nel primo originale"*. This original version, in Machiavelli's writing, had allegedly been used as the text for Blado's edition of the *Discourses* which anticipated Giunta by several months. Both versions are substantially similar, and both print the work as organised into three books, of sixty, thirty-three, and forty-nine chapters respectively—each sequence being numbered separately. A prob- lem arises, therefore, from Guicciardini's *Considerations on the "Discourses" of Machiavelli*, where the chapters of all three books are referred to as a continuous sequence; and it has been suggested that this may reflect a state of the manuscript prior to that pre- pared for the press. This, though feasible, is scarcely provable: but it helps to reinforce the impression that the text, as we have it, has undergone revisions of various sorts.[2]

However, this kind of hypothetical game is not very illumi- nating. Far more convincing, in suggesting that it is well-nigh impossible to assess the *Discourses* as a total work of political literature, is a straightforward stylistic consideration. The structure of the *Discourses* is glaringly imperfect in a particularly un-Machiavellian way. Whatever Machiavelli's faults as a thinker, there can be no doubt that he wrote his works carefully, and structured them with deliberation. *The Prince*, as we have seen, was conceived as a totality, leading up to a dramatic and imposing conclusion. The *Art of War*, though divided by the nature of various military considerations necessarily allotted to different books, has a satisfactory unity as a work of literature, and, like *The Prince*, culminates in a passionate appeal to contemporary Italian rulers. Each of the eight books of the *Florentine History*—despite the fact that further books were projected, and that those completed often suffer from an internal imbalance—has a unity of its own: moreover, collectively they read as a convincing narrative, and culminate in a brief, but striking, vision of current Italian degradation. Alone, of Machiavelli's major works, the *Discourses* show signs of inadequate revision—not so much of the argument in individual chapters, where it is doubtful that Machiavelli would have made improvements, but rather in its overall structure, where he most certainly would. That some degree of systematisation was attempted by Machiavelli is evident from the fact that considerable sections of each of the three books of the *Discourses* either form organic units, or have been knit together by interrelated arguments, cross references, or the deliberate development of points arising in earlier chapters. However, scattered amidst these sections—or, more usually, after them—there are many chapters which either have no relationship at all to any other topic discussed in the *Discourses*, or which could have been placed more advantageously elsewhere in the work. The closing chapters of Book Three are especially striking for this quality of irrelation: while the last chapter of all provides an uncharacteristically flat and indeterminate coda for a work of such potential magnitude.

Questions concerning the date, composition, and purpose of the *Discourses* together constitute one of the more storm-ridden Machiavellian tea-cups. Machiavelli, in *The Prince*, mentions that he has discussed republics at length elsewhere, and this has been interpreted variously as referring to an early version of the *Discourses*, to a lost work on republics, or as being in itself a later addition to *The Prince*.[3] On the other hand, in the *Discourses* there are several references to *The Prince* which, of course, might argue a later composition for the *Discourses*.[4] Unfortunately, none of these textual arguments has much force, since there is no complete autograph manuscript for either work and since, in any case, it is abundantly clear that both have undergone some species of revision at different times. The only sure things are as follows: that *The Prince* was being written in 1513, as is established by Machiavelli's correspondence; that, while not devoid of Livian learning, it shows little evidence of the serious systematic reading of Livy revealed in the *Discourses*; that *The Prince* was revised at least to the extent of giving it a dedication to Lorenzo de' Medici in 1516; that the *Discourses* mention several events after 1513, but no incident later than February 1517; the Dedication of the *Discourses* is addressed to Cosimo Rucellai who died about the end of October 1519; and there is a reference in Book Two to the Emperor Maximilian I, who died on 12 January 1519, as though he were still alive at the time of writing.[5] If we add to this small stock of information the facts that the *Art of War*, which seems to have arisen from the *Discourses*, was more or less complete by November 1520, and that from 1520 onwards Machiavelli was largely concerned with the composition of the *Florentine History*, then a fairly straightforward canon suggests itself—*The Prince* (1513–16), *Discourses* (1513–19), *Art of War* (1519–20), and *Florentine History* (from 1520). However, the cross-references between all four works both obscure distinctions and largely eliminate the necessity for making them. It is difficult without the requisite manuscript evidence either to discern revised matter or to date it. And Machiavelli himself came to regard his major writings as forming an interrelated corpus enabling him to refer hypothetical readers, seeking more detailed treatment of a particular point, additional arguments, or cognate topics, from one work to another.

The argument about the dating of the *Discourses* only becomes a burning issue if one is wanting to establish some intellectual distinction between that work and *The Prince*, or to suggest that Machiavelli's thought underwent some essential development over the years. That Machiavelli developed, in terms of an increasing knowledge of historical sources, seems incontrovertible. That this change was intellectually significant is less immediately apparent; and the views that Machiavelli moved from some kind of republican idealism to princely realism, or that, conversely, he progressed from a narrow view of the political expediency of autocracy to a more broadly-based humanistic republicanism, are alike insensitive generalisations. It is true that, in his writing subsequent to *The Prince*, Machiavelli shows an increasing conviction not merely that ancient government was superior to modern, but that the Roman republic was best of all. Similarly, though his dependence on classical sources in the *Art of War* might well be regarded as no unmixed blessing, his range of historical reference naturally increased with time and study.

On the other hand, over a whole range of fundamental issues —his view of the practical purpose of historical studies; the argument by ancient and modern exempla; the stress on the priority of military organisation in political affairs; the general belief in the superiority of ancient governments and institutions; the polarity of *virtù* and corruption; the necessity for adapting means to existing circumstances; the emphasis upon the need for extraordinary actions; the condemnation of half measures; the contempt for Christianity as an ineffectual instrument of state; the stress on adaptability to changing fortune; and the conviction that, in an age of total corruption, only the rule of one great man can save a society—Machiavelli did not change. Nor did he ever change on these matters. His arguments in the *Art of War*, and the *Florentine History*, have substantially the same foundations. Nor did his mode of thought change: and here I refer not only to the use of parallel exempla which has usually been taken as the Machiavelli method, but to his actual dialectical procedures. In these respects Machiavelli made little improvement: and his last major work—though more realistic than his earlier writings —is scarcely more rigorous in argument.

What are the *Discourses*? Opinions range from the view that they are primarily a commentary upon the first Decade of Livy's *Histories*, to the view that they are primarily not a commentary upon Livy.[6] Attempts to arrive at some conclusion about the composition and structure of the work by the tabulation of Machiavelli's references to Livy have been no more successful than the attempts to establish a date from the exiguous clues mentioned above. It is true that such tabulation has failed through incompleteness and easily-avoidable errors of judgement; but it is open to doubt whether the most careful and thorough listing of Machiavelli's references to Livy—however desirable for other reasons—would yield the kind of information which has thus far been sought.

The problem which interested Machiavelli early in 1513 and which was to bother him thereafter was that outlined in the *Ghiribizzi* to Piero Soderini: how is it possible for people to achieve similar successes by diametrically opposite methods; and why does a hitherto successful politician or military commander experience defeat, despite his pursuing well-tried methods? The answer, he felt, was that though times change, people do not: "that man is fortunate who harmonises his procedure with his time, but on the contrary he is not fortunate who in his actions is out of harmony with his time and with the type of its affairs". Consequently, were men wise enough to adapt themselves to changing fortune they would enjoy continuous success. Unfortunately, says Machiavelli, they cannot, and so they are left at the mercy of Fortune.[7] In *The Prince*, Machiavelli elaborated upon this answer, suggesting that the situation was not entirely hopeless, and that it is just possible to conceive of a ruler with sufficient *virtù* to dominate Fortune. The *Discourses* constitute a further stage in solving the basic problem; but this has now grown in magnitude, and Machiavelli is less concerned with individual deeds, and more with the vicissitudes endured by whole states. He even thinks that he has found an answer: first in a more elaborate and formal historical theory which, though by no means discarding the idea of constant flux, suggested a more predictable pattern of change; secondly, by the continued belief that, in ancient times, several states had managed to survive and flourish over long periods of time; and third, by the realisation that, of those states, the Roman republic—if not the longest-lived—was incomparably the most extensive and most remarkable.

How Machiavelli arrived at these conclusions constitutes yet another of those unsolved mysteries, surrounding the *Discourses*, which have been debated by modern scholars with all the vehemence and ingenuity of a medieval disputation, though with considerably less rigorous logic. We know that at some point, certainly after 1514, and probably a good deal later, Machiavelli drifted into the circle of upper-class intellectuals who used to meet in the Orti Oricellari—the superb gardens laid out, late in the fifteenth century, by Bernardo Rucellai, where first he, and then his grandson, Cosimo, used to preside over informal discussions. Cosimo was one of the dedicatees of the *Discourses*; while the *Art of War* was largely dedicated to his memory. And amongst the many friends who participated in these meetings were Zanobi Buondelmonti, the other dedicatee of the *Discourses*; Battista della Palla; Luigi Alamanni, the poet; and Jacopo Nardi, and Filippo dei Nerli, the historians. The Oricellari discussions are represented by Machiavelli, in idealised terms, in the *Art of War* which purports to record a meeting where Cosimo Rucellai, Buondelmonti, della Palla, and Alamanni, question the distinguished soldier, Fabrizio Colonna, concerning his views on ancient and modern military *virtù*. Cosimo was dead by the time that the *Art of War* was published; but, curiously, the other three interlocutors were all very much alive when, in 1522, together with other members of the Oricellari circle, they were involved in a plot to murder the Cardinal de' Medici, and initiate a policy of reform in Florence. It would, however, be a mistake either to read too much republican idealism into a conspiracy largely motivated by personal animosities, or—more important—to read this revolutionary zeal back to the years prior to the death of Lorenzo de' Medici in 1519. Villari long ago pointed out that the circle was not originally antipathetic to the Medici who were, in fact, on friendly terms with many of its members: and he has since been seriously contradicted neither on this point, nor on his assertion that Machiavelli's attendance was "certainly no sign of alienation from the Medici cause, but rather indeed of the reverse". This matter is of some significance since both Nerli and Nardi have left testimony that Machiavelli undertook the composition of the *Discourses* for his friends at the Rucellai gardens; and Machiavelli himself, in his dedicatory letter to Buondelmonti and Rucellai, says that he does not know who has the lesser obligation—he to them "for having forced me to write that which I would never have written by myself", or they to him, should his work prove unsatisfactory. He also asks them to enjoy the good or ill which they have wished upon themselves. This seems unequivocal: but it has since been asserted that the work owes not only its genesis but its very ideas to the stimulation of this group. And here, once again, we are on treacherous ground: for there is no way of assessing this kind of debt.[8]

Moreover, it is unfortunate that those who favour such unprovable notions are also inclined to view *The Prince* as a work of political realism, and the *Discourses* as one of political idealism. This is not quite as crude as the older antithesis between Machiavelli the advocate of autocracy, and Machiavelli the republican zealot: but it is still related to it. More plausible possibilities concerning both the evolution of the *Discourses* and the nature of its "republicanism", may emerge from a consideration of the work itself.

That the *Discourses*, at one stage of its career, did take the form of a commentary upon Livy is clear. Almost every important general statement throughout the work—with the exception of the introductory chapters to Book One—is either illustrated by reference to Livy or, alternatively, is derived from some incident described by Livy: the order of the argument might differ, but the result is the same, and depends, in the first instance, upon a reading of the Roman historian. This is not to say that the general ideas were not already in Machiavelli's mind when he first worked his way through the Decades; but that Machiavelli should have propounded a general theorem, and then thumbed his way through Livy in search of illustrative material, would be an absurd hypothesis. His probable procedure is that briefly adumbrated in his letter to Vettori, describing the composition of *The Prince* in December 1513. Machiavelli, it will be remembered, took refuge from the cares of the world by immersing himself in study, and conversing with the ancients: "and because Dante says that, without retaining what one has comprehended, knowledge is not produced, I have noted that of which, by their conversation [that is, of the ancients] I have made capital". A. H.

Gilbert, following the tradition that the *Discourses* were begun before *The Prince*, has suggested that this "seems to be Machiavelli making notes on Livy's *History* for his own *Discourses*, out of which rose *The Prince*".⁹ It could equally well have been Machiavelli making notes on Aristotle, Cicero, Plutarch, Tacitus, Xenophon, Polybius, or a host of other authorities employed in *The Prince* and the *Discourses*. What matters is simply the idea of Machiavelli reading through the writings of the ancients, asking his vital question concerning "the reasons for their actions", and jotting down the answers as they occurred to him. The *Discourses* themselves show that Livy was one ancient whose conversation Machiavelli found especially profitable; and, incidentally, the fact that this particular "capital" is but lightly drawn upon in *The Prince* suggests that Machiavelli's detailed reading of Livy and, therefore, the writing of the *Discourses*, was largely subsequent to the composition of the smaller work.¹⁰

At some time Machiavelli got around to the task of fashioning a book from his notes on Livy, paying special, but by no means exclusive, attention to the first Decade. The task, as I have suggested, could not have been completed: but the text of the *Discourses*, imperfect though it may be, shows the beginnings of an attempt at a structured general work on politics, based upon the comparative historical analysis which Machiavelli considered to be the only way to discover practical remedies for contemporary difficulties. He is explicit in *The Prince* that one can learn about modern affairs from ancient history, and that the best way to formulate rules for political behaviour is by a systematic juxtaposition of ancient and modern parallel instances: the whole work is, indeed, an exemplification of this method. The *Discourses*, too, are conceived as an attempt to draw practical lessons from the past by a detailed examination of Roman government compared, when necessary, with modern practice; the *Art of War*, which developed from the *Discourses*, constitutes a continuous juxtaposition of Roman and modern military usage; and even the events narrated in the *Florentine History* are constantly elucidated by reference to ancient, and especially Roman, examples. In the dedication to *The Prince* Machiavelli writes that his knowledge has been acquired by "long experience in contemporary affairs and continual study of antiquity"; in the dedicatory preface to the *Art of War* his conviction that it should be possible to recover lost military *virtù* is based upon what he has both "seen and read"; and the dedication to the *Discourses* opens with the same assertion that he has set forth everything he knows and has learnt "from long experience and continued reading of the affairs of the world".[11]

Machiavelli was asking the "reasons" behind historical occurrences, and his purpose was to discover rules for the present. Though unable to finish his book, he made substantial progress in organising his notes into a coherent structure, and not only was able to lay down the general principles whereby his material could be arranged in three books, but also managed to work whole series of chapters into this projected scheme. He further provided prefaces to the first two books, together with sequences of introductory chapters which make clear his main conception —which was simply to explain how Rome developed into the greatest polity the world had ever known, and thereby demonstrate the faults of modern polities.

Machiavelli begins his first Preface by pointing out that, due to man's natural envy and tendency to blame rather than to praise, it is always no less dangerous to discover new ways and methods than it is to seek unknown seas and lands. Nevertheless, he has persevered through his natural desire to work on those things which he believes will be of common benefit, and has, accordingly, entered upon a road as yet untrodden by others:

> And if my poor ability, slight experience of present affairs, and feeble knowledge of ancient ones should render my attempt defective and of not much use, they will at least show the way to someone else who, with more *virtù*, more eloquence, and more judgement, will be able to carry out this, my intention: which, if it does not bring me praise, ought not to bring forth blame.[12]

Machiavelli expresses his astonishment and grief that, while antiquity is held in such honour that a fragment of old statuary may sell for a great price, the wonderful deeds of ancient kingdoms, republics, generals, citizens, and lawgivers are now rather admired than imitated. Indeed, so far are they avoided nowadays, that not a trace of ancient *virtù* survives. This is all the more amazing when one sees that in law and medicine men base their decisions upon the precedents and practice of the ancients, but "in constituting republics, in maintaining states, in governing kingdoms, in forming armies and conducting war, in ruling subjects, in expanding an empire, not a prince nor a republic is found who has recourse to the examples of the ancients". The reason for this dreadful state of affairs, says Machiavelli, is not so much the weakness into which the "present religion" has led the world; nor the evils caused by ambitious slothfulness; but rather the fact that there is no true understanding of history. People enjoy what they read, but fail to grasp the essential lessons. They never think of imitating the ancient examples, deeming such a procedure impossible: "as though the sky, sun, elements, and men have become different from the motion, order, and power they had in antiquity". So it has come about that Machiavelli, wishing to draw men away from this error has decided

to write—upon all those books of Titus Livy which have not been taken from us by the malignity of time—that which, according to my knowledge of affairs ancient and modern, I deem necessary for a greater understanding of them [the books of Livy]; so that those who read my statements may more easily draw forth from them that utility which one ought to demand from a knowledge of history.[13]

The main points arising from this preface—the assumption that it is novel to combine experience with historical knowledge and thereby establish rules for contemporary conduct; the passing sneer at Christianity; and the repeated assertion that imitation of the ancients is practicable—require no further elucidation here. The closing paragraph does, however, set something of a conundrum: what does Machiavelli mean by this suggestion that his

Discourses provide a key to understanding "all those books of Titus Livy which have not been taken from us by the malignity of time"? Moreover, he had ended his Dedication with a similarly mysterious comment: if Buondelmonti and Rucellai find his opinions pleasing, "I will not fail to pursue the rest of the history, as, in the beginning, I promised you".[14] Finally, in the opening chapter of Book Three, Machiavelli defines the particular problems with which he will be concerned thereafter, adding that "within such boundaries this third book, and last part of this first Decade, will be concluded".[15] The tenor of these passages is such as to suggest that Machiavelli, in his desire to make people read their history intelligently and purposefully, had intended—promised, even—to write a great work embracing the entire corpus of Livy's extant *Histories* of which the second Decade, comprising Books XI to XX, and everything after Book XLV, had, in fact, been lost. This, like everything else connected with the *Discourses*, has been turned into a little battlefield, with partisans heatedly debating whether Machiavelli really finished his scheme; whether he intended only to comment upon the first Decade; or whether this point is merely a red herring, and that Machiavelli intended to write on—and in fact did write on—all the extant books of Livy. Since the work is incomplete—in the sense that it has not been thoroughly revised for the press by its author—there can be no absolute answer to these questions. But at least one might accept what Machiavelli himself says: which is plainly that the work, as it has emerged from his attempts at organisation, is primarily concerned with a thematic analysis of the First Decade of Livy. Of course, he uses material from the other Decades when they exemplify one of his general theorems with especial vividness: but this no more renders the *Discourses* a study of the whole of Livy than references to modern examples made it a study of contemporary Europe. The number of citations from, or references to, the first Decade is just double that of such references to the rest of Livy combined; and these, in turn, just slightly exceed Machiavelli's references to near-contemporary affairs.[16] The *Discourses* are precisely what Machiavelli says they are: an attempt to elucidate the first four hundred and fifty years of Roman history in such a way that a modern reader might see why Rome was great; how it remained for so long incorrupt; and why, by contrast, modern Italy was so contemptible.

Machiavelli, in his Preface to the second Book of the *Discourses*, elaborates further upon the study of the past.[17] Men, he says, always praise ancient times and find fault with the present: it is a common human foible, and we see this as well in old men's recollections of their youth, as in matters of history. There are various reasons for this psychological commonplace; but principally, Machiavelli suggests, it comes about because we do not know the whole truth about ancient affairs. People usually conceal those things which redound to the discredit of the past, while magnifying others which may bring them glory. Moreover, writers are so subservient to the fortune of conquerors that they not only exaggerate their valorous deeds, but also amplify those of the vanquished—so that later generations have reason to wonder at the prowess of their predecessors. Machiavelli stresses that he is not speaking here of the arts, where clear testimony survives concerning ancient excellence; but rather about matters pertaining to the life and habits of men, where the evidence is less apparent. So it may be admitted that people sometimes err in praising the past and criticising the present: the more so since, in viewing the past, two principal motives for disgust with contemporary affairs—fear and envy—do not operate. Nevertheless, none of this is to say that it is always wrong to praise the past. The truth of the matter is that human affairs are never stable: states, well founded, may continue for a time to improve, so that a man living in a period of ascent would clearly be mistaken were he to praise the past rather than the present; just as he would be correct if living in a period of decline.

All this is consistent, and not without psychological acuity: but Machiavelli, lapsing into one of his conspectus views of universal history, continues that

the world has always been in the same condition; and that, in it, there has been as much good as evil; but that this evil and this good have varied from province to province; as one sees from the knowledge one has of those ancient kingdoms which differed from one another on account of the differences in customs; but the world remained the same. There was only this difference, that whereas the world first placed its *virtù* in Assyria, it then placed it in Media, then in Persia, and at length it came to Italy and Rome; and, if after the Roman empire there has not ensued an empire which has endured, nor where the world has kept its *virtù* all together, nevertheless one sees it to have been distributed amongst many nations where men lived virtuously [*virtuosamente*]; such as the kingdom of the French, the kingdom of the Turks, that of the Soldan, and, today, the people of Germany; and formerly that Saracen tribe which did such great things, and occupied so much of the world after having destroyed the eastern Roman empire. Thus, in all these provinces, after the Romans had fallen into ruin, and in all these peoples [*sette*] there has existed, and yet exists, in some part of them that *virtù* which is desired and praised with true praise.

Thus anybody born in a region where *virtù* may yet be found, would be mistaken were he to praise the past as against the present: but no Italian who is not an "ultramontane" and no Greek who is not "a turk" can help criticising his own times and lamenting the passing of ancient glories. For their present state represents the utmost in degradation; there is nothing which is not corrupt; there is no observance even of religion, of laws, or of military institutions; all is "bespattered with every kind of filth"; and, worst of all, those who sit in the judgement seat, ordering everybody about, and expecting to be adored, are the most vice-ridden of all.

This is one of Machiavelli's first attempts at coming to grips with the background to the corruption of modern Italy and the inevitable comparison with Roman *virtù*; and it is not a satisfactory solution to his problem. What we have here is little more than the medieval idea of the translation of Empires writ large; and Guicciardini, in his *Consideration* of this preface, is quick to point out the absurdity of such a conception as that of a fixed amount of good and evil which does not fluctuate, but merely moves from one nation to another. Whole areas of *virtù*, says Guicciardini, especially in the arts and in military affairs, do not merely change their abode but, in truth, are extinguished sometimes for hundreds of years.[18] It is doubtful that Machiavelli expected his remarks to be interpreted quite so literally: but the quantitative presentation of what was, basically, an impressionistic view of world history, begged such adverse criticism. Machiavelli himself came to re-think the problem in the *Art of War*, where his views of modern achievements—even of the much-admired Swiss and Germans—led him to different, but no less implausible, conclusions.

Having digressed in this way Machiavelli returns to his main point, but, while reiterating that people are frequently misled in their admiration for the past, he points out that he, too, might well be adjudged one of those who overpraises the Romans at the expense of the present, were it not for the plain fact that "the *virtù* which then prevailed, and the vice which now prevails, are clearer than the sun". And he will be bold in setting forth what he has come to understand about those ancient times, so that young men, reading his writings, may be induced to shun vices and imitate virtues whenever Fortune presents them with a suitable opportunity: "because it is the duty of a good man to point out to others that good which through the malignity of time and fortune he has not been able to put into effect; so that those, more favoured by heaven, may be able to effect it". The purpose of the exercise is to encourage others to cure the political diseases which Machiavelli himself can only diagnose and prescribe for—an attitude of mind, as we shall see, even more in evidence in the *Art of War*.

There are, in fact, two assumptions basic to the *Discourses*. The first is that history remains the same throughout all ages, because it is compounded of the deeds of men who always have had the same desires and passions.[19] Thus it is possible, by studying parallel situations, either to discover the remedies previously employed successfully or to devise new remedies where the ancients failed. The possibility of making such rules is, of course, also at the root of *The Prince*: but the argument in the *Discourses* is more fully worked out through Machiavelli's second assumption—that the greatest example for active politicians is that of the Roman republic. It is often debated, says Machiavelli, whether Rome's greatness was due more to *virtù* or Fortune: but in his opinion there can be no doubt, "because if there has never been found a republic which has made the gains that Rome did, this comes about because there has never been found a republic so constituted as to be able to make such acquisitions". The reason for this was twofold: Roman military *virtù*; and the constitution given to Rome by its first lawgivers. It was this kind of military and civic *virtù* which produced good fortune, not the other way round. And the *Discourses* are intended to demonstrate how these qualities were evolved in Rome, how they functioned, and how they might be emulated.

The scope of Machiavelli's scheme for the *Discourses* is set forth in the opening chapter of his first Book: "those who read how the city of Rome began, and by what lawgivers: and in what manner it was constituted, will not marvel that so much *virtù* should have been maintained in that city for so many centuries; and that afterwards there should have arisen the empire into which that republic developed". Rome had the natural advantages of a fertile site and easy access to the sea, and it enjoyed a great succession of victories; yet for centuries it resisted the corruption which might easily have resulted from such continuous prosperity. That it did resist was due to the stringency of the laws imposed by Romulus, Numa, and other early rulers, which enabled the city to maintain itself full of such *virtù* as never adorned any other state.

> Because the things done by Rome, and which are celebrated by Titus Livy, resulted either from public or from private counsel, either within or without the city; I shall begin by discoursing upon those things, happening within and by public counsel, which I deem worthy of greater notice, adding to them all their consequences; to such discourses this first book, or rather this first part, will be limited.

This is the first statement by Machiavelli on the division of his material, and he is reasonably consistent both in the Preface to Book Two where he introduces his new subject by repeating that his previous discourses had dealt with internal affairs and that he is now moving on to the augmentation of the Roman Empire— in other words, to external matters; and again, in the first chapter of Book Three, which has the function of a preface, introducing discourses limited to the remaining topic listed earlier, "how the deeds of individual men made Rome great, and brought about many good results in that city".

In imposing some kind of system upon his *seriatim* notes on Livy, Machiavelli was helped by another of those ancients whose conversation he so delighted in, but whom he never mentions by name. This was Polybius—one of the most intelligent, judicious, and original of all ancient historians, whose great *Histories*, covering the affairs of the Mediterranean world from 221 to 144 B.C., is unified by the conception of the development of Rome to world dominance. The work of Polybius is marked by a comparative analysis of different governments; a cynicism which regards religion as a mere instrument of policy, and Fortune as the only transcendental factor in political affairs; a reasoned contempt for mercenary forces; a firm belief in the efficacy of national troops trained carefully "under the laws and customs of their country"; a sound appreciation of the purposes of war; an understanding that history, in order to be meaningful, must take into account the reciprocal interests, or conflicts, of many nations —that it must, in fact, be "general history"; the certainty that his researches and studies demonstrate the supremacy of the civil and military governance of Rome; and, above all, an overriding conviction of the practical value of historical study to the statesman who, not knowing the causes and sequence of political events, "may be compared with a physician who neglects to inform himself of the causes of those distempers which he is called in to cure".[20]

The interest which such a historian must have had for Machiavelli is immediately apparent; and the Florentine's debt ranges from the straightforward summary of Polybius's account of

Roman encampments, included in the *Art of War*, to the conception of "general history" which—probably more than
difficulties imposed by Medici patronage—led Machiavelli to
traverse so widely over Italian affairs in the *Florentine History*.
But Machiavelli's debt is largest in the *Discourses* where he
borrows both information and ideas from the Greek historian.
This use of Polybius has been drawn into the battle waged over the
Discourses' chronology.[21] It is pointed out that, whereas Latin
editions of the first five books of Polybius's *Histories*—the only
ones to have survived intact—were available from the late fifteenth
century, the fragmentary sixth book, which is much exploited by
Machiavelli, is not known to have been printed in Latin till 1520.
Could Machiavelli have read Greek? it is asked. Was there a Latin
translation in manuscript? Is black white? There could have
been a manuscript translation of the sixth book to hand; one of
Machiavelli's numerous learned friends could have provided him
with a version; and it is even possible that a printed edition
existed—unless we are to take the view that the only books
available to fifteenth- and sixteenth-century readers were those
which are now known to survive in modern libraries. Whether
or not Machiavelli could read Greek—and it seems likely that
he could not—he certainly had read Polybius, including the vital
sixth book, by the time he got down to organising the *Discourses*
into the shape known to posterity: and unless fresh evidence is
discovered, there is nothing more to be said on this topic.

It would be a mistake to suggest that Machiavelli only came
to think about Rome's greatness in general terms after reading
Polybius. Belief in the supremacy of Rome's constitution and
military organisation was the favourite intellectual pabulum of
Renaissance historians and political thinkers; and in Florence
it had, naturally, come to mean the supremacy of the early,
uncorrupted, republic. The kind of general sentiments expressed
by Machiavelli in the *Discourses*, the *Art of War*, and the *Florentine
History*, may be encountered in the trite pages of a host of
fifteenth-century humanists. Even the idea of regeneration based
upon a conscious imitation of Roman civil and military practice
was a commonplace nearly a hundred years before Machiavelli

put pen to paper.[22] Nevertheless, it seems to me that the impression made by Polybius on Machiavelli must have been considerable. It is one thing to read about Roman achievements in a humanist compilation; quite another to read a careful analysis of the reasons for those achievements, by a historian who actually witnessed much that he narrates.

It has been argued by Walker that the introductory chapters to the first book of the *Discourses* were especially inspired by Polybius; but a list of thematic correspondences goes beyond the introduction and is even more striking than Walker suggested.[23] One might note the following: the general stress on the value of history; the account of the origin of states; the composite theory of cyclical and degenerative changes in government—monarchy, tyranny, aristocracy, oligarchy, democracy, and finally anarchy; the perfection of Rome's balanced, or mixed, constitution; the relative significance of the consuls, tribunes, senate, and populace; the comparison between the Roman and Spartan constitutions; the note taken of the fact that whereas the constitution of Sparta was created complete, the Romans only arrived at perfection by experiment and evolution; the conclusion that the Spartan constitution was better for a non-expansionist state, while the Roman was superior for the founding of an empire; the stress on the great lawgiver, as exemplified by Lycurgus; and the importance assigned to religion and, more especially, to what Polybius terms "superstition" in preserving the fabric of Roman *virtù*. This is a formidable list; but there is yet more to be added. The very tone of Machiavelli's first preface, with its insistence on novelty, has its counterpart in the opening of Polybius's *Histories* where the author excuses himself from writing on the fact that "the knowledge of past events affords the best instructions for the regulation and good conduct of human life", on the ground that every other historian has enlarged upon this topic. Indeed, says Polybius,

the subject itself which I am engaged to treat may well exempt me from this task; since it is of a kind so new and singular, that it cannot fail to excite the attention of every reader. For what man is there so sordid and insensible, that he would not wish to be informed in what manner, and through what kind of government, almost the whole habitable world, in less than the course of fifty-three years, was reduced to the Roman yoke? An event of which there is no example in any former time. Or who, on the other hand, is so passionately fond of any other kind of speculation, or of any branch of science, as to think it more worthy of his care and pains than this inquiry?

... The Romans, disdaining to confine their conquests within the limits of a few countries only, have forced almost the whole habitable world to pay submission to their laws, and have raised their empire to that vast height of power which is so much the wonder of the present age, and which no future times can ever hope to exceed. And this is the event which I design to explain, in the following narration: and from thence it will be evident what great advantages may be derived from an attentive and close perusal of political history.[24]

Is it possible that Machiavelli could have read unmoved a work which, with a magisterial command of political verities, exhibits "the councils, strength, resources, upon which the Romans supported those great designs, which rendered them the masters of the world, both by land and sea"?[25] This was, after all, Machiavelli's own theme: he was not interested in the narrative of Roman history, but rather in the underlying causes of political success—and failure. Polybius furnished Machiavelli with many suggestions, especially in the fragmentary sixth book which constitutes not narrative but an analytical study of the development of Rome's constitution, and a detailed critical evaluation of Roman military institutions. These are the principal subjects of the first two books of the *Discourses*: and it is unlikely that this could have been entirely coincidental. Nor can one ignore the closing fragments of Polybius's sixth book, where the Greek historian, surveying Roman world supremacy, ponders as to the future. All things, he writes, are subject to decay and change, and, since these changes obey the laws he has already established, it is, therefore, possible to guess the fate of Rome:

For when a state, having passed with safety through many and great dangers, arrives at the highest degree of power, and possesses an entire and undisputed sovereignty, it is manifest that the long continuance of prosperity must give birth to costly and luxurious manners, and that the minds of men will be heated with ambitious contests, and become too eager and aspiring in the pursuit of dignities. And the imagined ignominy of remaining in a subject state, will first begin to work the ruin of the republic; arrogance and luxury will afterwards advance it; and, in the end, the change will be completed by the people; when the avarice of some is found to injure and oppress them, and the ambition of others swells their vanity, and poisons them with flattering hopes.[26]

In Machiavelli's view the well-balanced Roman republic collapsed into a tyranny rather than the anarchy of the multitude which was as far as Polybius was prepared to prophesy. But the doom-laden vision of inevitable corruption, even in the world's greatest state, was too much in accord with Machiavelli's own feelings not to have impressed upon him that Polybius was a historian to be reckoned with. And, finally, it must be noted that the whole spirit of Polybius's enquiry into the constitution of different states was explicitly *realistic* in the sense so frequently attached to Machiavelli's work. It will be remembered that, in *The Prince*, Machiavelli expresses contempt for those who have depicted republics and principalities which have never been seen or known. He may have read Polybius before or after writing this; but whenever it was he would have enjoyed the Greek historian's refusal to discuss the Commonwealth of Plato "how much so ever it may have been celebrated by philosophers". Just as untrained athletes are refused entry to public games, so, says Polybius, this untried theory cannot be admitted without having "first shewn its strength in some real action". However beautiful it might appear, to compare it with the republics of Sparta, Rome, and Carthage, would be no less absurd than to "compare a statue with a breathing, living man".[27]

That Polybius had much to say to Machiavelli seems undeniable: but Machiavelli had his own contribution to make, and,
taking Polybius's suggestions as a theoretical starting point, and
Livy's narrative as raw material, he set about constructing a new
exposition of Rome's greatness, which would be relevant to his
own age. In the *Discourses*, ideas already hinted at in *The Prince*
began to take more definite shape; and they served as the basis
for most of Machiavelli's subsequent thinking. Both the *Art of
War* and the *Florentine History* have their roots in this discussion of Roman military and civil organisation: the former
arising from the long sequence of chapters on warfare in Book
Two of the *Discourses*, and the latter developing from the ex-
ploratory comparisons, throughout the *Discourses*, between the
cities of modern Italy and the republic of Rome—or, in absolute
terms, between modern corruption and ancient *virtù*. It is in the
Discourses, too, that this political polarity—*virtù* and corruption
—only implicit in *The Prince*, emerges as Machiavelli's major
preoccupation. The idea of cyclical change did not, in itself,
satisfy Machiavelli who, having described it, largely by paraphrasing Polybius, goes on to point out that very rarely does any
republic pass through the whole sequence. Theoretically, he
admits, a republic might go through these transitions endlessly:
but, in practice, they undergo such upheavals that they fall
prey to another, better-constituted, state long before they can
finish the course. It was not so much the formalism of cyclical
change which impressed itself on Machiavelli's mind, but rather
the inevitability of decay even in the best-constituted state.[28]

Republican Rome, as Machiavelli argues, owed its prolonged
success less to Fortune than to *virtù*, a quality, as ever, undefined
but compounded of many ingredients: a balanced constitution;
sound military organisation, especially noteworthy for its dependence on national troops; intelligently planned expansion relying
only initially on conquest but far more on colonisation; respect for
religion and for the laws; and, above all, that other undefined
Machiavellian blessing, "liberty", indicating self-government
for the benefit not of a small group but of the state as a
whole. Yet all republics are smitten by disorders for which there

is no certain remedy, and "it follows that it is impossible to con-stitute an everlasting republic, because its ruin may be caused in a thousand unforeseen ways". Even mighty Rome ended in degradation.[29]

How it came about that a model state could sink into corruption is a question which Machiavelli does not answer satisfactorily. To be sure, he does try to cope with the problem, and finds an ultimate solution in human ambition. Men are so constituted that they may desire anything and everything: but, of necessity, they cannot satisfy such desires completely. Thus, since desire always exceeds the power of attainment, men are permanently discontented both with what they possess and with what they do not possess. From this circumstance arise the vicissitudes of their fortune: some desire more than they have, while others fear the loss of what they have acquired, and this leads to enmities, war, the ruin of one province, and the rise of another. Machiavelli introduces this general reflexion as necessary for understanding how the Roman plebs were not content with the security afforded by the creation of tribunes, but grew ever more ambitious: "from this arose the disease which brought forth the contention concern-ing the agrarian law, which was, in the end, the cause of the republic's destruction". This law—which attempted to regulate both the amount of land any citizen could hold, and the dis-tribution of territories taken in war—aroused the antipathy of the nobles, and led to constant friction. The matter was shelved when the Roman armies conquered territories further and further afield; but it flared up again in the time of the Gracchi, "and being then woken up, it completely ruined Roman liberty". This came about because factions developed within the state; mutual antagonisms led to open conflict, and this eventually resulted in civil war between the Marian party led by Caesar, and Sulla's party led by Pompey: victory went to Caesar "who was the first tyrant in Rome; so that never again was that city free".[30]

Another fundamental cause of Rome's decay, diagnosed by Machiavelli, was the prolongation of military commands. This began, he says, with the appointment of Publius Philo as pro-consul in order that he might bring a particular campaign to a successful termination. In taking this step the Senate was acting in the public interest; but ultimately it led to the ruin of the republic.

> Because the further afield the Romans went with their armies, the more necessary this prolongation [of military commands] seemed to them, and the more they used it. Which brought about two inconveniences: one, that a smaller number of men was trained in military command, and because of this military reputation was restricted to few: the other, that a citizen, being in command of an army for a very long time, won it over and made it partisan; because that army, in time, forgot the Senate, and acknowledged him as its head. Through this, Sulla and Marius were able to find soldiers who would follow them against the public weal: through this, Caesar was able to take over his fatherland. Had the Romans never prolonged magistracies and military commands, they might not have attained such power so rapidly; and if they had made their acquisitions more slowly, they might have come yet more slowly to servitude.[31]

The third factor in Rome's decline, which may be disentangled from Machiavelli's *Discourses*, is concerned more generally with the moral fibre of the nation. Slowly and imperceptibly corruption set in as the Romans—having conquered Africa and Asia, and reduced almost the whole of Greece to obedience—"had become certain of their liberty", and it seemed that there were no further enemies they need fear. This sense of security led the Roman people, first to award the consulate on grounds of a candidate's charm [*grazia*] rather than his *virtù*, and then to descend yet further by giving the honour to those with the most power; so that good men were excluded from office, and corruption was rife.[32]

Machiavelli is, as so often in crucial arguments, very cavalier about matters of chronology: so that, while the problem of the agrarian laws troubled Rome from as early as 486 B.C. until the time that they came to a head with the Gracchi in 133 B.C., the prolongation of military commands began, in Machiavelli's own view, with Publius Philo in 326 B.C., and culminated nearly three hundred years later with Caesar. Moreover, the main conquests described by Machiavelli as the cause of Roman sloth, were completed by 146 B.C. with the fall of Carthage. Now, obviously, if one is going to take this Olympian view of history, it is possible to explain any situation by reference to any one of a vast complex of other situations. This is not to say that such long-range judgements need be invalid: but they tend to be unsubtle, and are always very facile. Of this difficulty Machiavelli never became aware: but there was another problem posed by his scattered diagnosis of Rome's fall, of which he was uncomfortably cognisant. The agrarian laws which helped the process of corruption arose from, and exacerbated, the divisions between the populace and the nobles. Yet Machiavelli had already been at pains to argue that it was precisely such class dissension which led to good laws; and good laws led to good education; and good education led to the production of so many instances of *virtù*. Machiavelli realises that there is a contradiction here, and strives to overcome it. Though his views on the agrarian laws seem incompatible with his views on the value of class conflict, he will not, he says, shift from his opinion:

> Because it is the ambition of the great men [*grandi*] which, if not crushed in a city by various ways and means, soon brings that city to its ruin. Hence, if the quarrels over the agrarian law took three hundred years to make Rome a slave, she would, perchance, have been brought into servitude much more quickly had not the plebs, both with this law and with their other demands, always checked the ambition of the nobles.[33]

What Machiavelli is saying is that it is the rich who cause the ruin of a city: the agrarian law kept their ambitions at bay for three hundred years: and Rome would have been ruined earlier without that law. Why, then, attribute the decay of Rome to the agrarian law?

That is a good question. Here is another. If military expansion leads inevitably to corruption, why are Rome's large-scale acquisitions deemed intrinsically praiseworthy, as they are throughout the *Discourses*? Machiavelli tells us that Rome's whole purpose was the acquisition of empire and glory, not tranquillity. Indeed had Rome sought only tranquillity she could never have achieved her world-wide power. Nor, Machiavelli is very firm in stressing, could she, or should she, have acted otherwise. All human affairs are in a state of constant flux and it is impossible for a polity always to remain at peace; even if it tries to keep out of trouble, another polity will impinge upon it, and conquest will become necessary in self-defence. Thus Rome's four hundred and fifty years of aggrandisement are seen as a necessary condition of survival.[34] But, as Machiavelli explains, the further that Roman armies went afield, the longer became the military commands; and this, he argues, was another cause of corruption. The same is true of the conquests themselves, which led to a sense of security and a loss of civic *virtù*, thus paving the way to decadence. All this might well be seen as fitting into Machiavelli's general dictum that "in all human affairs he who examines them well will see this: that one can never eliminate one inconvenience, in such a way that another doesn't arise"; there is no issue which is absolutely clear-cut; and good is inextricably mingled with evil.[35] This is very true. But, again, it is too facile an explanation of historical processes. Indeed, when pushed to extremes—as in Machiavelli's account of Roman decay—it becomes so all-inclusive as to be valueless for political analysis.

There is yet another question which must be asked, for it is the question, above all others, which Machiavelli set himself to answer: how might this corruption have been prevented? Machiavelli himself raises the doubt that, since the controversies between people and nobles ultimately resulted in the destruction of Roman liberty, might not a constitution have been framed whereby such divisions were excluded? The answer we have, in part, already seen. Rome could have kept itself small by excluding foreigners and eschewing conquest, so that a few nobles would have been able to control the plebs. However, it was one of the conditions of the city's health that the people should be armed and that the population should increase: which meant, in turn, that the people were strong and had the opportunity to stir up troubles. Thus Rome could not have been constituted other than she was.

Corruption is always inevitable. It might, however, be deferred: and this, says Machiavelli, can be achieved by periodic renovation —changes which take institutions, and religions too, back to their origins: "hence those are best constituted, and have the longest life, which by means of their institutions [*ordine*] are able frequently to renew themselves: or which, by some accident, unconnected with the aforesaid institution, come to such renewal. And it is clearer than daylight that, without renewal, these bodies do not last."[36] As an instance of a purely external circumstance which delivered a salutary shock to Rome, Machiavelli cites the capture of the city by the Gauls in 390 B.C., which stirred the Romans— who had grown lax—to pull themselves together, renew the ordinances of their ancient religion, punish malefactors, and once again esteem the *virtù* of the citizens. But, far better than such shocks, is internal reformation which may come about either by some law, or by the *virtù* of some outstanding citizen. The introduction of the plebeian tribunes, and the institution of the censorship, were instances of the former; while Brutus's execution of his own sons for conspiring against the republic, and the punishment by death of the popular, but ambitious, Manlius Capitolinus, were instances of the latter. In particular, it is the tremendous severity of such personal actions which cause citizens to shun vice; but they need to be of sufficiently regular occurrence to allow no time for men to change their habits and break the laws. Were a state to have a continuous supply of great men whose example could renew the laws—not merely checking decay, but actually drawing the state back to its origins—it might, in truth, be everlasting.[37]

But there's the rub. No state can guarantee this kind of succession, and, in a sense, we are back to the *Ghiribizzi* again. States, like men, would enjoy continuous good fortune were they able to adapt themselves to changing circumstances: for this is what periodic regeneration would amount to. But, like individual men, they cannot do this. States must decline, and Rome was no exception. Republics, in Machiavelli's view, are more likely to produce a succession of great men than a princedom: but even in Rome this succession dwindled till, in the time of the younger Cato, the situation was too far gone for anything to be done about it.

Yet even this is not entirely true, as Machiavelli indicates elsewhere in the *Discourses*. There could always be recourse to the extreme measures recommended in *The Prince*. When the state is sinking into corruption it can be revived only by the *virtù* of one man—not by the *virtù* of the public as a whole [*dello universale*].[38] Institutions which function well when the state is healthy will be inappropriate when the state is corrupt. It is, therefore, necessary to reconstruct them, either in the early stages of decay, or when the state is already decadent. The first course is virtually impossible, in that it presupposes somebody who can both see an inconvenience long before it is manifest to others, and can then persuade people to take action for which they do not perceive the need. The second way is just as difficult, for normal methods will no longer suffice. Indeed we are here faced with a situation where conventional morality, as in *The Prince*, has been turned upside-down. "Normal methods have become evil," says Machiavelli.

It is necessary to resort to extraordinary methods, such as violence and arms, and to become—before anything else—prince of that city, and to be able to dispose of it in one's own way. And because to reconstitute political life in a city presupposes a good man, while to become prince of a republic by violence presupposes an evil man; it is very rarely found that a good man will wish to become prince by evil methods, though the end might be good; or that a bad man, having become prince, is willing to do good, for it will never occur to his mind to use properly that authority which he has acquired wickedly. From all the aforementioned things come about the difficulty—or impossibility—of maintaining a republic, or creating one anew, in corrupt cities. Should one have to create or maintain one there, it would be necessary to reduce it more towards royal government than towards popular government; so that those men who, by their insolence, cannot be controlled by the laws, might be held in check by an almost-regal power.[39]

Rome, of course, did try this. Its solution was first Caesar, and then the empire for which, on the whole, Machiavelli has bitter contempt. But, as always, Machiavelli has a little safety clause tucked away in another place to cover his inconsistencies. The answer here is that it is prodigiously difficult to convert a state suited to republican government into a monarchy. It can be done, but it will be "without proportion and not lasting". Rome was suited to republican government, not monarchy.[40]

Were there any real lessons to be learnt by contemporaries from Machiavelli's examination of republican Rome? One of the main difficulties they would have encountered is that Machiavelli himself was unable to make up his mind as to the cause of modern corruption. He returned to this problem frequently, but never answered it to his own, or to anybody else's, satisfaction. That the Western world had gone to the bad since the fall of Rome was obvious. Everybody said so—especially the Italians who had a vested interest in the matter. But why had this happened? For Machiavelli the problem was especially complicated by the existence, in his mind, of a little pocket of *virtù* north of the Alps. This comprised his idealised German cities which, he thought, had maintained some vestiges of ancient excellence. They had achieved this, in the first place, by being isolated—so that there had been no chance of contamination by the customs of the French, Spanish, or Italians, "which nations are, all together, the corruption of the world".[41] Another reason for the uncorrupted nature of German political life, was that the cities maintained perfect equality and would not tolerate the kind of "gentlemen" who plagued Italy—parasites who lived on the revenues of estates and produced nothing useful for the community as a whole. However, the main reason for Germany's *virtù* was the same as that which for so long kept Roman society in a healthy condition: "goodness and respect for religion". By goodness Machiavelli

means, quite clearly, moral probity, especially in public affairs—
as he demonstrates by citing an extraordinary story about the
honesty of Germans who paid their taxes promptly and fully,
without coercion or any need for an official check, solely because
they were on oath to do so. The Germans nevertheless are outside
the mainstream of Machiavelli's discussion. Why they should be
outside is not at all clear. We see these republics maintaining
their civic *virtù* in the midst of corruption, and, one might think,
it would be worthwhile trying to emulate them. Yet their
practice is totally unlike that of Rome: they are small, isolationist
and non-expansionist. In a sense they are like Sparta. But Sparta,
too, is discussed only to be dismissed in favour of Rome. Certainly,
in magnitude it could never compare with Rome's achievements;
and as soon as it attempted to establish an empire it failed dis-
mally: but it did preserve its freedom for eight hundred years—
twice as long as Rome—and it is Machiavelli himself who tells us
this. Would states not do better to keep themselves to themselves?
Elsewhere, in *L'Asino*, Machiavelli is convinced that they would,
and that it is grasping ambition which has led to so much modern
corruption: "Athens and Sparta, whose name was once so great
in the world, only fell into ruins when the powers about them
were subdued; but, at the present day, each city of Germany lives
secure, through having less than six miles about them."[42] What
then of Rome? What then of its quest for empire and glory?
This is all very confused: but far worse is Machiavelli's attempt
to explain the genesis of modern corruption.

Machiavelli devotes a series of chapters in the first book of the
Discourses to the importance attached by the Romans to religious
ceremonies and observances, and he expresses his belief that princes
and republics wishing to maintain themselves uncorrupted "must
above all else maintain uncorrupted the ceremonies of their
religion, and hold them always in veneration", for there is no
surer indication of a country's ruin than to see divine worship
despised or set at nought.[43] Machiavelli's principal view of
Roman religion seems to be that it was easily manipulated for
political purposes and was especially useful as a means of in-
culcating military *virtù*—an idea borrowed from Polybius, but

much distorted in the process. In Book Two of the *Discourses* Machiavelli asks how it could be that the ancients were greater lovers of liberty than the peoples of his own day. The cause, he says, is the same as that which now renders men less vigorous [*forti*]:

> which, I believe, to be the difference between our education and the ancient education, based upon the difference between our religion and the ancient religion. Because our religion, having shown us the truth and the true way, makes us esteem less the honour of the world; whereas the Gentiles—esteeming it greatly, and having placed therein the highest good—were more fierce in their actions. This one can appreciate from many of their institutions, beginning with the magnificence of their sacrifices, as compared with the humility of ours where there is a certain pomp more delicate than magnificent—but no fierce or vigorous action. With them neither pomp nor magnificence were lacking in their ceremonies, but added to these was the act of sacrifice full of blood and ferocity, with the slaughter of a multitude of animals. And this spectacle, being terrible, made men likewise. The ancient religion, besides this, did not count men blessed unless they were full of worldly glory; such as captains of armies, and rulers of republics. Our religion has glorified the humble and contemplative men more than the active. It has placed the highest good in humility, abjection, and in contempt for human things; theirs placed it in greatness of spirit, in bodily strength, and in all the other things fitted to make men most powerful.[44]

Christianity demands of its adherents the fortitude to bear suffering, not to achieve great things. As a result of this the world has become weak and has fallen prey to the wicked who are able to manage affairs securely, seeing that the generality of men— seeking only paradise—think more about bearing their injuries than about avenging them. Yet, says Machiavelli, though it seems that the world has become effeminate and that heaven is disarmed, this has come about from the baseness of men who,

interpreting Christianity according to sloth [*ozio*] and not according to *virtù*, have not considered how it permits us to exalt,
honour, and defend our fatherland. So, says Machiavelli, it is this
kind of education, and false interpretation, which has caused the
lack of republics such as flourished in days of old, and which
accounts for the fact that one sees less love of liberty. "Still",
Machiavelli concludes this extraordinary farrago, "I rather
believe that the reason for this is the Roman empire which with its
arms and greatness wiped out all republics and all self-governing
communities."

If that last sentence seems extraordinarily inconsequent, it is
only because the whole argument is one of Machiavelli's most
shapeless. He begins by ascribing modern corruption to Christianity which has led to pusillanimity. He contrasts this with a lurid
picture of pagan ritual which is not merely totally inaccurate as
far as the Romans were concerned, but is excessively naïve. Is one
really to believe that blood sacrifices—even had they been
favoured in Rome, which they were not—had aught to do with
civic rectitude, love of liberty, and military *virtù*? Machiavelli
then shifts his ground: the fault is not in Christianity but rather
in its base interpreters. This would read less like an apologetic
afterthought had it not been preceded by a categorical statement
that Christianity *does* exalt other-worldliness, and *does* require
fortitude in suffering rather than in bold action. Finally, there is an
anti-climactic assertion—quite unprepared-for in the preceding
text—that the Romans were after all to blame. And just in case
one might think this some kind of a slip, Machiavelli continues, in
the rest of the chapter, to describe how the Romans ruthlessly
crushed other self-governing communities and destroyed their
virtù.

Where on earth does this leave his argument, not merely on
this particular point but in the *Discourses* as a whole? The entire
work is supposed to impress us with the magnitude of Roman
virtù: the Romans fought; they conquered; they expanded;
and they renewed themselves. They also slipped inevitably into
corruption; they destroyed *virtù* in others; they eventually lost
their own; and they effectively prevented *virtù* from flourishing

thereafter. But what was it all for? Machiavelli does not tell us. The expansion of Rome is depicted as a kind of historical necessity: in four hundred and fifty years of relentless conquest, Machiavelli can find nothing better to say of Rome than that it did all this in order to survive, and in doing so destroyed the *virtù* of other states struggling for their own liberty. Were Machiavelli not so ardent a worshipper at the shrine of ancient Rome, his *Discourses* might easily be interpreted rather as a satirical indictment than as a laudation of the republic's history.

Machiavelli's view of politics was largely determined by his own frustrating experience. He had been a civil servant, a diplomat, and a circumscribed administrator. He had suffered from the ineptitude of his superiors, and had witnessed the efficacy of decisiveness, force, and fraud. Florentine politics had, perforce, been a limited *ad hoc* sequence of expedients, designed principally to keep things going: though garnished with an ill-articulated idealism concerning what the republic might have been, and the role it might have played in Italian affairs. And Machiavelli's representation of the Roman achievement in the *Discourses*—though inflated to global proportions—is conceived simply as a model answer to the perennial problem of maintaining power in a hostile world. That this struggle for survival is, in itself, worthy of the admiration expressed by Machiavelli, is open to question: but the *Discourses* provide a depressingly accurate picture of most political behaviour when stripped of its slogans, catch-phrases, and facile ideologies. Rome's four hundred and fifty years of expansion emerge from Machiavelli's pages as a kind of compulsion with no logic other than that of self-perpetuation; as a mindless, automatous activity; as less of a human polity, and more of an ant-hill.

4

A Literary Interlude

THE DATING OF Machiavelli's works, as we have seen, presents a number of insoluble problems. The evidence is usually inadequate or ambiguous; and, for the most part, we have to be satisfied with a series of terminal dates. We know, for instance, that *L'Asino* was being written around 1517; and that *La Mandragola*, probably written after 1513, was being rehearsed for performance in Rome by April 1520. All else about the composition of these works is largely conjectural and, on the whole, unhelpful. The straits to which we are reduced in such matters may be judged from the efforts of a noted authority to date the *Mandragola*. A reference in the play—"Do you think the Turk will land in Italy this year?"—is presented as a remarkable, hitherto unnoticed, revelation that 1518 was the precise date of composition, because it was the one year when the fear of Turkish invasion was "so great that the Pope ordered special prayers to be said".[1] However, since not merely Italy but the whole of western Europe had been in a state of agitation since the accession of Selim in 1512—and since panic that it was necessary to wrest the initiative from the Infidel, by organising a crusade, had been endemic for centuries, and since the Turkish threat had become a dramatic commonplace long before Machiavelli's time—little can be gained from this kind of hypothesis. And the same authority's subsequent arguments from an undated printed edition and a manuscript headed "Jesus, 1519", get us little further.[2] The truth is that we don't know when a good deal of Machiavelli's writing was accomplished. The best that we can do is to assign his works to feasible periods, and deal with them as becomes convenient.

The composition of *L'Asino* can be approximately dated by a reference in a letter, of 17 December 1517, by Machiavelli to the poet Luigi Alamanni. It appears that Machiavelli had just been reading Ariosto's *Orlando Furioso*, and had found it fine throughout—indeed, sometimes wonderful—but complains that, though Ariosto speaks of many poets, "he has left me out like a dog, and has done to me in his *Orlando* what I shall not do to him in my *Asino*".[3]

L'Asino is a curious poem, clearly conceived as an allegory of Machiavelli's life since his fall from office, and as a comment on the contemporary situation in Florence. The work is along the lines of a parody of Dante, and, though stiff in style and eventually abandoned by the author after only eight chapters had been completed, sufficient survives to merit close attention. Machiavelli speaks in the guise of a man metamorphosed into an ass, and the poem is structured like a flash-back to the circumstances leading up to his metamorphosis—though the fragment ends before this point has been reached.[4] The writer tells how, lost in a wild forest, he was met by a beauteous damsel attended by a herd of animals which, she reveals, are men transformed by Circe the sorceress. A similar fate assuredly awaits the writer, but the damsel, who is one of Circe's maidens, first leads him to a palace where, without great ado, they become ardent lovers. The following evening, after her day's work is done, she rescues Machiavelli from the gloom caused by a day of political reverie, and takes him to see the vast throng of animals; and the eighth chapter reports his conversation with a singularly fat pig which, though "all besmirched with dung and mud", refuses a proffered opportunity to change back into human shape, and eulogises at great length on the virtues and advantages of its present condition. The autobiographical nature of the poem is evident as are the author's customary preoccupations. The wild dark forest is Machiavelli's present miserable mode of life; the love affair is the typical passion which, from time to time, was supposed to make him forget his plight; and the animals are, presumably, contemporary portraits.

In the first chapter, Machiavelli writes that—though he no

longer regards "bites and blows" as he has done formerly, and
though he has been quiet and patient for so long, and though he
has tried to advance himself—he cannot but resume his earlier
inclinations. The present age, he writes, is so grudging and evil
that a man cannot help seeing bad more readily than good, and,
therefore, he, though out of practice, is going to spread some
poison by speaking ill. The world has grown bad, as he will
amply demonstrate. All this is very much in the mood of despair
and bitterness which must constantly have afflicted Machiavelli
after the spectacular lack of success enjoyed by *The Prince*. As he
expresses it, in the second chapter, he was lost in these dark woods
through his "scant judgement, vain hope, and false opinion"—
though he could not confide this to the maiden because he was
seized by such shame and self-pity.[5] Machiavelli lays on the com-
passion for his own plight with a trowel, putting into the maiden's
mouth such temperate sentiments as: "Amongst modern people,
and amongst ancient, no one has ever sustained more ingratitude,
nor greater pain: this did not happen to you, as it does to some,
through any fault of your own, but because bad luck was opposed
to your good deeds."[6] Nevertheless, she advises him to bear the
blows of Fortune with a face unmoistened by tears, so that eventually he may enjoy better times. And in the following chapter
Machiavelli tries to take her advice, declaiming that he will not
accuse the heavens, nor moan about his bad luck, because, as he
is so fond of saying in his letters, he is "more accustomed to evil
than to good". He decides to give himself up to Fortune—
doubtless comforted first by the maiden's assurances that his
suffering will be celebrated by historian or poet, and then, more
effectually, by the pleasures of the table followed by those of the
bed where, "in tasting the ultimate of all sweets", he swooned
away prostrate on his mistress's breasts.[7]

    This mild erotica, and the contrast which ensues in the next
chapter, are reminiscent of the new-found love described in his
letter to Vettori of August 1514. There, though the affair was
supposed to have freed him from all memory of his troubles,
and to have encouraged him to abandon serious political thought,
he soon relapsed into the writing of the *Discourses*. Here, in

L'Asino, after his night of grand passion, Machiavelli is left alone to ponder his fate: and, sure enough, within a few moments, he has plunged back into the gloomiest political speculation. Villari, writing of the fifth chapter of *L'Asino*, says that it is not poetry, "but rather paragraphs of the *Discourses* put into verse".[8] Provided that we add *The Prince* to this description, nothing could be more apt.

His mind, he says, began to wander, and—as is usual when one's mind wanders—Machiavelli soon found himself pondering the same old problems in the same old ways. Why has Fortune sometimes caressed and sometimes bitten the noble and famous peoples of ancient times? What is the cause of variation in worldly affairs? We are back, virtually, to the *Ghiribizzi* of January 1513; and the answers Machiavelli now gives to his questions are substantially the same as those supplied in *The Prince* and the *Discourses*. Insensate ambition is the root cause of the decay of states—"the powerful with their power are never sated".[9] Venice collapsed because, heedless of others' ruin, she attempted deeds beyond her strength. Athens and Sparta, too, once world-famous, succumbed through similar attempts to over-extend their power. Contrast this, says Machiavelli, as so often elsewhere, with contemporary Germany and one sees each city living there securely though possessing less than six miles of the surrounding territory. Florence itself, he continues—alluding to the siege by the Emperor Henry VII in 1312—had once been able to face any danger without fear; whereas now, having extended its territories enormously, it fears everything. And he compares all these vain political aspirations to the folly of Icarus—archetype of overweening human ambition.

It is true, Machiavelli adds, that the duration of a state depends upon whether its laws and ordinances are more, or less, good. Kingdoms, encouraged by *virtù* or necessity—basic Machiavellian political yeasts—will always rise to the heights; but, on the contrary, a city which has good laws, but bad customs, will always suffer distress and, ultimately, destruction. The familiar cycle of corruption is next described in terms later to be repeated, almost verbatim, in the *Florentine History*.[10] Empires begin with a Ninus, and end amidst the decadence of a Sardanapalus. *Virtù* leads to peace; peace leads to indolence; indolence leads to destruction; and then, after the land has been subject to lawlessness for some time, *virtù* may return. This cycle always has been, and always will be: evil follows good, and good follows evil. Machiavelli, moreover, reiterates another of his key ideas, originally set forth in *The Prince*, that conventional sin and conventional virtue are by no means identical with political values.[11] It is thought by some, says Machiavelli, that kingdoms are destroyed by usury or some such carnal sin, and that, conversely, they are preserved by fasting, alms, and prayers; other men, more discreet and wise, recognise that such evils are insufficient to ruin a kingdom, while such virtues are insufficient to preserve them:

> The belief that God fights for you while you are standing idle, or on your knees, has corrupted many kingdoms and many states. Prayers are certainly necessary; and he is completely insane who forbids the people their ceremonies and devotions, because from these, in truth, union and good order may be harvested; and on these, in turn, depend good and happy Fortune. But there should be no one of so little intellect, that he believes, if his house is being ruined, that God will save it without any other prop—because he will die beneath that ruin.

Reliance on piety and the normal moral virtues are, as always for Machiavelli, a sure way to political disaster; and the value of religion is seen, not in any intrinsic truth, but rather in its political and social efficacy.

The remaining three chapters of *L'Asino* are taken up with Machiavelli's visit to the animals, the description of their condition, and the final porcine harangue. Most of this is now very arid reading though, doubtless, it would be more telling were we able to identify the various satirical portraits. Nevertheless, at several points the allegory is so thin that Machiavelli's bitterness towards Florence and the Florentines is easily read; as, for example, when his mistress displays the lions who had once been magnanimous and courteous men—"but few of them are from your city" she says laconically.[12] Machiavelli studies the animals, recognising people he had once known, now, for the most part, metamorphosed into rabbits and goats—that is, the cowards and the self-indulgent; many who had formerly seemed to him very Fabiuses and Catos now appear as sheep and rams; while, of others who sit in high places, "how many eagles turn out to be mere kestrels!"[13]

The fat and filthy pig enables Machiavelli to give a further edge to his satire though, as so often in his writing, he loses control and his intentions become confused and contradictory. The pig is offered the chance of resuming human form, but refuses it in an impassioned speech castigating the folly of human aspirations and greed of gain. Some of the beasts have performed deeds of valour without hope of triumph or other glory, as the Romans once did; and others have preferred to gain glory and liberty in death, rather than live imprisoned and enchained. No, the pig most emphatically does not wish to become human again! All this is too obviously a satire on the vanity of sullied human ambition; and, more especially, it is a condemnation of those Florentines who cannot even emulate the nobility of beasts in their quest for liberty. But the point surely should be that the Florentines are now no better than animals and, like the pig, prefer this bestial state rather than assert their true humanity. Machiavelli has got himself well and truly lost; and he breaks off with the pig returning happily to his mud-bath.

L'Asino, though an interesting and important fragment, has never been regarded as anything more than that. But with the Mandragola one is on rather more difficult ground. A great deal has been made of this play. Symonds, writing from cloud-shrouded moral heights, saw it as indecent, "sinister and repulsive", yet indubitably powerful. It is, he says, a "study of stupidity and baseness acted on by roguery", while "credulity and appetite supply the fulcrum needed by an unscrupulous intelligence". And again, "moving in the region of his fancy, the poet adds Quod erat demonstrandum to his theorem of vileness and gross folly used for selfish ends by craft". The whole play, for Symonds, was a terrible indictment of the society which could accept it as an "agreeable work of art". The *Mandragola* he saw as a "piece of scientific anatomy, a demonstration of disease, executed without subjective feeling. The argument is so powerfully developed, with such simplicity of language, such consistency of character, such cold analysis of motives, that we cannot doubt the verisimilitude of the picture." And, says Symonds, "Society, far from rising in revolt against the poet who exposed its infamy with a pen of poisoned steel, thanked the man of genius for rendering vice amusing."[14]

Symonds was badly hemmed in by the moral preoccupations of his time, and by a rigid preconception of what constituted the Italian Renaissance and Machiavelli's place therein. But this mode of self-indulgent literary response, which can discern hidden meaning in a laundry list—provided only that it emanate from the household of a great man—is, unfortunately, still with us. As far as the *Mandragola* is concerned, things have scarcely improved since Symonds's day. Ridolfi is almost equally fanciful, and a good deal more hyperbolic. He assures us that, if there were a purpose behind the play, it could hardly be merely to make people laugh, "when the comedy has far more the effect of making people think". Moreover, Ridolfi continues—taking flight from an unacknowledged suggestion in Villari, whom he is always so ready to criticise adversely—"there is a glimmer of tragedy, though far off, which chills the laughter of the comic farce until a smile or a grin comes to chase the sighs away again". Machiavelli is, of course, the greatest Italian everything ever:

There have been few Italian authors, even among the greatest, able to reach the heights in more than one literary genre. Machiavelli was supreme or left a profound mark on almost all those which his genius explored. An incomparable political and historical writer, he wrote only one novella, but that of outstanding merit. He wrote only one play arising spontaneously from his own inspiration, not from the importunity of friends or worked up for an occasion on the basis of Latin models; and with it he produced the best comedy in the whole of the Italian theatre, where even Ariosto had had only moderate success—the best play any modern author had written up to then, and perhaps the best Italian play of all time.[15]

In fairness to Ridolfi it must be pointed out that he has since modified this opinion; and his most recent critical assessment of the *Mandragola* is that it is not merely the greatest comedy in Italian, but also in "all other literatures".[16] Such views would be laughable, were they not commonly accepted as authoritative. The epithet *great* has become almost inseparable from the *Mandragola* in literary commentaries. "One of the greatest, perhaps the very greatest of Italian comedies", writes one noted critic, assuring us that the play enables Machiavelli to "stand with Aristophanes and his company"; adding that the comic poet's observation in *Mandragola*, though "remorseless", is the work "of an intellect impartial yet constructive, and with the warmth of human contact".[17] Leaving aside the fact that the meaning of the last phrase is obscure, claims of this kind are surely irresponsible; and it is doubtful whether they would be entertained were the author of the play John Smith rather than Niccolò Machiavelli.

The story of the *Mandragola* concerns the desire, ultimately satisfied, of Callimaco to climb into bed with Lucrezia, the beautiful young wife of aged Nicia—an unbelievably stupid lawyer whose principal desire in life is to beget a son. Ligurio, a parasite, devises a plot whereby Callimaco, masquerading as a doctor, will advise Nicia to administer a potion of mandrake to his wife. This will render her fertile, but will cause the death of the first man to have intercourse with her, since he will "draw upon himself all the infection of the mandrake". A supposed dupe, therefore, will have to be found to sleep with the wife who has, moreover, to be persuaded to the unseemly business. For this purpose a rascally cleric, Fra Timoteo, the girl's confessor, is bribed to advise her to do her husband's bidding, and—with the connivance of Sostrata, the girl's mother—he easily prevails. The story, naturally, depends on a good deal of disguising, and Callimaco—acting as an unsuspecting lute-playing dupe—is introduced into Lucrezia's bed by the beguiled husband. Once between the sheets he transacts his business with great panache, and has scant difficulty in persuading the virtuous Lucrezia to accept him as her lover on a more permanent basis; and the play ends with Nicia inadvertently contriving means for the adulterers to continue as they have begun.

Tales of this kind were a commonplace, not only in the Italian *novelle* but throughout Europe in the Middle Ages and early Renaissance, and it can be matched both in its cynicism, immorality, and anti-clericalism, by a variety of stories from the *Cent Nouvelles Nouvelles*, as well as in the work of Ser Giovanni and Masuccio. Certainly there are a host of ingenious tales in the *Decameron*, very similar in tone to the plot of the *Mandragola*, which would afford equally effective, or better, material for comedy in the theatre.

The *Mandragola* is really little more than the presentation of a *novella* through the medium of the Roman comedy from which Machiavelli imperfectly derives his dramatic technique; and it has some of the virtues, as well as the limitations, of its sources.[18] Machiavelli could write clear, crisp repartee, and he seldom misses an opportunity to nudge our ribs at improprieties and double-meanings as, for example, in the very last scene of the play, when Nicia, having been cuckolded, formally introduces Callimaco to Lucrezia as the very man who will provide them with a "staff" to support their old age; and again, in Fra Timoteo's first appearance, when a barely-penitent widow, after hinting at all kinds of malpractices committed with her late husband, alludes to her terror of the Turks and their devilries— "I have great fear of that impaling," she says, before rushing off to join somebody in the church.[19]

Machiavelli is also successful at organising opportunities for funny stage business. The disguising theme, sempiternal stage trick, is well handled; and it would require a singularly inept actor not to make something of Callimaco's face-twisting, teeth-gnashing, and eye-screwing attempts at altering his physiognomy.[20] Another effective idea, which has long since passed into the arsenal of farcical devices, is the pretended deafness of Nicia, culminating in a brilliant exchange when the idiot lawyer, forgetting his feigned affliction, speaks out of turn. Timoteo, who has seen through the attempt to assay the extent of his dishonesty, expresses sardonic surprise at the remarkable recovery and, when Ligurio asserts that St Clement has shown Nicia favour, promptly suggests that they set up a votive image at the church to start a commotion there, so that he, too, might share in Nicia's gain.[21]

Amusing the play, undoubtedly, is. But one might justifiably expect more than a few witty sallies and a scattering of comic situations from the "best Italian play of all time". And Machiavelli, as is his wont, promises a good deal more in his prologue than he subsequently fulfils. The matter, he says, might seem too light for a man who wishes to appear wise and serious; but he excuses it as an attempt to make his miserable lot more agreeable, "since he has been prevented from demonstrating his other virtues with other enterprises—there being no reward for his labours". Even now the only rewards he anticipates are sneers and adverse criticism; and this, without any doubt, is why the present age has degenerated from ancient *virtù*. Since everybody finds fault with everything, nobody will strive to create a work of true merit. But the author gives warning—as in the first chapter of *L'Asino*—that he too can speak evil, "and this was his first skill", and he esteems no one despite his having to act "*sergieri*" to those who wear a better cloak than he.[22]

The familiar autobiographical lament of the man whose abilities are not recognised, and whose efforts go unrewarded, together with the scapegoat corruption of the times, are strongly reminiscent both of Machiavelli's letters and of *L'Asino*, and lead one to expect that this is going to be a play of ideas. *Mandragola* is, however, a disappointment. Ideas there are; but, as in *L'Asino*, they are extrinsic rather than intrinsic to the work. A number of telling observations and Machiavellian *bons mots* are scattered about indiscriminately, no attempt being made to co-ordinate them either to the development of character or to the unfolding of the story.

Ligurio, who dreams up the entire plot for Callimaco, is entrusted with one or two machiavellisms. It is he who echoes the conspiracy chapter of the *Discourses* when pointing out that the stupid Nicia, even were he to suspect that all is not well, simply would not have time to spoil their schemes.[23] Ligurio, too, discussing the open half of his plan with Nicia, comments on the difficulties of dealing with friars who know both their own sins and those of others—and are thus not to be relied upon, even in dirty work. And he warns Nicia not to spoil everything by careless talk, "because one of your sort who stays all day in his study, merely understands these books, and has no grasp of worldly affairs"—a sentiment much in tune with Chapter XV of *The Prince*, and ere long to be regarded, by hostile critics, as the very heart of Machiavellism.[24]

Callimaco, though lust-ridden and resourceless, is also accorded a few apophthegms. Having found Lucrezia's reputation greatly exceeded by the truth, he comments that this is "something which happens very rarely". Elsewhere he observes that even a parasite such as Ligurio may be trustworthy, provided either that a project works to his advantage or that he fears one's vengeance.[25] Above all, in his soliloquy on the extremities to which lust has driven him, Callimaco seems to be Machiavelli himself taking stock of his own situation, and echoes the *Discourses* in his belief that good and evil are inextricably mingled. Fortune and Nature balance each other, with every benefit bringing a concurrent disadvantage—"the more my hope has grown the more my fear has increased". And what is it all for? How little good does one find in things compared with what one anticipates from them? But on the other hand, the worst that can happen is to die and go to hell; and how many others have died, and how many worthy men are in hell? So Callimaco, like Machiavelli, bolsters up his courage with brave words in the face of adverse Fortune, only to crumble again at the fresh onset of desire.[26]

The effect of this appraisal of Fortune is, however, vitiated since we have already encountered Nicia, whose ineffable and quite incredible stupidity is the fulcrum of the play, also giving vent to a Machiavellian outburst, and even taking up the vital point made in the prologue.[27] In Florence, he complains, there isn't a man who isn't "*cacastecchi*"—literally "shitsticks". *Virtù* is not appreciated in the slightest. Without political power in the state a man is disregarded, and is "good for nothing but going to funerals, or to wedding receptions, or to sit all day on the Proconsul's bench to fritter away the time". These sentiments, in themselves, are an interesting if obvious comment on Machiavelli and Florence: but the scene in which they are delivered is of no consequence to the story; the character, into whose mouth they are thrust, is inapposite; and the only response they elicit from the servant Siro—a classic stage stooge who seldom utters more than half a dozen consecutive words throughout the play—is merely "*Non dubitate*". Here, as in the eighth chapter of *L'Asino*, Machiavelli has lost control. If the point, as seems intended in the prologue, should be that ability is no longer regarded in Florence, then why has it been entrusted to Nicia who is so patently unworthy of respect? We are, in fact, left with the impression that only worthless fools, such as Nicia, disgruntled by a false estimate of their own ability, are ignored—and quite rightly—by the state. But this is certainly not the point of Machiavelli's letters, nor of his historical and political writings, nor of *L'Asino*, and nor of the prologue to the *Mandragola*.

However, the most striking instance of Machiavelli's haphazard approach to characterisation and internal balance is his treatment of Fra Timoteo who, despite his late appearance in the play and secondary role in the plot, is given more psychological depth, and is provided with a greater number of, and more important, machiavellisms to propound than any other character. His first cynical aside is an anticipation of Callimaco's lament that advantage and disadvantage are inextricable, Timoteo merely observing that women are the most charitable and also the most troublesome of people, it being "true that there's no honey without flies".[28] More interesting, though, is his soliloquy after Ligurio has bribed him to participate in the plot to cuckold Nicia. Timoteo had quickly seen through the stratagem whereby Ligurio sounded out his dishonesty, but was not concerned at the deception. The real question is who deceives whom? Whatever the issue, the friar will benefit; both Nicia and Callimaco are wealthy and, in different ways, ripe for plucking; the whole business is so dangerous to all parties concerned that secrecy is bound to be maintained; and, however things turn out, Timoteo will not repent of it. The only possible difficulty is posed by Lucrezia's virtue; but, says Timoteo, he will be able to cozen her by means of that very goodness.[29] The arguments he employs for this purpose are, appropriately, derived from the crucial observation of The Prince. Things which, from a distance, seem terrible, unbearable, and bizarre, may seem humane, endurable, and familiar when looked at more closely. "Where a good is certain," quibbles Timoteo, "and an evil uncertain, one must never abandon the good through fear of the evil"; and he emphasises his point with a neat sophistry—it is the will not the body which sins. Thus, since Lucrezia's purpose in lying with a stranger is not to gain carnal pleasure, but to "fill a seat in paradise" and to please her husband, there can be no sin. The Bible itself, he concludes with consummate hypocrisy, tells us that the daughters of Lot, believing themselves alone in the world, committed incest with their father, "and because their intention was good, they did not sin".[30]

Timoteo later displays the obverse of this particular Machiavellian coin when, musing upon his own implication in the plot, he is constrained to the opinion that man is just as likely to fall into misfortune by being too accommodating and too good as by being too wicked—an idea Machiavelli had previously considered in the nineteenth chapter of The Prince.[31] This speech is also interesting for the curious slant Machiavelli gives to the friar who, elsewhere in the play, is the butt of obvious jests concerning clerical greed, and who has, indeed, already been quick to profit from Ligurio's immoral schemes. Yet here we are presented with an unwarranted implication that the friar is rather a victim of the bad company "which leads men to the gallows", than a true protagonist of evil. "God knows," he laments, "I wasn't thinking of hurting anybody." He was merely busy in his cell, saying the holy offices and conversing with worshippers, when "that devil of a Ligurio" came in and made him dip his finger into sin. Now he has plunged not only his arm but his entire body into it, and has no idea where he will end. This is not, clearly, the pricking of conscience, for Timoteo's real fear is lest anybody should discover his part in the sin: but it does present an unresolved conflict within the friar's character. And this is further compounded at the beginning of the fifth act. The friar hasn't had a wink of sleep all night, so anxious is he to learn how the plot is proceeding. To occupy the time he has busied himself with all kinds of peripheral holy activities: saying matins; reading a life of the Fathers; going into the church to light a lamp which has failed; and changing the veil of a miracle-working image of the Madonna:

> How many times have I told these friars to keep her clean! and then they are astonished that devotion is falling off. I remember when there used to be five hundred images here, and today there aren't fifty. This is our own fault—because we haven't known how to maintain her reputation. We used to go in procession to her every evening after compline and had lauds sung for her every Saturday. We were always making vows here, so that new images would be seen—we used to encourage men and women in confession to make vows to her. Now none of these things are done—and then we wonder why things grow cold! Oh how little sense these friars of mine have!

Gibes at the degeneracy of the Church were common enough; but Machiavelli, though unclear as to the ultimate cause of its corruption, lays the blame—as we know from the *Discourses* —largely upon the follies and laxity of the clerics themselves. They set a disgraceful example to Christendom; and it is precisely this notion which, put into Timoteo's mouth, further enhances the friar's self-awareness, and distances him yet further from the characters in *Mandragola*.[32]

Timoteo is also assigned the last word in the play, when, having ascertained that he will be getting paid for his services, he invites the choice company—cuckold, adulteress, lecher, pander, and procuress—into his church to say "the usual prayer". One is reminded of that later "Machiavellian" drama, *The Jew of Malta*, when Ferneze, the Christian arch-hypocrite, having triumphed by trickery, ruthlessness, and bad faith, ends the play with a sancti- monious couplet:

So march away, and let due praise be given
Neither to Fate nor Fortune, but to Heaven.

Neither the moral detachment, the profligacy, the general
air of corruption, nor the laughter at stupidity exploited by
vice, were peculiar to Machiavelli. To discern penetrating
comment on the human condition in this easy-going mixture of
stylised and predictable situation comedy is a pointless exercise.
Whether one wishes to classify the *Mandragola* as a great—nay,
the greatest—Italian play of all time, is purely a matter of taste.
But it must be a taste which considers it irrelevant that the action
of the play lacks tension of any kind; that dramatic technique
scarcely ever rises beyond the simplest dialogue, with one character acting as a question-and-answer stooge for another; that
the tone of the play fluctuates independently of, and often at
odds with, the enactment of its story; that characterisation is
rudimentary, haphazard, and inconsistent, with even protagonists
going through their motions like automata; and that, of penetration into human motivation and emotion, there is absolutely
nothing apart from the conclusion that some people are dupes,
some are astute, and all—especially clerics—are venal.

In view of the wealth of meaning frequently read into the
play, it is odd that its most choice Machiavellian irony has seldom,
if ever, been commented upon. The idea that the mandrake
affords a sovereign remedy for sterility in women, was common
throughout the Middle Ages. But Machiavelli, who cites the
story of Lot's daughters, from *Genesis*, to such great effect,
could scarcely have been unaware that the ultimate source for the
mandrake myth was in the same book of the Pentateuch when the
plant appears ambiguously related to barren women becoming
once again fertile—amidst connubial complexities exceeding by
far the naïve cuckoldry of the *Mandragola*. Modern audiences may
not appreciate the jest: but it is unlikely that the biblical allusion
would have been lost upon Pope Leo X when the play was acted
before him in the spring of 1520.

5

The Art of War

WHEN, IN *The Prince*, Machiavelli moves from a consideration of various governments to the necessary activities of the single ruler, he sets down his belief that the foundation of all states subsists in good laws and good arms, and that the former are dependent upon the latter. We have seen the same assumption in the *Discourses* where the entire edifice of an idealised Roman republic is erected upon the foundation of a great citizen army. And in his next major work, Machiavelli—having made clear his views on good government—concentrates upon the means whereby conditions might be established which would enable such a government to develop from the ruins of contemporary Italy.[1] Good laws stem from good arms; good arms are those trained to wage war successfully; and war, for Machiavelli, is an art which may be taught adequately to princes, soldiers, and politicians by an arm-chair theoretician: "for as much as every science hath his generality, upon the which a good part of it is grounded".[2]

We do not know exactly when the *Art of War* was being written: but—since Filippo dei Nerli wrote to Machiavelli in November 1520, complaining that he was anxious to receive *The Life of Castruccio Castracani*, and, more especially, the *De re militari* which was also desired by the Cardinal de' Medici—it would appear that the work was completed by that date.[3] In any event, it was published at Florence by the following autumn, and earned quick popularity first in Italy, and then in France where a translation appeared in 1546. In England, too, Peter Whitehorne's version—thrice issued, in 1562, 1574, and 1588—

remained the only published translation of any work by Machiavelli till 1595. However, with the growing notoriety of *The
Prince*, and its own obsolescence, Machiavelli's treatise on war
came to be less and less regarded in any assessment of the author's
political ideas; and it was not till the nineteenth century that there
was a serious attempt both to relate the *Art of War* to the rest of
Machiavelli's work, and to estimate its contribution to the
history of military theory. In recent years, opinions have ranged
from almost total contempt for its lack of prescience, to an
uncritical admiration which sees it as the "first classic of modern
military science". Both of these extreme verdicts are unhistorical;
and neither is valid.⁴

The *Art of War* is cast in the form of a dialogue supposed to have
taken place, a few years previously, in the famous Orti Oricellari.
The host, Cosimo Rucellai, has invited a group of friends—
including Zanobi Buondelmonti, Battista della Palla, Luigi
Alamanni, and a silent observer, Niccolò Machiavelli—to meet
the renowned professional soldier, Fabrizio Colonna: and, after
refreshments, they all repair to the shadiest part of the garden
where conversation begins, innocently enough, with remarks
upon the beauty of the trees laid out in antique fashion. Fabrizio,
however, cannot forbear commenting that it would have been
better for Italian princes to emulate the ancients in "things strong
and sharp, not in the delicate and soft: and in those that they did in
the sun, not in the shadow: and to take the true and perfect
manners of the antiquity: not those that are false and corrupted:
for that when these studies pleased my Romans, my country fell
into ruin".⁵ Were modern citizens to imitate the best qualities
of the ancients—to honour and reward *virtù*, not to despise
poverty, to esteem the good discipline of warfare, to love one
another, to live without faction, and to value private interest
less than public—then indeed might they plant trees and happily
enjoy their shade. Cosimo, prompted by all this, asks why
Fabrizio has not seen fit to emulate the ancient virtues in his own
military profession: and the scene is thereby set for a long discussion of the art of war. The dialogue form is handled in
elementary fashion, and, apart from some variety in the first Book,

soon lapses into increasingly long speeches by Fabrizio, till it becomes virtually a monologue—the brief questions of the interlocutors serving a function similar to the chapter headings of the *Discourses*. Fabrizio is obviously a mere ventriloquist's dummy: Machiavelli pulls the strings; but the script is provided by the ancients.

The idea both that the ancients, and especially the Romans, were the supreme exemplars of military prowess, and that classical treatises constituted the supreme systematic discussion of warfare, was peculiar neither to the Renaissance nor to Italy. Many writers were regarded as valuable repositories of this particular variety of wisdom, but the most popular and comprehensive of such treatises were the five books of the *Epitome Rei Militaris*—composed late in the fourth century A.D. by the otherwise obscure Flavius Vegetius Renatus—dealing respectively with the levying and training of recruits, the composition of the legion, the tactics of land warfare, sieges and fortifications, and naval combat. Another favourite author was Sextus Iulius Frontinus whose *Strategemata*, written very late in the first century A.D., dealt with stratagems employed by commanders before, during, and after battle, and concluded with sieges and defences of cities—all illustrated by short historical anecdotes. The manuscript traditions of these authors were extensive, comprising Latin, Italian, French, and English versions: and, with the invention of printing, their works gained even wider currency during the late fifteenth century, editions being issued either separately or as part of omnibus volumes on military matters.[6] But this dissemination of manuscripts and printed editions is only a small part of the story.

Machiavelli, as is well known, incorporates great gobbets of these, and other, ancient authorities into the speeches of Fabrizio Colonna, protagonist of the *Art of War*.[7] This is important on three counts. First, in employing such a technique, Machiavelli is following in the footsteps not merely of his Italian predecessors, Valturius and Cornazano, but also of such transmontane and "medieval" barbarians as Christine de Pisan, the authors of *Le Livre de Iouvencel* and of *Le rosier des guerres*, and indeed of almost every writer who had attempted to deal with military affairs.[8] Secondly, this classical tradition comprised every one of Machiavelli's major "discoveries" in the realm of civil-military relations, and purely military organisation. And thirdly, these political and military ideas had not escaped the attention of commentators—even as early as the thirteenth century.

One might well pause, in lauding Machiavelli's "marvellous innovations and intuitions" when one reads, in Egidio Colonna's *De Regimine Principum* (1280), of the need for all citizens to serve in the armed forces of a state, and of the necessity for constant military training to prevent harmful dependence on mercenaries and the decay of *virtù*.[9] These ideas were medieval and early Renaissance commonplaces, borrowed principally from Vegetius, and adapted to contemporary circumstances. The anonymous author of the *Pulcher tractatus de materia belli*, late in the thirteenth century, similarly extols the virtues of native troops, condemns the vices of mercenaries, advocates constant military training, and complains—in positively Machiavellian terms—that the youth of his own day, when compared to their predecessors, were soft and unused to the rigours of war: all must harden themselves by regular training in times of peace when, through citizens' pursuit of wealth, military virtues tend to rust away like iron disused.[10] The subsequent successes of foreign condottieri in Italy served to heighten the indignation of many thinkers at the decline of military *virtù*; while the rise of native Italian mercenary captains brought scant comfort: for it became apparent that the old citizen armies represented a vanished age not only of military prowess, but also of civic spirit. Throughout the fifteenth century, humanists—including such illustrious writers as Palmieri, Landino, Alberti, and even Pope Pius II—continued to rail against the mercenary system, propose the resuscitation of the native militia, and advocate military training in time of peace. And Patrizzi was expressing a conventional attitude when he argued that citizens were not intrinsically deficient in military capacity and that it was the duty of government to supply the organisation whereby the military instincts of the citizens could be fostered and encouraged.[11]

Sentiments of this kind, concerning the importance of military training, were not peculiar to politically-minded *littérateurs*: they were even drafted into the humanist programme of education, and thus enjoyed the widest possible circulation. All the great educationalists of the fifteenth century advocated systematic physical exercise, including archery, fencing, and military training to develop muscle, agility, and fitness for war. Skill in the practice of arms was even regarded as necessary for civic duty, so that each citizen would be able to participate in the defence of public liberty and independence. And in the very popular treatise *De ingenuis Moribus*, written by Petrus Vergerius about the year 1404, we find the following striking injunction:

Arms and methods of warfare change from age to age. The chariot of the Homeric Greeks, the legion of the Romans, have both disappeared; the chief arm of today is cavalry. But whatever the method or the weapon of the time, let there be ample practice for our youth, with as great variety of exercises as can be devised, so that they may be ready for combat hand to hand or in troop, in the headlong charge or in the skirmish. We cannot forestall the reality of war, its sudden emergencies, or its vivid terrors, but by training and practice we can at least provide such preparation as the case admits.[12]

Perhaps the most interesting fifteenth-century theories on military matters are those of that underrated scholar, Flavio Biondo, the unwieldy bulk of whose labours has tended to deter commentators from his own day and ever after. But his historical work was plundered, often unacknowledged, by later writers— including Machiavelli—and if they do not read as excitingly, they may at least be excused on the grounds that they anticipate the famous Florentine by some sixty years. His ideas on the nature and purpose of military organisation are partly set out in the *Roma Triumphans*—written in the mid-fifteenth century and first published about the year 1472.[13] Biondo was sneered at by contemporaries for his bad Latin style, and has been condemned subsequently for his interest in the detail of Roman archaeology and institutions, on the ground that this is merely "antiquarian"

—a word much favoured as a pejorative by those who prefer unsubstantiated flights of theoretical fancy to evaluation of evidence. However, Biondo's studies were motivated by a coherent theory of history: human institutions tend, with time, to decay; and it is the duty of statesmen to stave off the process of degeneration by restoring institutions to their first principles, taking, as their ideal model, the constitution of ancient Rome. However, if the historian's reconstruction of Roman institutions is to be of practical value for contemporary society, it must be accurate; and texts are, therefore, to be collated and evaluated. Biondo's work was in intention, if not always in effect, a far cry from the selective misuse of sources which links the work of many elegant humanist historians more closely with their medieval antecedents than with modern historical techniques.[14]

In the realm of military affairs Biondo's study led him to the conclusion that the *virtus bellica* of the Roman people was the basis of their political supremacy and of the security in which their arts and industry could flourish: and he stressed that this was no innate quality, but had been sedulously cultivated by universal recruitment and systematic training. The kind of decadence which had followed the collapse of Roman institutions and customs, and which was now prevalent in Italy, is described by Biondo in his immense *Histories*, where he displays an original appreciation of the mutilation of ideas which results from mutations in language. Even when modern authors use Roman terminology, he complains, they do not comprehend its meaning. The basic principles of Roman warfare have been corrupted by ill-informed theorists; while military practice, now in the hands of condottieri, is similarly debased. These mercenaries ignore the all-important training of recruits; they have no idea how to make camp; in battle they are disorganised; they transform war into a puerile game; they are such cowards that they take flight at the first reverse; the vanquished lose not their lives but merely horses and baggage; and, thus, even the overthrow of a great army can be accomplished without bloodshed. This could almost be Machiavelli speaking, but for two details: Biondo's ideas emerge from a comparative examination of historical sources, and an attempt to cope with philological complexities, never attempted by Machiavelli; but they are expressed in a cumbrous Latin which compares badly with Machiavelli's muscular aphorisms, and colourful Tuscan. It is, in some ways, a classic exemplification of the trite Renaissance debate concerning *Res* and *Litterae*—matter *versus* manner: and posterity, as so often, has given a sharp thumbs down to the laborious scholar, while lauding the achievements of the stylist.

Against this background—classical sources, medieval and Renaissance techniques of compilation and respect for authorities, and politico-military ideas—it is possible to see Machiavelli's *Art of War* for what it is. And this—though partially redeemed by some typical insights, and an attempt to take heed of contemporary military practice—is something considerably less impressive than its apologists have claimed.

Machiavelli's starting point, in the proem addressed to his friend Lorenzo Strozzi, is the assertion that—contrary to popular opinion—the civil and military modes of life are by no means discordant. Nowadays, says Machiavelli, it is true that as soon as a man enters the army he is transformed in dress and speech, and, deeming civil manners effeminate, seeks only to frighten everybody with beard and blasphemies. But if we consider ancient practice we find that the two modes of life are intimately connected: for all the arts and laws of man would be in vain were they not protected by force of arms.

And if in whatsoever other orders of cities and kingdoms there hath been used all diligence for to maintain men faithful, peaceable, and full of the fear of God, in the service of war it was doubled; for in what man ought the country to seek greater faith, than in him who must promise to die for the same? In whom ought there to be more love of peace, than in him which only by the war may be hurt? In whom ought there to be more fear of God, than in him which every day committing himself to infinite perils hath most need of this help? This necessity considered well, both of them that gave the laws to empires, and of those that to the exercise of service were appointed, made that the life of soldiers, of other men was praised, and with all study followed and imitated. But the orders of service of war, being altogether corrupted, and a great way from the ancient manners altered, there hath grown these sinisterous opinions, which maketh men to hate the warlike service, and to fly the conversation of those that do exercise it.

This state of affairs can, in Machiavelli's opinion, be remedied: what he has seen and read has convinced him that it is not impossible to bring military practice back to ancient methods, and to restore something of its former *virtù*. Accordingly he has written his treatise on the art of war; and, if it be deemed presumptuous that one who has never professed arms should write on military matters, Machiavelli neatly excuses himself: "for as much as the errors that I may happen to make by writing, may be without harm to any man corrected: but those the which of them be made in doing, cannot be known without the ruin of empires".[15]

Machiavelli, in the arrangement of his material, follows Vegetius: though he dispenses with the Roman's concluding section on naval warfare, incorporates modern examples and slight modifications due to recent technical innovations, and distributes his discussion over seven books. The first deals with the character of professional soldiery as compared with native militia, and, having decided in favour of the latter, goes on to examine methods of recruitment and the qualities requisite in a soldier. Book Two is devoted to arms and armour, the comparative merits of infantry and cavalry, the importance of training and discipline, and various types of military manœuvres. There follows, in Book Three, an examination of Roman, Greek, and modern Swiss battle formations; a proposed ideal battle array; a brief account of a model battle; and a theoretical post-mortem in which the various tactics are explained, and, in particular, the slight role assigned to artillery is justified. The next Book is especially concerned with the military commander: his choice of ground for battle; various tactics he might employ before, during, and after the combat; his relationship with his men; and some of the qualities he should possess. The order of march in enemy territory is discussed in Book Five, together with topics such as the organisation of supplies; arrangements for distributing booty and pay; and further advice on the tricks of the trade—ambushes, scouting, river crossings, and escapes from difficult positions. In Book Six, Machiavelli considers the problem of encampment, giving a detailed account of a model camp, its disposition, government, and supply system; and then continues with more information on tricks, tactics, and ruses. The final Book is mainly taken up with methods of fortification, siege, and defence: but it ends with miscellaneous matters, including a list of maxims for warfare, more qualities of a good commander, a lament on modern corruption, and an exhortation to the princes of Italy to remedy this.

The whole work constitutes a kind of *reductio ad absurdum* of the Machiavelli method: the comparison between what has been seen with what has been read; experience with study; contemporary examples with historical precedents. For modern material Machiavelli relies partly upon his own knowledge of the Florentine militia, where his comments are useful; and partly upon his inadequate knowledge of the recent warfare in Italy, where his inferences are fallacious. To furnish apposite historical *exempla* for his arguments Machiavelli makes good use of his reading of Livy; and he scores over his fifteenth-century predecessors by drawing upon the admirable Polybius for information concerning Roman arms in Book Two, and, at greater length, for the background to the perfect encampment in Book Six. But Machiavelli's greatest, and most obvious, debts are to Frontinus and, above all, to Vegetius, whom he paraphrases or translates at considerable length: and for much of the book we might as well be reading any fifteenth-century compendium as Machiavelli's the *Art of War*. On the other hand, whatever sources were used for its information and ideas—largely, indeed, because of them—the *Art of War* is crucial for an understanding both of Machiavelli's political theory of regeneration through military *virtù*, and of his limitations as a thinker. And its value, in these respects, is enhanced because it is the only one of Machiavelli's major works published in his lifetime; so that we can feel reasonably assured that the text represents what the author was thinking, and how he wished to express himself.

The dramatic contrast between ancient *virtù* and modern corruption was Machiavelli's permanent preoccupation; and, since this contrast was nowhere more manifest than in military affairs, it is natural that the *Art of War* should be especially concerned not only to describe it, and prescribe for it, but also to account for it. Cosimo Rucellai, having listened to a long diatribe against Italian decadence, asks Fabrizio if he can explain how such cowardice, discord, and negligence in warfare have come about. The condottiere's reply constitutes Machiavelli's fullest, specific exposition on the reasons for the growth and decay of *virtù*: and the confusion of this argument exposes Machiavelli's inability to define his own terminology.

Men, says Fabrizio, become excellent, and demonstrate their abilities, according to the way they are employed and encouraged by their king, prince, or republic. Thus where there are many political powers "there rise many valiant men, and where be few, few". Africa, and Asia, therefore, with few separate states, have produced a mere handful of great generals: whereas Europe, with many kingdoms and republics, has in the past produced countless excellent leaders. Moreover, Fabrizio notes, republics tend to produce more great men than do kingdoms:

> because in commonweals for the most part *virtù* is honoured, in kingdoms it is feared: whereby groweth that in the one virtuous [*virtuoso*] men are nourished, in the other they are extinct. Therefore he that shall consider the parts of Europe, shall find it to have been full of commonweals, and of princedoms, the which for fear that the one had of the other, they were constrained to keep lively the warlike orders, and to honour them which in those most prevailed.

Conversely, when governments are destroyed so their *virtù* also disappears: a state of affairs clearly seen in the ancient world where, with the Roman hegemony, there was left but one way to *virtù*. And when, at last, Rome itself became corrupt, "almost the whole world came to be corrupted: and the Scithian people were able to come to spoil the same empire, the which had extinguished the *virtù* of other, and knew not how to maintain their own".[16] Now Machiavelli was faced with a problem: after the break-up of the Roman empire, Europe was once again fragmented; yet *virtù* was not reborn. Why? The explanation advanced by Machiavelli is that, once customs have been spoiled, it takes time to recover them. This is hardly a satisfactory way to account for more than a thousand years of general corruption; and Machiavelli advances a further argument which had already been adumbrated in the *Discourses*.

Because the manner of living nowadays, having respect to the Christian religion, commandeth not the same necessity to men to defend themselves, which in old times was: for that then the men, overcome in war, either were killed or remained perpetual slaves, where they led their lives most miserably. The towns overcome, either were raised, or the inhabiters thereof driven out, their goods taken away, sent dispersed through the world: so that the vanquished in war suffered all extreme misery. Of this fear, men being made afraid, they were driven to keep lively the warlike exercises, and they honoured such as were excellent in them. But nowadays this fear for the most part is not regarded: of those that are overcome, few be killed, none is kept long in prison: for that with facility they are set at liberty. The cities also, which a thousand times have rebelled, are not destroyed, the men whereof are let alone with their goods, so that the greatest hurt that is feared is but a tax: in so much that men will not submit themselves to the order of war, and to abide always under those, to avoid the perils whereof they are little afraid. Again these provinces of Europe be under a very few heads, in respect as it hath been in times past: for that all France obeyeth one king, all Spain another, Italy is in few parts, so that the weak cities are defended with leaning to him that overcometh, and the strong states, for the causes aforesaid, fear no such extreme ruin.[17]

All this is patently the product of a mind compelled to fab-
ricate an *ad hoc* argument to support conclusions previously
assumed. Speak first, think later: this is, far too often, Machiavelli's dialectical procedure. The last part of the speech, concerning the current paucity of European states, is an obvious
non sequitur tacked on because Machiavelli has just remembered
that decadence comes not from fragmentation but through
hegemony, and that, therefore, the division of Europe after the
fall of Rome must be explained away as being not really a division
in comparison with earlier times—though how much earlier
these times must have been is left to the reader's imagination. In
any case, one would have thought that a Europe divided between
France, Spain, and Italy—and states not mentioned by Machiavelli, such as England, Germany, and the encroaching Turkish
Empire—was quite sufficient to provide all the wars anybody
could have wished for, both before, during, and certainly after,
Machiavelli's time. However, these inanities are as nothing compared with their disconnected introduction concerning the bane-
ful effects of Christianity. It was by no means rare in the fifteenth
and sixteenth centuries to condemn Christianity for certain of its
effects upon the classical heritage: indeed, Christian iconoclasm
became, with Gothic destruction, the normal mode whereby
historians of the fine arts, from Ghiberti to Vasari, explained
why there had been "Dark Ages".[18] Machiavelli's personal "Dark
Ages"—relating specifically to military corruption—extended
from the collapse of the Roman republic right up to his own
age: with a brief interlude of civic virtue in fourteenth-century
Italy. Christianity, he says, is to blame. One might well counter
that wars waged in the name of Christianity were at least as bloody
as their pagan antecedents: but, leaving aside this consideration,
when we come to examine the political conditions requisite for
the flourishing of *virtù*, Machiavelli's argument appears decidedly
eccentric. Wars would need to be almost perpetual, and to be
defeated must mean death, slavery, destruction of cities, and total
ruin: and thus warfare would be highly regarded, the warrior
honoured, good arms established, good laws ensue: and then
what? However, in modern times, due to the enervating effect of

Christianity, people do not fear war because it is no longer violent: hence military prowess is disregarded and dishonoured. Is the reader then expected to lament the passing of the good old days when the world was fragmented between ever-warring, cruel, and merciless provinces, and when one had to fight or die? Or is this farrago intended as a subtle panegyric on behalf of Christianity? Neither alternative can really be what Machiavelli intended: but, once again, as in his praise of blood sacrifice, we see him luring his argument into a hopelessly vulnerable position where he proceeds to ambush it himself.

This bizarre equation of military *virtù* with lavish effusion of blood will again be encountered in *The Life of Castruccio Castracani* and the *Florentine History*, where Machiavelli falsifies his sources deliberately, to substantiate his view of a temporary resurgence of *virtù* in the fourteenth century, and its total degradation with the mercenary armies of the fifteenth century. One can only ponder on the mentality of a man who enthused over the gory battles of antiquity, and described, with zest, the sanguinary feats of Castruccio, but expressed no joy either at the slaughter of mercenaries at Fornovo, the massacre of the French at Cerignola and Garigliano, the plenitude of death at Ravenna, the vast losses sustained by the French at Novara, and the costly thrashing administered to the Swiss at Marignano. There was plenty of killing in Italy during Machiavelli's time: but, seemingly, little *virtù*. At least there was no *virtù* amongst the Italians themselves; though a remnant was yet conceded by Machiavelli to the Germans and the Swiss.

Ever since Machiavelli's short mission to the Emperor in 1509, he had cherished an idealised estimate of the German city-states and the Swiss cantons—a conception based upon very scant firsthand knowledge of their government, but sustained, *a posteriori*, by the knowledge that the landsknechts and Swiss pikemen had for long been the most formidable fighting forces in Europe.[19] In each of his major works—and many minor ones, too—Machiavelli uses these non-corrupt citizen warriors as a stick to beat his errant countrymen. Of the obvious flaws in this idealisation Machiavelli cannot, or will not, take heed; and the *Art of War*, like the *Discourses*, makes use of German fighting qualities to give point both to Italian corruption, and to a possible cure for it. The only armies nowadays which are not a disorderly mob are the Germans and the Swiss: "consider Almaine, in the which, because there is many princedoms and commonweals, there is much *virtù*; and all the same which in the present service of war is good dependeth of the examples of those people: who being jealous of their states, fearing servitude—the which in other places is not feared—they all maintain themselves lords, and honourable".[20] This, of course, is the crux of the matter as far as the *Art of War* is concerned. The Italians are inferior in spirit, as well as in military prowess, to the Germans. But ultimately even the Germans are seen to be inferior to the Romans.

Modern corruption results directly from a decadent soldiery and a false conception of the purpose and practice of war. As it is now waged—says Machiavelli, making a point subsequently developed in the *Florentine History*—warfare ruins not only the vanquished but also the victors: "for that if the one loseth his estate, the other loseth his money and his moveables: the which in old times was not, for that the conquerors of the war waxed rich".[21] How, then, might good military practice be established? Clearly the answer lies, as always, in imitating the ancients: and Machiavelli is at pains to repeat throughout the work, that such imitation is not only desirable but also possible—provided that the state retains even a vestige of good quality. After all, he points out, certain aspects of ancient military usage have been successfully revived, for example, whereas decadent Italians require four horses for each man-at-arms, the Germans, like the Romans, use only one—and what the Romans could do, and the Germans still do, "we may do also; yes, in not doing it we err".[22] Similarly, since we see—from the success of the Swiss pikemen—that "so little a part of the ancient manner of arming, which is used nowadays, that is the pike, and so little a part of those orders, as are the main battalions of the Swizzers, do us so much good, and cause our armies to be so strong, why ought we not to believe that the other armours, and the other orders which are left, be profitable?"[23] The propagandist nature of the appeal becomes clearer as the work nears its conclusion, and Machiavelli, speaking through the person

of Fabrizio, admits in Book Seven that he has omitted a great
variety of topics from his discourse because he intended not to
describe an ancient army, "but how in these days a service of war
might be obtained which should have more *virtù* than the same
that is used: wherefor I have not thought good of the ancient
things to reason, other than that which I have judged to such
introduction necessary".[24] There is, however, one vital condition
to be met if such a military regeneration is to take place in Italy:

> Therefore I say, how that no deed that is done nowadays among
> men is more easy to be reduced unto the ancient manners, than
> the service of war: but by them only that be princes of so much
> state, who can at least gather together of their own subjects
> fifteen, or twenty, thousand young men: otherwise nothing is
> more difficult than this, to them which have not such com-
> modity.[25]

We are back to the situation of *The Prince*: when corruption is
sufficiently advanced, only the inspired, and inspiring, autocrat
can achieve anything. Modern states in general, says Machiavelli,
are in a sorry plight: but Italy is in the worst condition of all.

However, even for an effete race, Machiavelli discerns a faint
hope. Ancient examples show that "in every country, with
exercise, there is made good soldiers: because where nature lack-
eth, the industry supplieth, the which in this case is worth more
than nature".[26] Machiavelli bases his hope on Vegetius's assurance
that proper military training and stern discipline will enable a
small army to rout a vast, but ill-trained, host. Even where
troops are well-chosen and well-armed, says Machiavelli, they
will be useless if inadequately drilled. Fierce, but disorganised,
troops are weaker than timid troops who have been well-trained;
because organisation dispels timidity, while discord tames
ferocity—"for that an army is not made courageous because in
the same be hardy men, but by reason the orders be well appointed".[27] Both the Romans and the Greeks, employing small
but efficient forces, were able to vanquish the innumerable hosts
of their enemies, not by any innate ferocity, but solely through the

confidence engendered by training and discipline. And it is possible, given the right methods, for troops to master even the most complex manœuvres; and, with new recruits being guided by veterans, a whole province may become skilled in warfare. In ancient times nothing was deemed more fortunate in a commonweal than that there should be, in that commonweal, many men trained in warfare:

> because not the shining of precious stones and of gold maketh that the enemies submit themselves unto thee, but only the fear of the weapons; afterward, the errors which are made in other things may sometimes be corrected, but those which are done in the war—the pain straight way coming on—cannot be amended.[28]

The Germans and the Swiss, "whom only of the ancient warfare keep some shadow", follow this practice of training their citizens to defend the state: but in Italy, where the armies are composed of mercenaries, it is impossible to impose such discipline, and the inevitable decline has ensued—armies are neglected, laws decay, and, at last, whole states are reduced to the utmost weakness. It stands to reason, says Fabrizio, that men willing to serve in the army of an alien state are likely to be of the worst possible character: soldiers whose only concern is to wage war for profit rather than for a cause must needs be "ravening, deceitful, and violent", and must constitute as great a threat to those who employ them as to those against whom they are employed.[29] The condemnation of the mercenary is, nevertheless, implicit rather than explicit in the *Art of War*. Machiavelli is here more concerned to suggest a positive measure: and this, based upon his simplification of Roman custom, is the establishment of a part-time citizen militia. Since a standing army is rejected as dangerous, inconvenient, and costly, a citizen army seems the only way back to ancient *virtù*: though, in advancing this scheme, Machiavelli knows that he is open to criticism from two directions— that armed citizens could be dangerous to the state; and that the scheme had already been tried by Florence, prior to the return of the Medici, and had been found conspicuously wanting.

Fabrizio is manipulated to counter both attacks. To Cosimo's comments that an efficient militia, under an ambitious commander, might enslave the state, he replies by citing historical precedent: no citizen army, properly organised according to the laws, has ever damaged a state. On the contrary, the examples of Rome and Sparta—which retained their liberty for four hundred and eight hundred years respectively—demonstrate that armed citizens constitute a bulwark against corruption. All states must be armed in one way or another; and, obviously, hired foreigners are bound to be more injurious to the public welfare than native troops.[30] And if it be objected that inconvenience would arise from citizens periodically abandoning their own occupations for military training, the truth of the matter is quite the opposite: they would only need to assemble on holidays "to exercise them, the which thing doth not hurt, neither to the country nor to the men; but rather to young men it shall bring delight: for that where vilely on the holidays they stand idle in tippling houses, they will go for pleasure to those exercises, for that the handling of weapons, as it is a goodly spectacle, so unto young men it is pleasant".[31] Without a well-ordered militia nothing in a state can be secure: whereas, when it is established, states—formerly united but effeminate—lose their cowardliness while maintaining unity; and states, which were disunited and unruly, become united, and their ferocity—hitherto employed in disorderly fashion—is turned to the public advantage.

Cosimo's other objection is that the militia has been condemned by experts because the men were inexpert and were compelled to serve: matters are not easily learnt by adults, and nothing good is ever achieved by compulsion. Fabrizio admits that "lack of experience causeth lack of courage, and constraint maketh evil contentation"; but both courage and experience in troops may be supplied by the manner of arming, training, and organising them—all of which are to be the subject of his discourse.[32] With regard to constraint, however, Fabrizio is less convincing. The over-enthusiastic volunteer he rejects as unsuitable for the true dignity of military life; while, equally, forced conscription "will bring forth naughty effects". Thus there has to be posited a middle way—neither one thing nor the other—where men will willingly obey the commandment of a prince for whom they entertain such respect that they fear his anger more than the immediate discomfort of military service. Once again Machiavelli comes down firmly between two stools: if the men act through fear of their prince, it is difficult to see how this differs from compulsion; if, on the other hand, they act through a genuine sense of duty and civic responsibility then we are assuming that, prior to their military service, they have already been inculcated with that very *virtù* which it is the purpose of the militia to foster. Fabrizio is on surer ground when he abandons this impossible line of defence, and counter-attacks those "many wise men" who have condemned the Florentine militia on the basis of one lost battle. No army, he says, can ever be so ordained that it may never be beaten. Even the Romans suffered defeats; and the great Hannibal himself was vanquished. The important thing is to discover the reason for failure: and, in the present case, it will be found that the fault lay not in the conception of a militia but in the imperfect manner of its implementation.[33] The proper procedure would be to correct flaws rather than blame the basic idea: and Fabrizio returns to this argument towards the end of the *Art of War*, where it echoes the appeal in the final chapter of *The Prince*. The young men in the Orti Oricellari, says Fabrizio, have been moaning about the Florentine militia, but:

I say unto you, that if you had ordained it as I afore have reasoned, and it had given of itself no good experience, you might with reason have been grieved therewith: but if it be not so ordained and exercised, as I have said, it may be grieved with you who have made a counterfeit thereof, and no perfect figure. The Venetians also, and the Duke of Ferrara, began it, and followed it not, the which hath been through their fault, not through their men. And therefore I assure you that whosoever of those, which at this day have states in Italy, shall enter first into this way, shall be the first, before any other, lord of this province. . . . He then that despiseth these studies, if he be a prince, despiseth his princedom: if he be a citizen, his city.[34]

This is the political message of the *Art of War*: a strong state may be created by the first prince who will encourage the systematic military training of his own subjects. But the bulk of the treatise is taken up with an explication of the type of army which should, ideally, be created; and by a description of its disposition on the march, in camp, and in battle. Machiavelli, though dependent on classical sources, recognised the need to modify ancient usages to modern conditions, and, especially, to take account of the one factor with which the ancients did not have to contend— the devilish invention of firearms. This matter merits attention not because Machiavelli's critics have condemned his lack of foresight, or because his apologists have retorted that the man was not a prophet, but because it shows not merely a limited capacity for foreseeing the future, but rather a failure to understand the present.

For Machiavelli, as for every other theoretician, the ideal army was the Roman; and, in Book Two, he describes the heavy armour of its infantry and cavalry, arguing against his principal source, Polybius, that the Roman foot soldiers did not use any spear other than the *pilum* which they threw at their opponents before joining close combat. The Roman cavalry, says Fabrizio —this time following Polybius almost verbatim—was originally lightly armed; but experience led to their adopting heavier defences and a weighty spear: "with these armours as well on foot as on horseback, the Romans conquered all the world, and it is to be believed by the fruit thereof, which is to be seen, that they were the best appointed armies that ever were".[35] Fabrizio goes on to discuss the Germans and Swiss who, being obliged by poverty to fight on foot against the cavalry of their princely oppressors, had found an effective method by following the practices of the ancients, and, by using the pike, had demonstrated the vulnerability of mounted troops to determined and disciplined resistance. Nevertheless, such infantry—lightly armed, without shields, and encumbered by the pike which is useless for hand-to-hand fighting—had themselves been badly mauled by the sword and buckler tactics of the Spaniards in close combat at Barletta and Ravenna. Fabrizio concludes, therefore, with a suggestion Machiavelli had already advanced, years before, in *The Prince*, that the best modern infantry should combine the virtues of both the Germans and the Spanish.[36] In ideal terms this meant combining the virtues of Greek and Roman military organisation, as is made clear in Book Three where the perfect battle formation incorporates elements of both the phalanx and the legion.

Of cavalry, Fabrizio takes little heed. As a matter of fact, he believes that, with the current type of saddle and stirrups, unknown in antiquity, modern cavalry may well be superior to that of the ancients! This staggering admission is not, however, allowed to spoil the argument. The Romans were able to defeat the vast horde of horsemen amassed by Tigranes, despite their being armed in similar fashion to modern men-at-arms—a characteristic Machiavelli double-think—so it is safe to conclude that states relying more on cavalry than on infantry must be doomed. Cavalry may be gainfully employed in scouting, harassing the enemies' countryside, and cutting lines of supply: "but concerning for the day of battle, and for the fight in the field, which is the importance of the war, and the end for which the armies are ordained, they are more meeter to follow the enemy being discomfited, than to do anything which in the same is to be done, and they be, in comparison to the footmen, much inferior".[37]

In all this, Fabrizio makes scant mention of firearms, apart from one passing reference to the placing of artillery in drawing up a battalion, and two contradictory remarks on the value of the harquebus. He tells Cosimo, in Book Two, that military training should include running, wrestling, leaping, crossbow and long-bow practice, and drill with the harquebus—"a new instrument, as you know, very necessary".[38] How "necessary" appears at the end of the same Book where he advises that harquebusiers be included among the light-armed cavalry: "the which though in the other affairs of war, they be little profitable, they be for this most profitable—to make afraid the countrymen, and to drive them from a passage that were kept of them: because a Harke-butter shall fear them more than twenty other armed".[39] This is really Machiavelli's whole view of artillery in battle: it is noisy, dirty, and ineffective. Heavy artillery, he concedes, has certainly necessitated changes in the fortification of towns; but otherwise it is an over-rated, new-fangled nuisance, and more trouble than it is worth. Machiavelli had said all this in the *Discourses* to which, in fact, he refers in the *Art of War*.[40] He has nothing new to add, though he renders his point more dramatic by demonstrating it in an imaginary battle waged by Fabrizio in Book Three. Much has been made of this literary device by some modern commentators who hold that it is both unique and significant.[41] Unique, it may be: significant, it is not. In less than two pages Fabrizio's neatly drawn-up battle array, moving with clock-work precision—thanks to their rigorous training, perfect discipline, and a chess-board terrain conveniently supplied by Machiavelli—overwhelms its clumsy and inept opponents. There are three principal stages in the battle: first, an exchange of but one artillery salvo from each side, that of the enemy being especially harmless because its shot passes over the heads of Fabrizio's infantry; then, an indecisive cavalry engagement; and, finally, according to plan—after part of the enemies' cavalry has been lured into the ranks of awaiting pikemen—the main infantry combat where Fabrizio's heavily-armed swordsmen soon cut the lightly-equipped enemy pikemen to pieces: "see, they fly on the right corner, they fly also on the left: behold the victory is ours". And all this without even using the second and third lines of battle![42]

It is no wonder that poor Luigi Alamanni, the interlocutor in this Book, being invited by Fabrizio to raise any matter concerning the battle, felt obliged to complain that the whole affair was won in such a hurry that he was completely stupefied. He does, nevertheless, rally himself to the extent of propounding several penetrating questions. Why, he asks, did the artillery fire only once, and was thereafter never mentioned? "Me thought also that you levelled the artillery of the enemy high, and appointed it after your own device: the which might very well be, yet when it should happen, as I believe it chanceth often, that they strike the ranks, what remedy have you?" Finally, the undaunted Luigi argues, he has heard many contemn the armour and order of the ancients on the grounds that they would be useless against

artillery which breaks ranks and pierces armour, so that it seems
sheer lunacy to draw up a battle array which cannot be maintained, or to wear armour which affords no protection. Fabrizio,
in answer to this, asserts that he had doubts about letting his guns
fire even once; for it is more important to avoid being hit by
the enemy than to hit him; and, therefore, the best way to deal
with guns is to attack them rapidly, as he did with his own light
cavalry in the battle. The enemy, being thus forced to place men
in front of their own artillery, can fire no further salvoes. Gun-
smoke, too, is a nuisance to any well-ordered army, and he would
prefer not to use artillery at all: nevertheless, since it has such a
reputation nowadays, he would place it on the wings where it
could not blind his own army's front. With regard to the enemies'
shot passing overhead, says Fabrizio, this is what normally
happens, because it is so difficult to adjust guns to an elevation
suitable for hitting the infantry. Finally, there is the question of
suitable armour and battle formation: and to this there is no real
answer. The fact is that one must still use heavy armour and fight
in close formation, because these will enable troops to withstand
conventional weapons, and enable them to push back an opposing
infantry, withstand cavalry, and prevent their own forces being
broken. None of this will defend them against artillery: but,
Fabrizio asks rhetorically—returning to a point first made by
Machiavelli in his *Report on the Affairs of Germany*—who has
invented anything for that purpose even among the moderns?
It is thus pointless to condemn the ancients for practices not yet
improved upon. Artillery, therefore, does not prevent us from
following the well-tried methods of the past, nor from showing
something of the ancient *virtù*.[43]

None of this is coherently thought out. The enemies' artillery
fire passes overhead, and, moreover, blinds their own troops. Yet
it is imperative that their guns be captured by a swift and resolute
attack—even though this will, inevitably, cost lives. Such an
attack will be successful, however, because the enemy will oblig-
ingly fire all their guns at once and will be unable to reload in
time for a second salvo. But, if artillery is so useless, why the
doctrine of despair that one might as well stick to the ancient

methods because nobody has found any method of protection against gunfire in the field? And why does Machiavelli later admit that at least one tactic, favoured by the ancients—that of letting the wings of an army engage before the centre—has been rendered impracticable by the use of artillery? All this is on a par with another inconsistency which the usually-admiring Villari discerned in the *Art of War*: Machiavelli scorns cavalry, yet is constantly anxious to devise methods to deal with the charge of heavily-armed horsemen.[44] He despises artillery, too, because it undermines all his cherished preconceptions about how armies should function; and he can only cope with this modern threat by asserting—not demonstrating—that it is virtually useless.

Machiavelli's method in all things is to compare the results of his historical studies with his practical experience of affairs. With regard to the art of warfare, he was deficient in both respects. His account of the Roman army is an unreal projection into the past; and he assumes an attitude on the part of the Romans towards the function of cavalry which is quite at variance with that described by Livy, and, more important, by the acute Polybius who was himself an authority on military affairs and one of the most judicious historians of ancient times. How could Machiavelli not take heed of Polybius's comment after the slaughter of the Romans at Cannae?

> The Carthaginians upon this occasion, as in all the former battles, were indebted chiefly for their victories to the numbers of their cavalry. And from hence succeeding ages may be able clearly to perceive, that in time of war it is far more advantageous to have a great superiority of cavalry, with no more than half the infantry, than an army that is in all parts equal to the enemy.[45]

The Romans themselves certainly heeded the lesson of Cannae, and reconstituted their cavalry system; and the ultimate victory of Scipio over Hannibal at Zama was gained largely through the defection of Massinissa, with a great part of the Numidian horse, from the Carthaginian cause. Cavalry was rarely the main arm of the Roman army, but it was never regarded as insignificant. Likewise, it is difficult to see how anybody—despite the success of Swiss and German infantry—could maintain that the cavalry had had its day even in the Italian battles just prior to Machiavelli's *Art of War*.

The trouble is that Machiavelli was blinded to military realities by his colossal antipathy to the mercenary captains whom he deemed responsible for most modern ills. Italian warfare, as waged by these professionals, had largely consisted of elaborate cavalry manœuvres: and, if the fighting of the Quattrocento had not been quite as bloodless as was often alleged, it certainly lacked the totality of violence introduced by the French and Spanish into Italy. The disgraceful showing of the mercenary armies at Fornovo in 1495, when confronted by troops who really meant business, was enough to convince anybody that all was not well with Italian arms. But the lesson was not precisely that which Machiavelli drew from insufficient evidence. It is true, in the early sixteenth century, that horsemen no longer had things all their own way: but the Spaniards had demonstrated most forcibly that, used in conjunction with well-covered harquebus fire, the heavy cavalry charge could still be devastating. The answer to the challenge of modern warfare was not simply to relegate cavalry to a position of marginal significance in battle. Still less was it to pretend that guns had made no difference.

Machiavelli's experience of really bloody battles, such as delighted him in the safety of his study, was negligible. Despite his references to recent conflicts such as Ravenna and Novara, he obviously failed to comprehend that infantry had been cut to ribbons by artillery fire on these very fields. Still less did he take account of Marignano in 1515, when the issue had been decisively settled by the superior firing power of the French. Machiavelli did not need to be a prophet. He merely needed to take in the lessons of contemporary warfare. Of this he was, seemingly, incapable: and his views on artillery are scarcely more advanced than those of Flavio Biondo who had lamented the decay of the art of warfare, and could detect only one modern improvement over the ancients—the invention of the bombard. And even this, the old scholar had firmly believed, would in no way revolutionise warfare or out-date ancient military wisdom. Guns had come a long way since then: but Machiavelli, firmly ensconced in his antique strait-jacket, could not see it.

These then are Machiavelli's principal ideas on the art of war both in its political and its more purely technical aspects. They are essentially the ideas common to his predecessors, Italian, English, and French, for more than a hundred years; and their primary source—if anything which is in itself second-hand can be so termed—is Vegetius. Thirty-one years before Machiavelli's *Art of War* was published, readers in backward and barbaric England could have read, in a printed book, such Machiavellian aphorisms, as "who that will have peace let him learn to fight". They could learn that the reason for modern corruption and lack of valour was because "long peace rendereth the men which heretofor by long and continuous travail were wont to exercise the feat of arms, set nothing by this occupation: but now be put in delight, rest, and covetise of money, which the noble ancients praised nothing but honour of arms nor set nought thereby. And thus is chivalry set in negligence and, as it were, forgotten and not raught of." They could see, clearly exposed, the folly of relying upon mercenaries, and the advantage of training native troops: "for neither gold nor precious stones vanquish nor overcome not the enemies, nor make not the inhabitants to live in peace as doth and may do the might of worthy chivalry well taught". They could read how it came about that "so small a quantity of folk as the Romans were" could subdue great multitudes, thus proving that "better is a small quantity of folk used and well taught in feat of arms by continual exercise of all that thereof may fall in the doubtous hap of battle, than is a great multitude of rude folk nought knowing". And, above all, these English readers could be instructed that of all the arts and crafts in a land, the most commendable is "the art of fighting in exercise of war; for by that is the freedom of the land, place, or country, surely kept, and the dignity of the province is thereby increased: and the ancient worthy men, as it is said, sovereignly kept the same". To learn all this, the Englishmen would simply have had to peruse a copy of William Caxton's *The Book of Fayttes of Armes and of Chyualrye*, published at London in 1490, and itself only a translation of the compilation from classical authors executed by Christine de Pisan more than eighty years previously.[46] Indeed the French text had been given to Caxton by King Henry VII, so that it could be translated and put into print: "to the end that every gentleman born to arms, and all manner men of war, captains, soldiers, victuallers, and all other, should have knowledge how they ought to behave them in the feats of war and of battles".[47]

Machiavelli was not the first person to compile a treatise from the well-picked bones of the ancients: nor was he the last. But, more important than this is the fact that, popular as Machiavelli's *Art of War* undoubtedly became, it did not oust the well-established favourites from the field. Quite the contrary: there were many more editions and translations of Vegetius, in the sixteenth and early seventeenth centuries, than of the *Art of War*; while editions of the other classics were almost as popular.[48] Since the main principles underlying Machiavelli's military theory were well known long before the publication of his treatise, and since they were subsequently disseminated more widely in their original form than in his digest, it becomes legitimate to ask whether his work has anything other than a literary significance. Sir Charles Oman, in his *History of the Art of War in the Sixteenth Century*, thought little of Machiavelli, arguing that not one of the Florentine's practical recommendations bore any relation to subsequent developments in tactics and organisation: artillery did not remain negligible; cavalry was not outmoded; infantry did not continue in huge units like the legion; and the pike was not relegated to a position of inferiority as compared with the sword.[49] Some more recent apologists have rejected this harsh verdict, arguing that the true revolution in early modern warfare was due less to technical innovations than to changes in discipline and training, and the stale maxims of Max Weber have been pressed into service: "the kind of weapon has been the result and not the cause of discipline"; it was discipline and not gunpowder which initiated the transformation; the army of Maurice of Nassau was "one of the first modern disciplined armies"; "gunpowder and all the war techniques associated with it became significant only with the existence of discipline".[50] The argument is as spurious as it is specious. In the first place, even if attention is confined to Italy, it is clear that mercenary captains were attempting to organise an efficient infantry and a more adaptable cavalry system by the end of the fifteenth century; while in France, contrary to popular misconceptions, the change came much earlier, and even Christine de Pisan was able to write that the main difference between the Roman army, described by Vegetius, and modern forces, was that the ancients relied more on cavalry![51] Secondly, the merest glance at the course of early sixteenth-century battles—Cerignola, Ravenna, Novara, Marignano, Biccoca, and Pavia—must reveal that firearms were already doing deadly execution, helping substantially to decide the issue, and necessitating a thoroughgoing revision of tactics. Nobody studying the career of Gonsalvo de Cordova, for example, could think otherwise. Whatever the importance of Maurice of Nassau, it is absurd not to recognise that the face of war was changing radically, and rapidly, even during the fifteenth century; and that firearms—if not the only significant factor—were largely responsible.

But what has any of this to do with Machiavelli? Is it being seriously suggested that Maurice of Nassau's techniques, which bear scarcely any resemblance to Machiavelli's suggestions, are the result of some revolution in military thinking brought about by the *Art of War* published some seventy years previously? To link the inevitable evolution of sixteenth-century warfare with Machiavelli is the crudest kind of *post hoc ergo propter hoc* fallacy. And, in any case, as I have suggested, changes in military practice were afoot long before Machiavelli put pen to paper. Furthermore, since these changes had little to do with the theoretical writings, based upon the ancients, which were circulating before, during, and after Machiavelli's lifetime, and which were saying substantially similar things both to each other and to Machiavelli, the connection between the *Art of War* and modern military thinking remains obscure. Machiavelli had little new to say about warfare; and the model army which he did create from his own imagination was outmoded by the growing use of firearms even before he started writing.

The *Art of War*, like *The Prince*, ends on an exhortatory note with an appeal to the princes of Italy to abandon their effeminate habit, and restore ancient *virtù* by establishing the kind of military order advocated throughout the book. But the very last sentences of all, though uttered by Fabrizio, are manifestly Machiavelli's own lament at the miserable fate which had given him knowledge but no power, and is reminiscent of the Preface to the Second Book of the *Discourses* where Machiavelli had expressed the hope that others would be able to effect what he could only describe and recommend:

> Wherefor, I lament me of nature, the which either ought not to have made me a knower of this, or it ought to have given me power to have been able to have executed it. For now being old, I cannot hope to have any occasion to be able so to do. In consideration whereof I have been liberal with you, who being grave young men, may (when the things said of me shall please you) at due times in favour of your princes, help them and counsel them. Wherein I would have you not to be afraid or mistrustful, because this province seems to be altogether given to raise up again the things dead, as is seen by the perfection that poesy, painting, and writing, is now brought unto. Albeit, as much as is looked for of me, being stricken in years, I do mistrust. Where surely if Fortune had heretofor granted me so much state, as sufficeth for a like enterprise, I would not have doubted, but in most short time, to have showed to the world how much the ancient orders avail: and without peradventure either I would have increased it with glory, or lost it without shame.[52]

It is, however, not difficult to imagine what would have happened to Machiavelli's army, with its disregarded cavalry and negligible artillery, had it faced a force such as that of the Imperialists who triumphed at Pavia.

The popularity both of Machiavelli's *Art of War*, of other similar compilations, and of the ancient treatises themselves, raises problems concerning sixteenth-century attitudes towards established authorities, which it would be inappropriate to discuss here. But the fact which is immediately obvious is that in military matters, as in other spheres, theoretical writing of a general and comprehensive nature lagged far behind practice. The really important writing was of a more specific and technical kind—studies on military engineering, fortifications, and firearms—with an increasing emphasis on mathematics rather than on such human aspirations as training for good citizenship, defence of liberty, and freedom from oppression. A more recognisably modern attitude towards the military organisation of human beings did not emerge till much later in the sixteenth century, with the introduction of tactical tables, enabling commanders to juggle with their troops as an arithmetician juggles with figures.[53] This kind of thing was a long way from Machiavelli's idealism which, as we have seen, had its roots partly in the civic humanism of the Quattrocento with its profound yearning for a vanished age of *virtù*. Partly, too, Machiavelli expresses a truly chivalric attitude towards the function of military training and of warfare; and many of his sentiments may be paralleled not only in French compendia based upon sources similar to his own, but even in the articles of fifteenth-century tournaments at the courts of England, France, and Burgundy, where idleness was customarily condemned as the "mother and nurse of all vices", and where knights were urged to practise the arts of war in order the better to defend king, country, and Church.[54] Machiavelli was little concerned with Church; but otherwise his motivation was not dissimilar from the chivalric enthusiasts for feats of arms. The *Art of War* has much more in common with antecedent military theory than with subsequent military practice. Far from being the first modern treatise on warfare, it would be more properly regarded as perhaps the greatest—though certainly not the last—medieval compilation.

6

The Florentine History

SINCE THE FALL of Soderini, the disclosure of the Boscoli plot, and the failure of his first attempts to impress those in authority, Machiavelli had been gradually outgrowing the odium which attached to his name. Moreover, the situation in Florence itself was changing. Lorenzo de' Medici died in May 1519; and the new head of the family in Florence, Cardinal Giulio, was much more amenable to men of talent—even to Machiavelli who had been presented to him in the Orti Oricellari in March 1520. Machiavelli was becoming known once again. Already, early in 1518, he had been sent by some private citizens to Genoa, to protect their interests threatened by a bankruptcy there; and in July 1520, he was sent, in similar circumstances, to Lucca where the debts involved were of such magnitude that his mission—initially on behalf of private merchants—soon attracted the active interest of the Cardinal and the Signory.

Machiavelli was kept busy, but he found time to write his *Life of Castruccio Castracani*—a fantasy based very loosely upon the career of a real military dictator who flourished in fourteenth-century Lucca. Incidents from an early biography of Castruccio were combined with material from Diodorus Siculus's account of Agathocles, a ruler who had been deemed too wicked even for *The Prince*; and Machiavelli, giving free rein to his imagination, wove these materials into an extraordinary tale in which the hero became a gigantic figure of *virtù*. Castruccio's *virtù*, like that of Cesare Borgia, was a complex of physical address, military skill, ruthlessness, and political cunning, and his morality was dictated only by necessity. Yet, even here, Fortune's dominion over men was supreme: for she both provided Castruccio with his earliest opportunities and encompassed his death at the moment of his greatest triumph.[1]

The *Life of Castruccio Castracani* has been variously interpreted: and most recently it has been plausibly explained away as a test-piece in which Machiavelli demonstrated his skills as an historian.[2] One might well think that this light-hearted little biography, with its fantastic treatment of sources—culminating in a series of apophthegms attributed to Castruccio but obviously culled from Diogenes Laertius—would have been scant recommendation in this respect. But Machiavelli's friends were greatly impressed by its literary qualities, and Zanobi Buondelmonti wrote informing the author that he, and all his colleagues, had read the *Life* and thought it very good; though they suggested some revisions, especially in the list of aphorisms, and in the hero's death-bed oration. Moreover, Zanobi referred to the work as a "model of a history"; told Machiavelli that he ought now "with all diligence to write this history"; and mentioned the need for Machiavelli to return to discuss "that *fantasia* you know about".[3] All this confirms the view that the *Life* was a show-piece, and that negotiations were already afoot for Machiavelli's next step back to favour. This came on 8 November 1520 when he received a commission from the University to compose a record of Florentine history. His annual fee was to be somewhat less than half the salary he had received at the height of his political career: but it was sufficient to afford some measure of security; while the honour of being an official historian of the republic was worth more than the gold itself.

It was possibly at about this time that Machiavelli, along with other known political theoreticians, was asked by the Cardinal Giulio to make suggestions concerning the best form of government for Florence. Machiavelli replied with his *Discourse on Florentine Affairs after the Death of Lorenzo*, in which he blandly disregarded the lesser branches of the House of the Medici, and assumed that, with the death of the Pope and of Cardinal Giulio, Florence would be allowed to function, once again, as a republic. He, therefore, boldly suggested that the reason for the city's failure to establish a stable government was that it had never been either a true princedom or a true republic, and had been torn by party divisions throughout its history. The only stable polities, he wrote, had been princedoms or republics: that is the undisguised rule of a single man, or a system in which all classes have been represented. Other forms of government were defective. And since Florence was unsuited to the rule of one man, it followed that a republic would be the only solution to her difficulties.[4]

Machiavelli's proposed reforms, more than anything else he wrote, lay bare the astonishing gulf which existed between his acute observation of political realities when writing speculative and historical works, and his obtuseness and circumscribed imagination when it came to drafting a constitution for the here and now. Machiavelli, the shrewd cynic, who had recognised the venality of practising politicians, nevertheless assumes that the Medici will be motivated by the purest public spirit, and will be ready to educate the Florentines for republican rule. Machiavelli, the experienced ex-diplomat, who had endured the inefficiency and vacillation of a constantly-changing administration, now advocates a schematic, three-tier system—to accommodate the highest, middle, and lowest classes of the city—in which the executive power is to be organised in the following extraordinary manner. Sixty-five citizens of more than forty-five years of age are to constitute the new Signory:

> choose from the said number a Gonfalonier of Justice for two or three years, if it should not seem proper to set him up for life; the sixty-four citizens who are left are to be divided into two groups, thirty-two for each. One group is to govern along with the Gonfalonier for one year, the other group the next year; and so in succession they are to exchange. . . . The thirty-two are to be divided into four groups, eight to a group; and each group is to reside with the Gonfalonier three months in the Palace, and to assume the magistracy with the ceremonies that are customary, and to carry on all the business that the Signoria alone carries on today.[5]

The reason for Machiavelli's proposals—including a resuscitated Grand Council, and an unwieldy Senate—are likewise of this typically Florentine order: an elaborate system of checks and balances, all devised in the name of freedom; but, whenever put into practice, productive of a deadening complex of bureaucratic ineptitude. The Medici, in Machiavelli's view, were to establish the preconditions for the building of such a republic. While retaining effective power in their lifetime, the Pope and the Cardinal were to create free institutions which could take up the reins of government upon their demise. Characteristically, towards the end of this *Discourse*, Machiavelli allows himself to be carried away in a cloud of unrealistic fervour:

> I believe the greatest honour possible for men to have is that willingly given them by their native cities; I believe the greatest good to be done and the most pleasing to God is that which one does to one's native city. Besides this, no man is so much exalted by any act of his as are those men who have with laws and with institutions remodeled republics and kingdoms; these are, after those who have been gods, the first to be praised. And because they have been few who have had the opportunity to do it, and very few those who have understood how to do it, small is the number who have done it. And so much has this glory been esteemed by men seeking for nothing other than glory that when unable to form a republic in reality, they have done it in writing, as Aristotle, Plato, and many others, who have wished to show the world that if they have not founded a free government, as did Solon and Lycurgus, they have failed not through their ignorance but through their impotence for putting it into practice.
>
> No greater gift, then, does Heaven give a man, nor can Heaven show him a more glorious road than this. So of all the many blessings God has given to your house and to Your Holiness in person, this is the greatest: that of giving you power and material for making yourself immortal, and for surpassing by far in this way your father's and your grandfather's glory.[6]

As might be expected, these proposals, and others of like kind, weighed little with the Medici who continued to exercise their wonted authority, and thereby frustrated the ideals of their enemies, and created a body of hostile extremists who were soon to try their hand at plotting revolution. Machiavelli himself had no part in these schemes, but settled down to work on a task more suited to his capacities than such political activism or, indeed, than the drafting of paper constitutions. Not that he wasn't disillusioned with Florentine affairs: but he came to realise with increasing despondency that simple answers would not suffice; and that, even if they did, nobody would be fit to put them into practice.

I have been staying and am still staying on my farm to write the History, and I would pay ten *soldi*—I wouldn't say more— to have you by my side so that I could show you where I am, because, having come to certain particulars, I need to learn from you if I give too much offence, either by raising or by lowering things. But I shall keep on taking counsel with myself and shall try to act in such a way that, since I tell the truth, nobody will be able to complain.[7]

By May 1525, less than nine months after writing this letter to Guicciardini, Machiavelli had taken counsel with himself to such effect that he had been able to complete the first eight books of his *Florentine History*—up to the death of Lorenzo the Magnificent—and present them to Pope Clement at Rome. According to Donato Gianotti—in a letter written a few years after Machiavelli's death—Machiavelli had experienced difficulties in writing the later portions of the work, and had often said:

I cannot write this history from the time when Cosimo took over the government up to the death of Lorenzo just as I would write it if I were free from all reasons for caution. The actions will be true, and I shall not omit anything; merely I shall leave out discussing the universal causes of the events. For instance, I shall relate the events and the circumstances that came about when Cosimo took over the government; I shall leave untouched any discussion of the way and of the means and tricks with which one attains such power; and if anyone nevertheless wants to understand Cosimo, let him observe well what I shall have his opponents say, because what I am not willing to say as coming from myself, I shall have his opponents say.[8]

To write a history of Florence, commissioned by the Medici, without looking too closely into the means whereby their ancestors gained and retained power, was certainly a task requiring careful handling: but, on the basis of such slender evidence as these letters, there has been constructed a fantastic interpretation in which Machiavelli is seen as a lover of liberty, forced to devise all kinds of shifts and expedients in order not to depict the Medici as the barely-concealed tyrants he knew them to be. This is very dramatic: but it makes out Machiavelli to be much more of a high-minded idealist than is consistent with his writings in general, and this work in particular; it represents the task of evading Medicean issues as being excessively difficult, when it was but mildly so; it suggests that Machiavelli's style as an historian was cramped by considerations other than those which really did limit his capacities in this direction; and it simplifies our reading of a work which is highly complex. Indeed, in some ways, the *Florentine History* is the most enigmatic of all Machiavelli's writings: partly due to his own intention that it should be so; partly due to the limitations of his historical and critical techniques; and partly due to the mixed nature of the problems he set himself to solve.

The scope of the *Florentine History* is clearly, but disingenuously, set forth by Machiavelli in his proem. He had originally intended —so he says—to begin his narrative in the year 1434, when the Medici had taken their place as Florence's foremost citizens; since the earlier history of the city had been well treated by Leonardo Bruni and Poggio Bracciolini. But subsequent examination of these writings had revealed that they were concerned primarily with wars and external affairs, and had passed over domestic history—either through thinking it too paltry, or because they feared offending the descendants of those involved in civic strife. Machiavelli intends to redress the balance: "if any reading is useful to citizens who govern republics, it is that which shows the causes of the hatreds and divisions of the city, so that, having become wise through the perils of others, they may be able to keep themselves united".[9]

The history of Florence, says Machiavelli, is a record of the most complex internal dissension: class has fought class; party has striven against party. Surely such divisions warrant description, especially since, as Machiavelli shrewdly observes, men always desire to have their own names, and those of their ancestors, perpetuated—even by shameful deeds. He has, therefore, revised his original plan, and will write on the history of Florence prior to 1434—stressing the domestic affairs ignored by his predecessors, and only dealing with external affairs when they elucidate his principal concern—before treating of the Medici era, when he intends to give equal weight both to internal and external matters. He will, moreover, preface all this with an account of the ways in which Italy came to be divided under several powers, so that the development of Florence may be better apprehended.

All these things, Italian affairs as well as Florentine, will be completed in four books: the first will tell briefly of all the occurrences in Italy from the decline of the Roman Empire down to 1434; the second will carry its narrative from the origin of the city of Florence down to the war which, after the expulsion of the Duke of Athens, was fought against the Pope; the third will end in 1414 with the death of King Ladislao of Naples; and with the fourth I shall come to the year 1434. From that time on I shall describe in detail the things which happened within Florence and without, down to the present times.[10]

As a matter of fact, Machiavelli adheres only to the first half of his promise relating to the first four books which do, indeed, proceed from a general sketch of Italian history to a consideration of the evolution of Florence and its party divisions, culminating in the rise of the Medici. The latter half of the work, however, despite Machiavelli's assurances, largely eschews internal affairs. Books Five and Six are concerned with wars between Italian states, and briefly touch upon Florence only in relation to these. The next book opens with an inartistic apology for the large amount of space devoted to external affairs—Machiavelli excusing himself because, were he not to go into such matters, Florentine history would itself be less readily understood. This might, in general terms, be true enough: but the fact remains that Machiavelli moves on to a résumé of internal affairs, from 1427 to 1464, occupying but five-and-a-half chapters of which two—and those the longest—are devoted to a eulogy of Cosimo de' Medici. The rest of the Book deals partly with Florence under Piero, Cosimo's son, and partly with external affairs: ending with an account of the Milanese conspiracy and murder of Galeazzo Sforza in 1476. The Eighth Book is, however, the most ill-balanced of all. Of its total of thirty-six chapters, nine are devoted to the Pazzi conspiracy of 1478; twenty-six describe the ensuing wars in which Florence was involved; and one, the last, is entirely taken up with a character-sketch and eulogy of Lorenzo the Magnificent, terminating in a brief apocalyptic message concerning Italy's ruin.

This scarcely adds up to the history of Florence Machiavelli has promised us: though it is impossible not to sympathise with his determination to avoid writing at length about Medici techniques of government. But there are other limitations to Machiavelli's endeavours as an historian far more fundamental than this desire to pass over long tracts of domestic history which would, objectively, demand study. The trouble is that Machiavelli, as in everything he writes, sets out with a whole series of ready-made ideas which history must, perforce, substantiate. Thus the *Florentine History* is patched together from a variety of sources which are in no way evaluated comparatively, but are treated in an arbitrary, unilinear fashion, with Machiavelli following now one and now another author, as it suited his notional purposes. His work is, therefore, no more an analytical record of events and their causes than the *Discourses* are an objective study of Roman government, or the *Art of War* an original treatise on military affairs. What we have, instead, is a highly selective, idiosyncratic, and often wilfully-inaccurate narrative serving as the raw material with which Machiavelli illustrates his politico-historical preconceptions. His treatment of the literary sources of Florentine history is thus basically similar to that accorded to Livy in the *Discourses*, and to Vegetius, Frontinus, and Polybius, in the *Art of War*.

In criticising Machiavelli in this way, it must be remembered that he does not stand alone in his view that history is nothing more than what has been written down before; that one may select from this material whatever is most convenient; that whatever is most convenient is that which instructs; and that that which instructs does so according to preordained truths of universal applicability. Where Machiavelli differs most dramatically from his predecessors is that his universal truths extend only to human political affairs. Another difference is that, however fallacious his method—which pretends to be inductive and is demonstrably not so—Machiavelli's preconceptions do have their roots in his own experience. He had formed a number of ideas about political behaviour, based not on academic theory but on empirical observation: so that, on the whole, his political and historical expectations do less violence to the evidence than those of any previously published historian attempting a work of similar scope. On the other hand it is a pity that Machiavelli was never able to proceed beyond these intuitive insights, and carry his empiricism into the study of literary and documentary evidence. This is no mere unhistorical criticism. Guicciardini, a younger contemporary, was able to use sources in a manner far more "modern" than Machiavelli; while even Flavio Biondo, whose vast compilations Machiavelli plundered for much of his material, had shown himself better aware both of the need to evaluate divergent documentary evidence, and of the techniques requisite for this purpose, than his infinitely more imaginative, dynamic, and literate successor.

In a curious way, too, despite his selective, and sometimes dishonest, use of evidence, Machiavelli is rarely able to dominate his sources. Though heavily paraphrasing, cutting, and compressing earlier narratives, and transmuting much literary dross into characteristically taut and telling language, he too frequently incorporates their basic content without considering either their implications or relevance to his argument. In such a patchwork, similar events are sometimes presented with flatly contradictory interpretations, while other actions are passed over with inadequate comment; so that it often becomes difficult not merely to discover what Machiavelli's ideas really are, but what his ideas are not. And this air of ambiguity and evasiveness, pervading the *Florentine History*, is due as much to an uncertainty of technique as to any consistent attempt by Machiavelli at masking his opinions. For evidence of this one has only to consider the use made of set orations—either in direct or reported speech.

Machiavelli, according to Gianotti, intended to utilise speeches, put into the mouths of the Medici's opponents, to express opinions which he preferred not to utter directly. But if this were his intention Machiavelli was not specially successful at implementing it. The use of set speeches to convey ideas in narrative histories was a favourite Renaissance device, and was particularly adapted by fifteenth-century humanists from classical models—notably Thucydides. When introducing his use of speeches, made either before or during the Peloponnesian War, Thucydides had written that "it is hard for me, and for others who reported them to me, to recollect the exact words: I have, therefore, put into the mouth of each speaker the sentiments proper to the occasion, expressed as I thought he would be likely to express them, while at the same time I endeavoured, as nearly as I could, to give the general purport of what was actually said".[11] What was good enough for Thucydides was good enough for the humanists; and Renaissance histories are filled out with orotund oratory expressing, if not literally the views of the protagonists, at least the opinions which contemporaries expected of them: and Machiavelli, in using this method, was merely traditionalist. However, this poses problems: the ideas in an oration may simply be those of the original source as summarised by Machiavelli; or they may be fictitious, but used to give dramatic point to certain historical situations; and in either case Machiavelli may, or may not, agree with what is said. The context, it might well be thought, would afford a clue to the expected interpretation: but sometimes the context is, frankly, baffling.

With regard to his attitude towards the Medici, Machiavelli, for example, adapts a speech by Rinaldo degli Albizzi—from Giovanni Cavalcanti's *Istorie Fiorentine*—attacking the pretensions of Cosimo:

> He then demonstrated the dangers of disunion, and how there was no remedy conducive to union other than to eliminate Cosimo—because he alone, through the favours brought about by his excessive riches, kept them weak; and that he had been brought so high that, if nothing were done about it, he would become their prince; and that it was the part of a good citizen to remedy this by calling the people to the piazza, and to take back the government, and to restore liberty to his city. He reminded [the new gonfalonier] that Salvestro de' Medici had been able, unjustly, to bridle the greatness of the Guelfs to whom, through the blood shed by their ancestors, the government belonged; and that what Salvestro had been able to do unjustly against so many, he [the gonfalonier] could better do justly against only one.[12]

This, though not as potent as Machiavelli's earlier, unpublished, version of the text, is still strong medicine: but it is diluted by the fact that Albizzi has himself already emerged as an ambitious, power-seeking man who had, indeed, previously sided with the Medici in urging an unjust war against Lucca.[13] Machiavelli's handling of the situation suggests, therefore, a case of the pot calling the kettle black; and he enhances this effect with another speech, this time delivered after the unprofitable Lucchese war, by Niccolò da Uzzano, one of the leading Florentine elders. Niccolò is approached by Rinaldo's party to support action against the Medici whose evil-doing—contrary to Machiavelli's avowed intent—has previously been clearly exposed in the text of the *History*.[14] Uzzano closely examines the case against the Medici, pointing out that much depends upon the interpretation put upon Cosimo's undoubted generosity. "Tell me now," he says, "what law is that which forbids, censures, or condemns liberality, and love, in men? And though they are all charity, methods which men, aiming at the principate, may employ, nevertheless they are not believed to be so; and neither are we able to make them so understood—because our own methods have deprived us of trust." The fact is, he continues, that any action taken against the Medici would be highly dangerous and suspect: and, moreover, there is every reason to suppose that were the republic to be saved from Cosimo it would immediately fall prey to Rinaldo, which would be an even worse fate.[15]

There are three things to bear in mind here: first, that Uzzano's words—spoken by one of the few characters in the *Florentine History*, whom Machiavelli depicts as entirely sane and honourable—carry more conviction than the reported speech of Rinaldo; on the other hand Machiavelli himself, has, in undisguised terms, condemned Medici methods and ambitions as well as those of their adversaries; and lastly, the speeches—both of Rinaldo and of Niccolò—were not invented by Machiavelli, but are stream-lined versions of Cavalcanti. Thus one cannot have it both ways: if Machiavelli was deliberately and expertly arranging his set speeches to achieve a desired effect, then it must be an effect of ambiguity; if he intended to imply adverse criticism of the Medici then he has achieved this not by any ingenious and positive manipulation of his material, but only by the much cruder expedient of omitting most of their activities from his narrative.

Machiavelli's use of set speeches in general, though constituting a striking feature of his work, offers clear evidence that he is as much at the mercy of his sources as they are at his. Despite his brilliance at rendering turgid and repetitive rhetoric into his customary terse eloquence, Machiavelli is not adept at selecting material to convey ideas adequately. Even when he creates fictitious orations, it is by no means always clear whether or not he sympathises with a particular speaker. Such a criticism would, or course, be irrelevant if applied to any truly objective historian: but Machiavelli is explicitly seeking to instruct his readers, and it is difficult to take in lessons when no clear guidance is offered by the teacher. What, for example, is a reader to make of the impassioned speech concerning liberty—declaimed by the Signory to the tyrannical Duke of Athens—when he already knows that this same Signory, by its unreasonable persecution of the nobility, had created the very conditions enabling the Duke of Athens to seize power; and when, furthermore, the Duke is accorded a short address which reduces "liberty" to absurdity by unerringly probing the exposed nerve of Florentine corruption.

> He said that it was not his intention to rob the city of her liberty, but to restore it to her; because only disunited cities are slaves, while the united are free: and if Florence, by his government, were divested of factions, ambitions, and enmities, he would be restoring liberty, not taking it away; and since it was not his own ambition, but the prayers of many citizens, which had led him to undertake this burden, they would do well to content themselves with that which satisfied others. And as for the dangers he might encounter in this undertaking, he took no account of them—because it was not the part of a good man to avoid good through fear of evil, and it was the part of a coward not to attempt a glorious enterprise because of a doubtful outcome.[16]

This could easily be Machiavelli speaking: yet he makes it abundantly clear, before and after this speech, that he despises the Duke.

Wise words by the contemptible Duke of Athens; impassioned words by a culpable Signory; anti-Medici words by the suspect Albizzi; and tolerant words by the respectable Uzzano: we are here confronted by a failing similar to that encountered elsewhere in Machiavelli's work. It is the failing which betrays Machiavelli into depicting Cesare Borgia as a victim of Fortune, despite a palpable error of his own judgement; into elevating an incongruous aspect of pagan religion into a necessary cause of Roman military greatness; and into providing Fra Timoteo with twinges of conscience, self-awareness, and insights out of keeping with his importance and behaviour. Machiavelli has a tendency to set down ideas as they occur to him regardless of the logic which their context demands: he is afflicted, intermittently, by a lack of control, either of tone or of proportion.

Such are the principal defects which mar the *Florentine History* both as a work of Renaissance historiography, and as a vehicle for conveying Machiavelli's ideas. Yet, despite its flaws, the book remains vitally important to the student of Machiavelli. Although the speech technique is often ambiguous, there are other occasions when Machiavelli's meaning is made perfectly clear by the context of an oration. Machiavelli also employs the obvious, but convenient, device of prefacing each book of the *History* with a short general reflexion upon the nature of the problems arising therein, where he is expressly speaking his own mind. The subjects covered in these passages—on the need for colonies, the comparison between ancient and modern practice in civil and military affairs, the causes and results of discord in republics, the role of the lawgiver, the problem of historical repetition, the nature of corruption, the purpose of war, the dangers of conspiracy—are all classic Machiavellian preoccupations, and are often more concisely expressed here than elsewhere in Machiavelli's works. Moreover, there is still the "athlete's style, all bone and sinew", as Symonds put it—so that the work abounds in those pithy maxims, clever turns of phrase, pungent cynicisms, and shrewd sarcasms, which always make reading Machiavelli a more wholly satisfying experience than thinking about what he says. These maxims, too, run the whole gamut of favourite topics—*virtù* and Fortune, force and fraud, human nature, mercenaries, the papacy, tyranny, republics, and everything else. The *Florentine History* is thus valuable both for the light it throws on many of Machiavelli's key ideas and for the obscurity it casts over others: a paradox which will emerge from a consideration first of the historical assumptions underlying the *Florentine History*, and then of its three major themes—corruption, the Medici, and the art of war.

Machiavelli's view of history here is substantially similar to the theory enunciated at greater length in the *Discourses*. Provinces, he writes in the introductory chapter to Book Five, normally pass from order to disorder and then back again. The nature of worldly affairs is never stable, so that as soon as perfection is achieved—there being no room for improvement—decline is inevitable; while, conversely, when provinces have declined to a level beyond which it is impossible to sink, they once again begin to rise. Thus good always lapses into evil, and evil becomes good. All this had been a commonplace of historical thinking from ancient times; and it was an attitude especially favoured in the Renaissance which, of course, saw itself precisely as a period of ascent following long decline from the fall of Rome through to the abyss of the Dark Ages. The idea appears in many guises, perhaps the most noteworthy being in the field of culture history where it culminates in Vasari's attitude towards Michelangelo whose achievements, being the God-given perfection of all the arts, can only be followed by decay: just as the ancient arts, having attained their zenith, fell into total corruption.[17]

Machiavelli goes on to explain the fluctuation between good and bad polities as a sequence of necessary causes and effects, repeating, almost verbatim, his earlier reflexions in *L'Asino*: "*virtù* brings forth tranquillity; tranquillity, laziness; laziness, disorder; disorder, ruin; and likewise from ruin there grows order; from order, *virtù*; and from this, glory and good fortune".[18] This, incidentally, enables Machiavelli to give a clear answer to the age-old controversy concerning the relative merits of arms and letters: philosophy and literature constitute the most in-sidious means whereby states, having achieved peace, become corrupt and are seduced, via indolence, into discord. "Provinces, by these means, come to ruin, whence, men having become wise through sufferings, they return again to order"—unless, adds Machiavelli, recalling the rarely-completed historical cycle described in the *Discourses*, they are overwhelmed by some "extraordinary force". This unilinear cause-and-effect structure of ideas is typical of Machiavelli, occurring in a wide variety of contexts of which cyclical change in states is but the most obvious. It is also the most fundamental: for its two extreme terms—corruption and *virtù*—are the poles not only of Machiavelli's historical process, but also of his entire political conception. And while the Roman republic, as analysed in the *Discourses*, represents the state in a period of *virtù*, so contemporary Italy, and especially Florence, represents the ultimate in corruption—and it is with this that the *Florentine History* is principally concerned.

In the *Florentine History* Machiavelli provides both his most succinct clue to the two extreme conditions of states and his most elaborate description of one of them. Towards the end of Book Eight, when enumerating the extraordinary combination of opposites comprised by Genoese government, he points out that one can observe there, "amongst the same citizens, liberty and tyranny, the civil life and the corrupt, justice and licence".[19] Corruption is seen here in contradistinction to "the civil life" [*la vita civile*]: and how these are constituted may be seen in Book Three, where Florence, about the year 1372, is on the verge of ruin through party strife. A concourse of citizens, "moved by love of their country", present themselves before the Signory to whom they address a long speech, worth citing at some length since its context leaves no room for doubt that, on this occasion, Machiavelli is expressing his own deepest convictions.

The common corruption of all the cities of Italy, magnificent Signors, has corrupted and still corrupts our city; because from the time that this province escaped from the power of the Empire, its cities, not having a strong bridle to correct them, have their states and governments not free but divided into factions. From this have arisen all the other evils and all the other discords which have appeared in them. In the first place, there is found among their citizens neither union nor friendship other than amongst those who are privy to some wickedness committed either against their country or against private persons. And because in all men religion and the fear of God are extinguished, the oath and the pledge are as lasting as they are useful: men avail themselves of them not to observe them, but as a means to deceive more easily; and the more easily and securely the deceit succeeds so much the more glory and praise it acquires. By this means noxious men are lauded as industrious, and good men are blamed as fools. And indeed, in the cities of Italy all that can be corrupted, and which can corrupt others, is heaped together: the young are lazy, the old lascivious, and both sexes and every age are full of disgusting habits; which good laws, being marred by bad practice, do not remedy. From this stems the avarice observed in the citizens, and that appetite not for true glory but for shameful honours, on which depend grudges, enmities, dissensions, and factions; and from those come about deaths, exiles, afflictions for the good, and advancements for the bad. Because the good, trusting in their innocence, do not seek—as the wicked do— for those who will defend and honour them by extraordinary methods, and so come to ruin undefended and without honour. From this circumstance grows both the love, and the power, of parties: because evil men follow them through avarice and ambition, and good men through necessity. And what is yet more pernicious is to see how the movers and leaders of these parties justify their intentions and ends with a pious expression; because always, since they are all hostile to liberty, they crush it under colour of defending either the government of the aristocrats or of the people. The prize they desire from victory is not the glory of having liberated the city, but the satisfaction of having overcome the others and of having usurped the government; and having succeeded therein, there is nothing so unjust, so cruel, or avaricious, that they dare not do. Thus ordinances and laws are made not for public, but for private, utility; thus wars, peace, and treaties, are decided upon not for the common glory, but for the satisfaction of a few. And if other cities are full of these disorders, ours is more sullied with them than any other; because the laws, statutes, and civil ordinances, have always been ordained—and still are ordained— according to the ambition of that party which is left on top. Whence it comes about that always, when one part is driven out and one discord is exhausted, another springs up from them; because that city, which wishes to maintain itself with factions rather than laws, is of necessity divided within itself as soon as one faction is left without opposition: because it cannot be defended by those private means which had originally been ordained for its safety.[20]

The rigidly sequential character of Machiavelli's thought is here laid bare: his favourite conjunctions are "because", "by this means", and "whence arose". But more important are the ideas themselves, concerning the constituents of corruption: faction, disunity, lack of religion, faithlessness, indolence, debauchery, greed for personal gain, private animosities, murders, and expulsion. And the social system, in which these depraved appetites and habits flourish, is comprised of hypocrisy, lip-service to religion and liberty, legislation for private and party ends, and a foreign policy dominated by similar motives. These then are the diagnostics of political corruption—self-interest is rampant, and there is no conception of the common good. By inference, the *vita civile*—the state wherein civic *virtù* abounds—must comprise the opposites or negation of each and every one of these vices, and must be a polity where, as in Machiavelli's notional Roman republic, government was devoted to propagating the good of the generality of citizens.

The problem is, where does Italy, and especially Florence, fit into this historical pattern? Again Machiavelli gives an answer, in the discussion of cycles prefacing his fifth Book. He stresses that, though since Rome's fall nothing of comparable stature has risen from its ruins, several cities and governments, including Florence, once displayed such *virtù* that they were able to liberate Italy and defend her from the barbarians. However, their *virtù* was of a limited and inferior order, and resulted in a paradoxical situation: "there arose times which, if not tranquil through long peace, were at least not dangerous through the hardships of war". This came about, says Machiavelli, because one cannot describe as peace a period in which princedoms attack each other with armies: nor can one describe as war a situation in which men are not killed, cities are not given to the sack, and princedoms are not destroyed: "wars came to such feebleness that they were begun without fear, transacted without danger, and completed without injury". Thus *virtù*, which in other provinces was exhausted by long peace, was wasted in Italy by cowardice: "as will clearly be known from that which we shall describe from 1434 to 1494; where will be seen how, at last, the road was once again opened to the barbarians, and Italy again placed itself in servitude to them".[21]

This is really the crux of the *Florentine History*, and the key to the last four books which should have dealt with Florentine affairs under the Medici, but deal with almost everything else. Machiavelli's wish to avoid difficulties only partially accounts for this discrepancy. Much more fundamental is the fact that a study of Medici government could add little to Machiavelli's theme which remains essentially the same as that first sketched a decade earlier in *The Prince*, and continued in the *Discourses* and the *Art of War*. Why do states sink into corruption; how, if ever, might they be revitalised; and, above all, to what depths had all Italy—not merely Florence—already sunk? The full historical cycle would provide that states, having fallen to the nadir of degradation, may then expect to rise again. But, cautions Machiavelli, rarely do states ever complete the cycle by reasserting their *virtù*; for they are commonly overwhelmed by some "extraordinary force" before this can be achieved. This has been the fate of Italy. No leader has arisen to heal her divisions, and unite her factions: and she has succumbed to the power of the barbarians.

The story has, for Machiavelli, a peculiar and morbid fascination. The activities of Italian princes will not, he tells us, fill us with admiration, as do the achievements of the ancients. This is to be no record of bravery and prudence on the field of battle, nor of civic patriotism. It is rather an examination of the deceits and frauds whereby princes, soldiers, and heads of republics have maintained a reputation which they never merited. It is a study of the manner in which so many noble peoples have been held in check by such feeble and ill-managed arms: "this perhaps will be no less useful than to understand ancient history; because if the latter excites free spirits to follow them, so the former will excite such spirits to avoid and extinguish *them*".[22] This record of depravity includes everything that Machiavelli was prepared to say, or imply, for and against Medici government; and also most significant references—and there are many—to the absurd non-wars which in his view wasted Italian military *virtù* in the fifteenth century, and left the land prey to invaders.

The role of the Medici in Florentine history posed, as we have seen, a major technical problem: how could the tortuous activities of this family be presented in a manner fit for the perusal of a Medici pope? The conventional interpretation of Machiavelli's difficulty, and of his structural expedients, is not adequate to explain away what one encounters in a reading of the *Florentine History*. He does not always cope with his materials as adroitly as has sometimes been thought: but, in any case, it is by no means certain that he even wished to solve the Medici question in absolute terms. I have already suggested that, by the time Machiavelli came to deal with the period after 1434, he had other, bigger, fish to fry than an official civic history. His theme was the corruption and degradation of Italy—and the villains of the piece were not the Medici. Even if we choose to confine our attention— as Machiavelli did not—to the government of Florence, it would be naïve to represent Machiavelli as a subtle opponent of concealed autocracy, and as a republican zealot, striving after stratagems to veil his bitter hostility towards the government. Machiavelli's enthusiasm for republics was entirely speculative: the perfect republic had existed in ancient Rome; and, though a number of Italian governments had, in the past, shown a limited and intermittent capacity for vigorous and united action, only the Germans and Swiss, in recent times, had displayed even a semblance of ability. Italy was utterly degraded: and, in such a situation, salvation could only come from a great leader: a "kingly hand". If Italy were to be saved, it would be by another, superior, Cesare Borgia, not by a republic, however reconstituted: and in the *Florentine History* even this hope has, seemingly, been extinguished.

That the government of the Medici in Florence was a symptom of general and chronic corruption, rather than its cause, is everywhere apparent in the *Florentine History*. It is true that Medici methods are criticised, covertly and overtly, by Machiavelli: but it is equally true that he criticises their opponents. And this is the point. The Medici are presented equivocally: and, from a consideration of the possible administrative alternatives, nothing positive emerges. Apart from one or two very brief, and lightly

touched-upon spells, the history of Florence, as depicted by
Machiavelli, is a gloomy record of internecine strife, of which
the citizens' speech on corruption—already cited from Book
Three—is a fair representation. Machiavelli distinguishes in
Florentine society two distinct modes of conflict: that which
divides the city laterally—the struggle between the upper classes
and ill-defined strata of lower classes; and that which operates
vertically—party divisions, generally taking their origin in
family disputes amongst the nobles. Machiavelli's terminology
is very imprecise, and on only three occasions—all towards the
end of Book Two—does he come near to clarifying his view of
the class structure: when the Duke of Athens's punitive executions
"frightened the middling citizens [*i mediocri cittadini*] and only
pleased the nobles [*Grandi*] and the lowest class [*la plebe*]"; when
he discerns three separate, though concurrent, conspiracies
against the Duke—of the nobles, of the *popolani*, and of the
artificers; and when, concerning the subsequent turmoil, he
writes that the nobles hoped to defeat the *popolo* who were in
disagreement with the lower classes [*la plebe minuta*].[23] Unfortunately, Machiavelli's use of these, and of other terms, is inconsistent. At the very end of Book Two he writes that the people
themselves were divided into three sorts—the powerful, the
mediocre, and the base; and elsewhere we find the *popoli*, who
might otherwise be taken as the middle class between nobles and
workers, merging frequently with the far more extensive
moltitudine who, in turn, become identified with the mob activities of the lowest classes, for whom Machiavelli has an undisguised contempt.[24] The only sure thing is that no class, no party,
and no form of government, emerges unscathed from his
pessimistic scrutiny.

Curiously enough, the class least castigated by Machiavelli
proves to be the old nobility. Admittedly their feuds and factions
are mercilessly exposed, as is their lust for power which, whenever satisfied, resulted in civic servitude. On the other hand, they
alone had retained something of a military *virtù* and a greatness
of spirit not to be found in the ordinary people. Machiavelli's
treatment of the old nobility is most revealing of the limitations

of his "republican" sympathies. He discusses the matter in the introductory chapter to Book Three, when he reflects that conflict between nobility and people has been the eternal ground of discord in republics. It kept Florence disunited, just as it had similarly affected Rome: "if it be permissible to compare small things with great". But different results had accrued in these republics. In Rome the people wished to enjoy supreme honours in conjunction with the nobles; in Florence they desired only to exclude the nobles from government. In Rome conflicts of class had increased military prowess; in Florence they exhausted it. In Rome divisions had led from an equality of citizens to a considerable inequality; in Florence they reduced the city from inequality to a remarkable egalitarianism, levelling everybody down to their lowest common denominator. In Rome the people had acquired *virtù* through their association with the nobles in civil and military government; in Florence the people triumphed so completely that the nobles, compelled to abase themselves, lost all their former great qualities and became as despicable as their conquerors. Thus, "Florence became ever more humble and more abject"; *virtù* was extinguished; and thereafter, apart from a brief spell from the end of the fourteenth to early fifteenth centuries, the city—while as faction-ridden as in the earlier period—was without the military prowess which had hitherto saved it from total degradation.[25] This strange lament is almost the last reference to the great nobles in the *Florentine History*: and henceforth they are tainted and transformed by the pettiness and cowardice of the ordinary people. The leading Florentine families of the fifteenth century, one is forced to assume, were not of the same calibre—having all the faults but none of the virtues of their predecessors: and this is a judgement which must, inferentially, also be applied to the Medici.

If the great nobles pass early from the scene, the lower classes are ever-present: and theirs is a uniformly dishonourable role in the history of Florence. They are as quick to get involved in faction as their superiors; but, having no *virtù*, they either act capriciously or are preyed upon as mere dupes by astute politicians. Repeatedly one part, or another, of the people is shown to be

unworthy of responsibility. The people are of a slavish mentality
with no regard for their own freedom; the plebeians "naturally
delight in evil"; the people, especially "the most ignoble part",
subject Florence to such depredations that the most cruel enemy
of the city would have been ashamed; the favour of the whole
mass of people [*l'universale*] is won or lost by the most trifling
circumstances; the plebeians have fickle minds, "more concerned
about their own dangers than about others' liberty"; the lower
orders always join the party of malcontents; the multitude are
slow to resolve upon evil, but, when so disposed, the least accident may set them off; they cannot be relied upon in dangerous
enterprises; and, as if to make plain the incapacity of the people
in assessing a political situation, they are responsible for electing
the Duke of Athens to the sovereignty of Florence for life: a
decision speedily regretted, and only remedied by conspiracy.
They are as unfitted to control a state as were the nobles: for if
the latter were ministers of servitude, so the populace are ministers
of licence. Both extol the name, but not the spirit, of liberty:
and neither is prepared to live subject to laws or to men.[26]

What kind of government, then, would be needed to induce
such divergent interests to live subject to the laws? Clearly,
according to Machiavelli's definition of corruption, no administration favouring one section of the community at the expense
of others would suffice. Aristocracy, oligarchy, and democracy,
were all out of the question. Thus we are left exactly where we
were with the *Discourse on Florentine Affairs after the Death of
Lorenzo*: the choice is between the rule of a prince or of a republic.
And neither receives an enthusiastic press in the *Florentine History*.
In the entire book, the only ruler accorded almost unmitigated
praise is Theodoric whose activities, terminating in A.D. 526, do
not take us very far into Italian history.[27] For the rest, princes are
depicted as vindictive, faithless, and—especially in fifteenth-
century Italy—enemies of the *virtù* which they fear and extinguish
in others, since they lack it themselves.[28] The administration
of but one prince is studied in detail, and this—the vice-stained,
murder-ridden career of the Duke of Athens—is offered to the
reader as a dreadful exemplar of tyranny. Indeed, personal rule

is manifested throughout the *Florentine History* principally by insensate tyrants: but republican governments are seen to be scarcely less corrupt. The fact is that a republic needs to be perfectly organised, balancing out conflicting interests, so that the efforts at aggrandisement by individuals, being unsupported by faction, benefit rather than harm the community: "with such laws and ordinances many ancient republics, whose governments enjoyed long life, were endowed".[29] But with such laws and ordinances, Italian republics were not endowed.

It is impossible, in Machiavelli's opinion, to maintain any republic, even the greatest, in perfect unity of purpose; and Florence is the supreme example of a thoroughly incompetent political organisation masquerading as truly republican. It is always preaching liberty while attempting to subjugate its neighbours; and it is chronically faction-split and, hence, without *virtù*. The very word "liberty" recurs in the *Florentine History* as a mere catchword, now of one party, now of another, till little is left of its meaning—even for Machiavelli—apart from the idea of a city being free from foreign domination. This is a trifling and trite signification which might equally apply to any kind of internal government from tyranny to democracy.

Machiavelli has scarcely a good word for his native city, but contrives a great variety of bad ones: Florence is displeased with every government and divided by every accident; it cannot, even when prompted by the memory of recent discord, hold itself firm; it does not know "how to maintain liberty, but cannot endure servitude"; and in war it is saved more by the death of its enemies than through any merit of its own. Machiavelli repeatedly ascribes Florentine weakness to internal dissension; and his own attitude is most succinctly expressed by wise old Niccolò da Uzzano who points out that the city "is naturally partisan, and, having always lived in factions, corrupt".[30]

In one sense, therefore, Machiavelli's gloomy review of the totality of Florentine history does constitute an adverse criticism of the Medici, despite his dutiful funebrial eulogy for each member of the family, and his particularly elaborate tributes to Cosimo and Lorenzo. They had given no true stability to the government of Florence; they had ruled merely as one faction triumphant over others; and they had contributed no more than the other rulers of Italy towards defence against foreign invaders. On the other hand, Machiavelli depicts little better in earlier Florentine history, and nothing better in contemporary Italy. As he writes, in the introduction to Book Two: "many parts of the world, especially Italy, have become, in comparison with ancient times, deserts; and all this has come about, and still comes about, through there being in princes no desire for true glory, and in republics no institutions deserving of praise".[31] Corruption is omnipresent. For such a situation in the land as a whole Machiavelli had once argued the need for (and remote possibility of) a prince who would unite separate states and lead them against barbarians. More specifically for a corrupt republic, such as Florence, Machiavelli had consistently appealed for the one man— the great lawgiver—to set things aright; and, in the *Discourse on Florentine Affairs after the Death of Lorenzo*, he had even visualised the Medici in this exalted role. Now in the *Florentine History*, he sees nobody.

Yet, despite his profound pessimism, Machiavelli still entertained one faint hope for Italy's future—the same hope he had cherished from his early years in government service, through his period of disgrace, and during his slow, partial recovery of favour. Good customs and good laws are the result, not the cause, of good arms. This Machiavelli had maintained in *The Prince*, the *Discourses*, the *Art of War*, and elsewhere in his writings.[32] The Roman republic was the greatest polity in history; and its basis was the greatest national army that had ever existed. Military *virtù* had been extinguished in Italy during the shameful sham wars of the fifteenth century. Might it just be possible to resuscitate the Peninsula by diagnosing this dread disease so convincingly that somebody would, at last, take heed? The work was written for the Pope, and its immediate sequel was Machiavelli's attempt to organise a papal militia. In the *Florentine History*, as we have seen, Machiavelli's views are often difficult to determine, and are sometimes qualified out of existence. On only one subject does he write consistently, with unfeigned vehemence, and without any possibility of misinterpretation—that is upon the debased art of war practised in Italy during the fifteenth century. Here Machiavelli no longer makes any pretence at playing the historian: he writes as a propagandist.

Structurally the *Florentine History* falls into two separate works, each of four books, divided at the year 1434. This effect is intensified by Machiavelli's preoccupation with a steadily deteriorating art of war. In the earlier books he refers, occasionally, to the faithlessness of mercenary troops, to the superiority of a citizen army, and to the ineptitude of fifteenth-century warfare: but these are only foretastes of what he has in store. Book One, in fact, having brought the general history of Italy down to 1434, concludes with a brief résumé of the Italian states at that time. None of the principal powers had arms of their own: Milan relied upon commissaries; Venice, having achieved greatness by its own naval strength, attempted to expand landwards employing the arms of others; the Pope and the Queen of Naples "did of necessity what the others had done through ill-choice"; while Florence, its nobility destroyed and its government administered by tradesmen, was compelled to adopt the same bad policy. The arms of Italy were thus in the hands of those who fought solely for their own profit, and, since they were all in business together, those who employed them were generally the losers: "in the end they reduced war to such baseness, that any mediocre captain, in whom there had been reborn some shadow of ancient *virtù*, would have put them to shame—to the astonishment of Italy which, with so little prudence, honoured them".[33]

Machiavelli complains that, "with these slothful princes and these most contemptible arms", his history must be filled: though it takes him a further three books to reach this point again. But when he does, he is as good as his word; and his last four books read less like a history of Florence than as a further complement to the *Art of War*—giving the historical evidence for many of the theoretical assumptions in the earlier treatise. At least this would seem to have been Machiavelli's intention, though much of his "evidence", judged by any objective standards, must be deemed inadmissible. For it is in his treatment of warfare that the inductive method, always roughly handled, is most blatantly violated. Machiavelli had an audience to convince, and a preconceived thesis to prove; and he was not too fussy about academic niceties when going about his business. The thesis is stated at length in the opening chapter of Book Six, when the purpose of war and the use of victory are considered in terms borrowed directly from the *Discourses* and the *Art of War*. A state wages war to enrich itself and to impoverish its enemies.

> Ancient and well-ordered republics, in their victories, were accustomed to fill the treasury with gold and silver, distribute gifts to the people, remit taxes to their subjects, and entertain them with games and solemn festivals: but victories of the times we are describing first emptied the treasury, then impoverished the people, and did not secure you from your enemies. Which all came about from the disorder with which these wars were waged; because the vanquished enemy were despoiled but, being neither held prisoner nor killed, only deferred attacking the victor again for just as long as they had to wait for their leader to refurnish them with arms and horses. Moreover, since the ransoms and the booty were in the hands of the soldiers, the victorious princes could not avail themselves of new money for fresh expenses, but drew it from the very entrails of their own people; thus victory brought forth no other benefit for the people than it made the prince more ready to burden them and less regardful about doing it.

Thus, with victory affording scant advantage, and defeat slight injury, the whole business of war became ridiculous—profiting nobody, apart from the mercenaries, and resulting in that vitiation of *virtù* which eventually left Italy an easy prey to foreigners.[34]

Machiavelli misses no opportunity to pour scorn upon fifteenth-century generals, their troops, their battles, and their sieges. His favourite devices are to demonstrate how the advantages of a victory in the field were inevitably dissipated by faulty leadership or discipline; how even at a siege such as that of Foiano, where the defenders appeared to display exceptional ability for the times, they were aided by the glaring deficiencies of the attackers; how places "now abandoned as impossible to defend, were then defended as places impossible to take"; and, above all, how in those days the fiercest battles, sometimes fought throughout a day, were completely bloodless.[35] In reconstructing these combats, the propagandist obliterates the empirical historian, and Machiavelli is guilty of gross exaggeration, wilful misrepresentation, or total disregard, of his sources. For example, the battle of Anghiari in 1440, as described by Machiavelli is worthy of the Keystone Cops. Two great armies are drawn up, one on each side of a river, and attempt to get at each other across a single, narrow bridge. They push each other backwards and forwards all afternoon—the bridge being held first by one and then the other army—until at long last the Florentines manage to gain a footing on the opposite bank where they triumph over their enemies. And when it is all over, after four hours' stiff combat and a great victory, "not more than one man died; who expired, not from a wound or any honourable blow, but through falling off his horse and being trampled on".[36] This is a good story; but it is disturbing when one notes that Machiavelli's sources clearly state that as many as seventy men were killed and six hundred wounded, together with some six hundred horses shot down by the artillery. Similarly, the battle of Molinella in 1467 is described by Machiavelli as an encounter in which no one was killed, and only a few horses were wounded—despite the fact that contemporary sources suggest that several hundred troops were slain. Scipione Ammirato, writing later in the sixteenth century, was highly irritated by the constant errors in the *Florentine History*, and when detailing the various casualties at Molinella, as listed in the original sources, he especially notes Machiavelli's falsification and "customary sneers at the expense of hired troops".[37]

The simple truth of the matter is that Machiavelli had decided, years before while on active diplomatic service, that mercenaries were villains and cowards, and that wars waged with such troops must necessarily be void: and if the evidence failed to fit this hypothesis, then the evidence—not the hypothesis—would have to be altered. Machiavelli's military fixations and his methods are illuminated by the one fifteenth-century battle which he chooses not to falsify, but instead reports with enthusiasm. This is the victory of Roberto Malatesta over the Duke of Calabria in 1482: "and this engagement was fought with more *virtù* than any other waged in Italy for fifty years, because on the two sides more than a thousand men died there".[38] This is reminiscent of the sanguinary battles reported, with such relish, in the *Life of Castruccio Castracani*: *virtù* in war means real fighting, and plenty of killing. It also happens that this battle was one in which the infantry enjoyed a striking success against the opposing cavalry. And, by some strange coincidence, another of Machiavelli's hypotheses—dependent upon his personal reconstruction of Roman military practice—was that infantry must again be recognised as superior to cavalry before modern warfare can regain its lost *virtù*.

The eight books of the *Florentine History*, terminating with the death of Lorenzo the Magnificent in 1492, constituted Machiavelli's last major work. Though further books were projected, they were never completed: for events now drew Machiavelli back into active political life. Giulio de' Medici—now Pope Clement VII—was favourably impressed by the history, and increased Machiavelli's stipend. More to the point, the militant message of the work seemed to have made some impact on the dilatory pontiff: and nothing in Machiavelli's career is more ironic than the ensuing episode when he was sent by the Pope to Francesco Guicciardini, President of the Romagna, to discuss the feasibility of establishing a papal militia. Machiavelli had expressed his contempt for the Papacy as a temporal institution, not only in the *Discourses* and in his private correspondence, but even in the *Florentine History* itself where he had represented the Popes as having been, from earliest times, the root cause of Italian weakness.[39] Now Machiavelli was trying to organise an army on the Pope's behalf; while Clement, fresh from Machiavelli's pessimistic pages, was supporting his efforts by assuring Guicciardini that the matter was of great importance: "and on it depends the safety of the Papal states as well as that of the whole of Italy, and practically of the whole of Christendom".[40]

Guicciardini was not so impressed by the scheme which he deemed impracticable in the Romagna; the Pope himself soon lost interest; the idea was dropped; and Machiavelli returned to Florence where he was employed in various public services, including a mission to Venice in August 1525. During his absence he became once more eligible to hold office, and in the following May he was elected as Chancellor to a new magistracy, the Five Procurators of the Walls. For some time Machiavelli had been busying himself with an investigation of the fortifications of Florence, and now his position was formalised: though, as usual, little was done about his various recommendations.[41]

Machiavelli was, at long last, back in active politics: but he was no more able to persuade his superiors to action now than he had been when serving the Soderini régime. And events in Italy were moving rapidly to a disastrous conflict, as the Imperial forces gathered strength to strike at a league between the Pope, Venice, Milan, and France—with Florence, as always, dragged willy-nilly at the confederates' heels. On 6 May 1527, Rome was taken by the Imperial army and given to the sack. The Florentine administration, for too long a mere appendage of the Medici Papacy, promptly collapsed, and a republic was re-established. Niccolò Machiavelli, who had spent the time since his dismissal in 1512 assiduously winning his way back to favour, was again out of a job.

The office of Secretary to the re-constituted Ten of Liberty and Peace was vacant: but though Machiavelli's candidacy was strongly advanced by his friends, he was passed over as being politically suspect. Fortune had struck him yet another malicious blow. But it was of little moment. Machiavelli was already mortally sick; on 21 June, less than a fortnight after the election, he died; and, on the following day, he was buried at Santa Croce.

7

Realism

And such is that book, as I discovered, written by an enemy of
the human race. In it are set out all the plans of the enemy and
the methods by which religion, piety, and all types of virtue
could more easily be destroyed. For, although it bears the name
and style of a man, nevertheless, I had hardly begun to read
the book before I recognised that it was written by the hand of
Satan. . . . Not to keep you in suspense any longer, the book is
inscribed with the name of Machiavelli, a Florentine who is
utterly unworthy to have so noble a city as his fatherland.[1]

"THAT BOOK" WAS Machiavelli's *The Prince*, and Cardinal
Reginald Pole—exiled from his native land, his religion overthrown by the English Reformation, and his family exterminated
by Henry VIII—did not enjoy reading it. The bitter attack on
Henry VIII and Thomas Cromwell, launched in Pole's *Apologia*
to the Emperor Charles V, included the earliest surviving discursive condemnation of Machiavelli. The Florentine had flung
a good many gauntlets at the feet of conventional thinkers, and
Pole, picking up several of these, recognised as most dangerous
the assertion that political practice differed from generally-
accepted political theory. He accordingly put an apposite, but
refutable, defence of Machiavelli's attitude into the mouth of
Thomas Cromwell who was himself execrated as a messenger
from Satan. The advice to princes, given according to the law of
Nature and the opinions of wise men for the honour of the ruler,
advocated by Pole, was scorned by Cromwell who said that such
sentiments excited great applause in the Schools and from the

pulpit, but were of little use in practical affairs; for counsel must be appropriate to the place, the time, and the person. Indeed, says Pole, Cromwell would have been ready, had he lived in the days of Nero, to provide the Emperor with some reason of piety for murdering his own mother. He told Pole that, were he to enter into practical politics, he would soon see how greatly the real art of government differed from the speculations of Schoolmen. A short discourse by an experienced man was of greater utility than many volumes by inexperienced philosophers such as Plato whose ideal state had still not been created by man. If the art of government had to be learnt from books, then at least those should be read which adhered more to experience than to speculation.

Machiavelli would have appreciated this Aunt Sally defence of his efforts, though Pole's subsequent pious refutation would have been less to his taste, and would merely have confirmed his opinion that philosophers concerned primarily with ethical motivation had nothing sensible to say about politics. Machiavelli had dismissed the speculations of such people in the fifteenth chapter of *The Prince* when, it will be remembered, he asserted that, though "many" had written on the conduct of princes, he was discussing the matter again because he was consciously departing from their methods. It was his intention to write something useful rather than provide another ideal projection unrelated to practical affairs: for what people do is very different from what they ought to do.

The kind of literature from which Machiavelli was consciously diverging was not merely that of the ideal republic created by Plato and the ancient philosophers, though he must have shared Polybius's view that they were irrelevant in any consideration of real polities. It also comprised the vast corpus of medieval and Renaissance prince literature dealing specifically with the problems of kingship—countless treatises with such titles as *De regimine principum*, *De officio regis*, or *The governal of princes*—copied and recopied, translated, revised, enlarged, and adapted for century after century.[2] It was this kind of book which Machiavelli deliberately satirised in *The Prince*, using the traditional shape and form to express very different ideals. For up to and including the fifteenth century these works largely followed a set method and pattern. The primary question they ask is simply, "what should the prince do were he to preside over a perfect state?" They tell the prince what he should do and what sort of person he should be. There is, at the root of all their argument, a fixed belief in the inter-relationship between ethics and politics. They treat of states which existed for the propagation of the Christian ethic. They treat of universals, for the terrestrial state is, after all, only a fragment in a cosmic plan; and the duty of the ruler is to guide his state so that it may fulfil its part therein. In other words, their principal concern was to show the way to the good life. This certainly involved special instruction on virtues: but since political virtues were deemed identical with private virtues, all such advice dealt with perfect princes, living in perfect states, and dealing, externally, with other perfect states.

It is this kind of attitude that Machiavelli is especially concerned to refute. And he was not alone in asserting the need for practicality in political thinking, and in his rejection of purely imaginary projections. Realism was in the air: words like *reason* and *necessity* dominated the day-to-day administration of the Italian city states. Systematic thinkers and historians, too, apart from Machiavelli, assumed the priority of *ad hoc* solutions to political problems, over general rules of universal applicability from which one was supposed to deduce justification for political action. Francesco Guicciardini made such political realism almost axiomatic in his own writings. Again and again in his *Dialogue on the Government of Florence* he asserts that the only way to learn about politics is through experience. A government, he says, must be judged by its results: and he erects this idea into a general proposition, pointing out that all people, in fact, do this but simply will not admit it. Guicciardini, explicitly discounting the authority of philosophers, claims that he is going to speak "naturally", and writes that "we have not to look for an imaginary government which appears much more easily in books than in fact, as perhaps is the case with Plato's republic". Instead, it is his business to "consider the nature, the quality, the conditions, the inclinations, and, in a word, to sort out the vital characteristics of a city and of its citizens, and thus to find a government which we would really hope to be introduced according to our conceptions". Francesco Vettori, whom we know well as Machiavelli's correspondent, also felt that the old methods in political thinking had to go overboard: "speaking of the things of this world, without respect and according to the truth of the matter, I say that if one fashioned a republic as that imagined by Plato, or as the Englishman Thomas More pretended had been founded in Utopia, perhaps one could say that these were not tyrannic governments: but all those republics or princes of whom I know anything in history, or those whom I have seen, have seemed to me to savour of tyranny".[3]

That Machiavelli has come to be particularly identified with the divorce of political from private morality, with the doctrine of expediency in political action, and with the mode of justifying all political means on grounds of reason of state, is due less to his uniqueness than to the dynamic way in which he expressed these ideas. The interesting question is whether these realistic political writers, with Machiavelli as their prime exponent, were all that novel? It is still commonly believed that they were. But the matter is not as simple as a reading of Machiavelli's striking axioms makes it appear.

In one very real sense Machiavelli himself and later critics, impressed by his forceful style, were deceived by the apparent novelty of his political thought. Burckhardt and other nineteenth-century scholars were all too ready to accept the Italian Renaissance at its own evaluation in every sphere: and, though many of these ideas have been modified by more than a century of academic demolition work, the belief that the Renaissance invented "the state as a work of art" is still very much with us.[4] The plethora of treatises on ideal kingship must not obscure the fact that there were in medieval Europe several very highly developed states which, in their internal organisation, and their relations with other powers, showed themselves as aware of general political problems as of the technicalities of a constitutional and legal system. Medieval legal theorists and canonists did not merely employ "reason of state", or some synonymous term, literally, they also had a very clear conception as to its meaning: and used the idea that "necessity has no law" to justify the extraordinary acts to which a ruler might oftentimes resort through force of circumstances. This conception of "reason of state" has recently been convincingly elucidated by Gaines Post: and one can do no better on this point than to quote his own summary, given in a devastating footnote devoted precisely to conventional claims concerning the Florentine use of "reason" and "necessity", and the idea that it was first in Italy "that an objective treatment and consideration of the State and all things of this world became possible". Professor Post writes

I must point out once more that this kind of *ragione*, the *ratio publicae utilitatis*, etc., as we have abundantly seen, was as medieval as modern; *necessitas legem non habet* was a commonplace in the twelfth century; the legists and canonists often said that the prince could make new laws because situations, circumstances, and the times are constantly changing; and Terence was frequently quoted (*Phormio*, II. iv. 454): "quot homines tot sententiae". And why were the Florentines more "rational" about politics than medieval men in subjecting *ragione* to the moral law and God? Who was more sincere, who more cynical, in calling upon God? Finally, why say that the idea of *necessità* is opposed to or limits the use of *ragione*? After all, *necessitas* is a part of and enhances the force of "reason of State". Even the maxim, "Dove necessità caccia non bisogna consiglio" represents the medieval doctrine, that by reason of the safety of the State, when the necessity or danger was so urgent and imminent that delay in taking action could not be risked, there was no need of waiting for lengthy debate or the consent of all interested parties. Not only was this understood when Edward I and Philip IV taxed the clergy without waiting for the consent of Boniface VIII, but Thomas Aquinas stated it for a more ordinary immediate danger.

As for objectivity, can one really demonstrate that the Florentine concept of *ragione* was free from subjectivity, from irrationality, and piety? And who can maintain that *ragione di stato* today is objective or scientific? "Reason of State" has always been under the influence of all kinds of emotions of patriotism and religion, as well as the practical considerations of the self-interest of the government or the genuine safety of people and state.[5]

This, on the evidence adduced, seems incontrovertible. Nevertheless, there is still a qualitative difference between a theory which suggests certain areas of necessity, principally in connection with foreign affairs, and puts forward only general suggestions as to the manner in which such necessity is to be met, and a theory such as Machiavelli's which extends the area of necessity to almost everything, and which describes, in detail, the dark deeds which might be perpetrated by a ruler in such circumstances. There is a difference between Laurentius Hispanus— who wrote that "for the defence of the fatherland many things are lawful which are otherwise unlawful" and then went on to pose one of those extraordinary medieval hypotheses (of which Machiavelli is by no means free) in which a man who unavoidably kills his father while defending the *patria* should be rewarded, not punished—and Machiavelli, who tells us in detail and much more comprehensively what needs to be done.[6] We can see, in this instance, and in many others, an early awareness of a dual morality—expediency and normalcy—but it is never enunciated with such completeness and so starkly as in Machiavelli. It is, however, worth pursuing the question of dual morality in greater detail, so that Machiavelli's peculiar qualities may be more properly assessed.

We have already seen how, in general terms, medieval and early renaissance treatises on political morality tended to discuss the problem from an ideal standpoint. Nevertheless, there has rarely been a thinker so naïve as to fail to recognise that not everything on this miserable globe is perfect. Of course there were evil princes and wicked governments; and the problem inevitably arose as to whether even the best prince might be forced by circumstances into behaviour never condoned in private individuals. Is it reasonable to judge the actions of those engaged in

politics by the standards prevailing in private affairs? As early as
the end of the twelfth century, the jurist Azo had written that
"many things are lawful by reason of the public utility".[7] And
subsequently even Aquinas, while stressing that the prince must
have the moral virtues and be a good man, was forced to postulate that political morality might be different from private morality. "In the third book of the *Politics*", he grudgingly concedes,
Aristotle shows that "it is not the same without qualification to
be a good man and a good citizen, in any political organisation.
For there are certain political organisations, not properly organised, in which one could be a good citizen without being a good
man; but in the best political organisation, one is not a good
citizen who is not a good man."[8] The only trouble with Aquinas's
last qualification is that the best polities are very few and far
between.

The kind of moral problem touched on here arose from those
sections in Aristotle dealing with the extraordinary actions
sometimes necessary for political survival. More especially
Aristotle describes how in every form of state—oligarchies and
democracies as well as the more obviously dire tyrannies—
extreme measures, such as ostracism or even judicial murder,
were sometimes taken against overmighty subjects. States, he
writes, behave thus not only towards individual citizens but also
towards whole cities or nations, even breaking treaties for this
purpose: "the problem is a universal one, and equally concerns
all forms of government, true as well as false; for, although
perverted forms with a view to their own interests may adopt
this policy, those which seek the common interest do so likewise".[9]

This is the heart of the matter—the universal justification for
all kinds of political action. Rulers, says Aristotle, may practise
compulsion "and still live in harmony with their cities, if their
government is for the interest of the state".[10] So we can see that
the ethical norm accepted for private citizens may be inapplicable
to affairs of state when the common weal is involved, and that
those responsible for taking decisions on behalf of the state might
have to practise virtues different from those of their subjects.

This latter point, like so much else, is implicit rather than expl.
in Aristotle's *Politics*, but it was a worry to systematic thinke.
and came especially to the fore in the prince literature of the
fifteenth-century Italian humanists who may be regarded as the
immediate antecedents to Machiavelli.[11] These writers, like all
those concerned with good government, compiled long lists of
virtues for their princes—and very conventional they seem to be.
Yet, closer examination reveals significant cracks in the moral
fabric. Often very intimately involved in the exigencies of inter-
state relations, these humanists could simply not ignore the fact
that rulers were frequently faced by circumstances demanding
a decision where there was no clear issue between right and wrong
—where, in fact, a prince had to choose between evils, and had to
decide upon the lesser. And this, in turn, meant that the prince
would always have to take into account the results of his decision:
for a good result would clearly mitigate actions which might
otherwise be deemed immoral. Pontano, writing about 1490,
points out that "it is the act of a wise man, when two ills are put
before him, always to choose the smaller one; it has even been
permissible to lie for the sake of the state and of the king who is
the father of his people". The prudent man, he adds, "balances
utility and necessity with the true and with the false".[12]

Thinkers tied themselves in knots trying to make nice distinctions for such eventualities. Everybody, for example, from
Aristotle onwards, was mightily exercised by the fact that a
ruler, seeking only the good of the State, might have to take
measures which would incur the hatred of his subjects. Aristotle
is perfectly clear that princes should be neither hated, despised,
nor feared.[13] Yet they should be respected withal, and held in
reverence: and this combination was excessively difficult to achieve
in troublous times when coercive measures might be urgent.
Egidio Colonna, one of the most influential Aristotelians of the
late thirteenth century, contented himself with merely stating
that the prince "should not show himself too terrible and severe,
nor is it fitting to show himself too familiar, but he should appear
to sustain his part rather gravely and to be worthy of reverence,
something that cannot fittingly be done without virtue".[14]

Diomede Caraffa subscribed to the traditional view that princes should be loved by their subjects. But his advice on how to achieve this affection is singularly negative: when the prince is forced to impose extra taxes he should make it clear that he does so through necessity and against his will; and when he is constrained to impose penalties on his subjects and take away their property, he should make it equally clear that he does so for the sake of justice.[15] In other words Caraffa is merely telling a prince how to avoid being hated when doing unpleasant things. Patrizzi, too, had to face up to this problem of the prince's dignity in difficult times, particularly in the execution of justice, and he concluded that "severity is very suitable to a king; it presents a certain majesty, and increases his dignity, and renders him, as it were, a divine being among mortals, not merely venerated but even adored by men". He adds that this quality is "very useful in carrying on all kinds of activity and especially in giving judgement and in punishing offenders"; and he makes his point quite clear by including a quotation from Menander to the effect that "salutary severity is superior to the empty appearance of clemency".[16]

We are here tottering on the brink of Machiavelli's expediential world where conventional vice might become political virtue, and where conventional virtue might result in political ruin—a topsy-turvy situation perhaps most in evidence when thinkers faced up to the existence of beneficial deception. Pontano's view that, for the good of the state, it might sometimes be necessary to tell lies, was widely accepted. The prince is advised, by Patrizzi, always to appear in command of men and situations so that, even in dire circumstances, his people should never learn from his demeanour that they are near ruin: "hence it is proper that by simulating and dissimulating he should often show the contrary of truth". Most explicit of all was Platina who maintained that even private citizens might dispense with normal morality when the common good is involved. It is obvious, he says, that every person has a greater obligation to his native land, to his family, and to citizens of the same nation and language, than to aliens and foreigners. The law of nations, therefore, is not to be kept with robbers and pirates, nor with those warring against us. Against such enemies, citizens—even though they might break a sworn oath—can commit no fraud.[17]

I do not want to give the impression that any of this amounted to more than scattered observations amidst a mass of conventionality. None of the writers cited had worked out a consistent doctrine of political necessity, involving a specifically political morality. They merely had glimpses, from time to time, that the traditional ethical commonplaces had to be bent or cracked a little in order that political advice might have some relationship to actuality. They could not entirely ignore the obvious: but, despite equivocational expedients such as those mentioned, their attempts to formulate a theory of political morality, accommodating their ideally good prince to reality, were only partially successful.

Yet there was a way to systematise the real, as well as the ideal, political world. Princes and states were, admittedly, full of imperfections; and worst of all these imperfections, by general consent, were tyrants and their tyrannies. These were certainly not to be emulated by any prince. They were examples of surface flaws in the grand plan of the universe, and were all destined for a sticky end. The ways and means of the tyrant were discussed, therefore, only to show a prince what he must, at all costs, avoid. And, wondrous to behold, it is precisely in their discussions of how princes should not behave, what states should not be, and how states should not act, that political writers from Aristotle onwards touched upon how princes do behave, what states really are, and how states really do act.

Aristotle himself, in the fifth book of the *Politics*, gives a striking account of tyranny—so cogent that it has often been regarded as a direct source for Machiavelli's own thoughts on the prince. But, after all, Aristotle's views on most topics, either in his own words or those of his myriad commentators, were part of the common intellectual baggage of medieval and renaissance Europe, and anyone writing on similar problems was almost bound, consciously or unconsciously, to echo something of his terminology, categorisations, and arguments. Aristotle outlines two modes of procedure for the tyrant. The first is entirely oppressive and aims merely at crushing and humiliating his subjects so that they can never have the strength or spirit to overthrow him. The second is far more subtle and follows the principle that, though the tyrant must always retain sufficient power to rule his subjects "whether they like him or not", in all else he should "act or appear to act in the character of a king". To this end the tyrant is advised to take care of the public revenues so that it appears to everybody that taxes are collected for state purposes, and that money is not wasted in profligate spending. The tyrant should, however, adorn and improve the city, as though he were a guardian of his people. He must contrive also to appear not harsh but dignified, so that men revere rather than fear him; and therefore "whatever virtues he may neglect at least he should maintain the character of a statesman, and produce the impression that he is one". In the indulgence of his pleasures the tyrant should be moderate "or at any rate should not parade his vices to the world"; when he has to use force he should make it appear merely as "fatherly correction"; and he should refrain from outrages against his subjects. Above all, the tyrant should show himself to be religious: "for if men think that a ruler is religious and has a reverence for the gods, they are less afraid of suffering injustice at his hands, and they are less disposed to conspire against him, because they believe him to have the very gods fighting on his side". In sum, were the tyrant to follow these instructions his power would be more lasting: "let his disposition be virtuous, or at least half virtuous; and if he must be wicked, let him be half wicked only".[18]

Thus Aristotle. And thus Aristotelians thenceforth. The ruses of the tyrant were listed in slavish, and often mindless, imitations throughout the Middle Ages and the Renaissance, and little would be gained by examining these in any detail. The writers consistently fail to recognise that, in describing the more subtle activities of the tyrant, they were frequently describing the behaviour of many non-fictional contemporary rulers. But there is one especially apposite example of the genre which is illuminating through its genuine relationship to political actuality. This is the treatise, on the government of Florence, by the *bête noire* of Machiavelli's young manhood, Girolamo Savonarola.[19] In his foreword, Savonarola says that in treating of the government of Florence he would write in Italian, rather than Latin, for "more general utility". Even more than Machiavelli he was writing as a political propagandist concerned with giving practical advice: he was putting forward a programme of constitutional reform. Savonarola divided his work into three books: a discussion of what he deemed the best government for Florence; an exposé of the worst government; and suggested methods whereby the Florentines might avoid the latter and establish the former. For Savonarola, of course, the worst government is that of the single evil man, the tyrant, uniting all the worst people who are, in any case, always more numerous than the good—a comment on human nature with which Machiavelli would largely have concurred. The end of government for Savonarola, as for Machiavelli, is the "common good"; but under the bad man nothing common remains and the people are saddled with a ruler who is difficult to remove because always on his guard. Yet the tyrant, as from time immemorial, is doomed to disaster despite his attempts to maintain himself by the traditional evil expedients.[20] These are carefully listed by Savonarola and include an observation later to be exalted into a political virtue by Machiavelli: that to maintain himself the tyrant will do anything necessary for that purpose, whatever it might be. In other words, Savonarola recognises that this particular type of ruler has, perpetually, to resort to extreme measures. The tyrant must always seek to abase the powerful in his state, and to eliminate potential rivals—even killing them if necessary. He has, in time of plenty and tranquillity, to provide his people with spectacles and festivals, so that they think more about themselves than about him. Especially must Savonarola's tyrant appear religious and devoted to sacred practices though, it is stressed, all this only amounts to "external things". This tyrant wages war for effect and reputation, even when wars themselves are not otherwise necessary. He spends money on palaces and on patronage, but only to make himself, and himself alone, glorious. He always wishes to be first in everything and, "when by his own *virtù* he cannot do this, he seeks to be superior by frauds and by deceits".

The qualities of the Savonarolan tyrant are not new to us. They are, in the main, Aristotelian and seemingly culled from traditional sources. Nevertheless, Savonarola's comments on tyranny were inspired more directly by the actions of the recently overthrown Medici power in Florence. He was writing to show the evils of such a régime, and how they were to be avoided. His list of vices masquerading as virtues emancipates itself from the merely platitudinous because it is consciously related to a real and recent sequence of events. Political realities were not always the same as political ideals, and Savonarola recognised that the single ruler, seizing power illegitimately, must necessarily adopt extraordinary means to maintain himself. It was reprehensible, and was to be avoided by all right-thinking people: but it could, and did, happen.

Machiavelli really took only one more step—albeit a rather long one. The special morality which even conventional thinkers had been forced to accord to their good prince, in order that he might preserve the common weal in times of emergency, pointed the way. Machiavelli simply recognised that the kind of prince and the kind of polity, described by writers like Savonarola as an immoral abomination, was no mere perversion but rather the norm. Thus the ruses of the Aristotelian tyrant, striving to maintain himself in an hostile world, became the basis of a moral code for the Machiavellian new prince, seeking the same end amidst similar difficulties.

Machiavelli's bold new morality is, obviously, most dramatically displayed in *The Prince* where he deliberately uses a traditional literary form—complete with concluding rhetorical flourish— to give point to his grim observation that new princes, seeking to create new states out of corrupt material, must employ the methods generally associated with tyrants. It was difficult for any practical-minded politician to deny that Italy was divided and inept; that any new ruler would be bound to come into conflict with every kind of selfish vested interest; and that such a prince would have to deal with other cities seeking by all means to frustrate his designs, and with other, far greater, nation-states whose only interest in the Peninsula was loot. "If we make a good examination of the beginnings of kingdoms," wrote Francesco Vettori, "we will find that all of them were taken with force or skill."[21] But in such a political morass could any new prince, striving to maintain or increase his state, remain spotless? It is astonishing that some critics, even to this day, persist in castigating Machiavelli for writing an immoral, or at best amoral, "textbook for usurpers" or a "handbook for tyrants". This is as sensible as complaining that one doesn't fall about laughing at a performance of Mahler's *Kindertotenlieder*, or that Greek tragedy tends to be tragic.

Active politics have always been recognised as involving the moralist in difficulties. The medieval legalistic doctrine, "necessity has no law", was devised precisely to help meet this problem. From at least the twelfth century, jurists, decretalists, and canonists had made a clear distinction. On the one hand there was the ruler who, though good, might none the less on some occasions resort to extraordinary modes of behaviour because pressure of circumstances forced him into a position where delay for consultation, or failure to act in what might normally seem an arbitrary fashion, would result in danger to the state. On the other, there was the tyrant who acted in an arbitrary fashion continually, not from necessity, but from motives of personal gain or whim. This could, in practice, be a very nice distinction indeed: and how far you might deem a ruler tyrannical would depend largely upon how badly you were affected by his various arbitrary acts. However, taken in conjunction with customary views about the desiderata of a good ruler, and the qualities of a bad one, one can see that the distinction was not without meaning and value.

Machiavelli himself retains the distinction. He, too, speaks in impassioned terms about the tyrant: citing with approval the traditional view that nearly all tyrants come to miserable ends.[22] In the *Florentine History* he examines the career of the Duke of Athens, whose insensate lust, greed, cruelty, and inevitable failure, provided an object lesson in the kind of tyranny described in the nineteenth chapter of *The Prince*—where a ruler whose actions are directed solely towards the satisfaction of his own base desires, and not towards the good of the state, earns himself universal hatred and contempt. However rulers behave, they "cannot avoid being hated by someone": but they should, therefore, avoid being hated by everyone; and, more particularly, they should seek to retain the friendship of the most powerful element in the state whether this be the army or the people. The Duke of Athens's mistake was that he alienated everybody and won the approval of nobody save the very lowest of the working classes.[23]

But the Duke of Athens was an extreme case, and his rule would have been regarded as tyrannical by any conventional thinker. The difference between Machiavelli and his predecessors is this: that he extends enormously the area within which any ruler, striving to create or maintain a state, may be expected to operate. For Machiavelli political affairs were always in a state of emergency. Necessity is the norm not the exception. This would, in fact, be the correct focus for adverse moral criticism of Machiavelli, were it relevant: not that *The Prince* advocates anti-ethical procedures, but that such procedures—modified to suit differing circumstances—are regarded as normal in all Machiavelli's discursive writings. It has, from time to time, been argued that the extreme views of *The Prince* are peculiar to that work, and that, were Machiavelli's other books equally well known, he might never have earned so malodorous a reputation from posterity. All the evidence suggests the contrary. There are minor exceptions to Machiavelli's gloomy view of the world of affairs, but these are principally in the past. Of modern states, only the Germans preserved any semblance of ancient *virtù*; and, in the main, the corrupt world of Renaissance Italy was, for Machiavelli, the world of politics *in toto*. Even Rome, when Machiavelli's position is closely examined, loses most of its lustre: the city was, after all, founded on homicide; its laws had to be most rigorous to keep men from erring; it required periodic purges in order that its vigour could be maintained; its internal health and wealth depended upon over four centuries of uninterrupted aggression and expansion, which effectually stifled *virtù* elsewhere in the world and prevented it from ever flourishing again; and, eventually, despite everything, it sank into corruption just like every other polity since the dawn of time.

History, for Machiavelli, tends always to be the same because it is compounded of the deeds of men—and men always have the same passions. When one considers how these passions are generally depicted by Machiavelli, it does not become difficult to understand his gloomy view that political affairs are perpetually desperate; for his estimate of human nature is as low as any theologian could have wished. General reflections on the depravity and venality of mankind are scattered throughout Machiavelli's works. In *The Prince* men are fickle, selfish, bad, easily deceived by appearances, and, since they only do good under constraint, are to be governed more by fear than by love. The *Discourses*, too, are full of such comments and even begin by alluding to the dangers of innovation due to the envious nature of man. Evils are multiform, but they all come down to one basic sin: human ambition. By nature, says Machiavelli, men are more prone to evil than to good; they are ambitious, suspicious, and unable to gauge the limits of their own fortune; greed blinds them to danger; their appetites are insatiable, always desiring what cannot be obtained, and discontented with what is already possessed; indeed, so overweening is their ambition, that they cannot—in satisfying present desires—foresee future evils.[24] *L'Asino* similarly attributes all the misery of the world to human ambition; while the *Mandragola*, in so far as it may be read as a serious comment on anything, seems to suggest that everybody is looking for personal gain, be it lust or loot. Even the *Art of War*, though a technical treatise and little concerned with moral generalisations about human nature, contrives two passing thrusts: one at the ignorance and little diligence of men; the other at men's love of property which is as great as their love of life itself.[25] Finally, there is the *Florentine History* where Machiavelli's pessimism is at its most profound: for here it is not tempered, as in *The Prince*, by some hypothetical hope of a warrior-saviour; nor, as in the *Discourses*, by the supposition that a great lawgiver might be able to constitute a state wherein people could be educated towards a life of civic *virtù*. Machiavelli's study of the history of Florence, and of the other Italian cities, has confirmed his worst suspicions about modern corruption; and his narrative is a dark sequence of deceit, murder, greed, inefficiency, conspiracy, corruption, and—dominating everything—insensate human ambition. And in this historical context Machiavelli's cutting remarks on human nature—though substantially similar to his earlier criticisms—have a keener edge than in his more theoretical, and more idealistic, political work. Men, he sneers, are more likely to strive after things they cannot obtain than to accept things which are within their reach; the more authority they enjoy the worse they use it, and the more insolent they become; they are never satisfied with recovering lost possessions, but always wish to seize those belonging to others, and to gain revenge; they are never satisfied, and having gained one thing they immediately seek something else; they are always more ready to covet the possessions of others than to preserve their own; they seldom suffer as much from the loss of their own things, as from not having appropriated someone else's; and, repeating a dictum from the *Discourses*, they are far more readily disposed to evil than to good.[26]

It will immediately be apparent from this catalogue of human vices that Machiavelli, contrary to the more old-fashioned view of him, had a deeply-rooted morality. The very fact that he felt obliged to castigate his fellow creatures for their short-sighted and venal ambitions makes this clear, as does his admiration for the German states. This political fiction, created in his own mind as a little pocket of decency in a corrupt world, shows the store Machiavelli set by people leading secure lives, free from internal disturbance and from external threat; and by such qualities as respect for religion, the keeping of oaths, unselfish regard for the welfare of the community as a whole, contentment with a moderate sufficiency, and condemnation of those who produce nothing for society. These were the Machiavellian virtues in the best of worlds. The difficulty was that Machiavelli's experience of practical politics, together with his knowledge of history ancient and modern, had convinced him that such qualities were rare, and that they could only be introduced into a corrupt society—if ever —by force. Political action, to be successful, must be apposite to the time and the place: and given the circumstances of modern Europe such action could not be of the kind regarded in conventional circles as normal. The situation was, in short, a state of necessity. And thus Machiavelli extended the area of medieval *necessitas* to embrace almost all political activity. Emergency is permanent; choice must always be between evils; the situation constantly demands salutary severity; beneficial deception is perpetually required; and, above all, since such behaviour is likely to incur hatred, it must be masked by all the wiles of the Aristotelian tyrant: extreme measures are to appear under the guise of probity, piety, and equity.

Machiavelli did something else to the old dictum that "necessity has no law". For him necessity had many laws, but they were different from all other rules of conduct: and, as I have suggested, Machiavelli took ideas which had long been in common currency —either as shamefaced and apologetic hints as to what naughty deeds rulers might occasionally be forced into, or as the stock-in-trade of efficient tyrants—and demonstrated that these were, in truth, the very laws of necessity.

This position is most clearly enunciated in *The Prince*, where Machiavelli, in dealing with modern Italy—the most corrupt corner in a corrupt world—argues that, unless a ruler is prepared to abandon conventional ideas about morality, he can accomplish nothing save his own ruin. He must be prepared to lie, to cheat, to use servants as scapegoats for his own unpopular policies, to break treaties when they cease to be advantageous, and even to exterminate rivals, if by so doing he can preserve the state and bring order to it. The prime example, adduced by Machiavelli, is Cesare Borgia whose ruthless methods were necessary to rid the Romagna of the plague of petty tyrants whose pernicious greed and perversion of justice is also described and deplored in the *Discourses*.[27] There can be no doubt that their overthrow was welcome to the inhabitants of the Romagna, and that it could have led to the creation of a powerful papal state. Yet, in order to achieve this beneficial purge, Cesare had resorted to every kind of deception, violence, and, in the end, to the cold-blooded stranglings at Sinigaglia. The end was good: the means judged by any normal standpoint were bad. But since the end could not have been achieved otherwise, those means come within the area of Machiavellian necessity.

Thus a good end—and for Machiavelli there are few better ends than the creation of a secure state in the midst of corruption—might necessitate acts of violence. And here we are on common ground with the *Discourses*. When the material is absolutely corrupt only the single man of outstanding *virtù* can possibly renovate it: but this requires a brutality which presupposes a bad man, while a good end presupposes a good man. To find a good man prepared to employ evil means to achieve a good end is extremely difficult. It can be done, but is so rare that it scarcely ever works out satisfactorily: for, though such a person may bring law to the state, relapse will almost certainly follow his death.[28] In this instance Machiavelli is discussing the reconstitution of a corrupted republic. Elsewhere in the *Discourses* he discusses the prodigious difficulties of creating a completely new state, and once again he is unequivocal on the adaptation of means to ends. The prototype of the creator of a state is Romulus, who founded Rome, the greatest of all polities. To achieve this, Romulus needed to be alone in authority and he had, perforce, to murder his own brother Remus, and to acquiesce in the death of Titus Tatius his colleague. Now, says Machiavelli, this would appear to be a very bad precedent, justifying any ambitious citizens who employ violence against those who oppose their own authority. Indeed, such an opinion would be true were we not to consider the end which prompted Romulus to commit murder.

One must take this as a general rule: that never, or rarely, does it happen that any republic or kingdom is well ordered from the start, or when it is completely reformed without regard for its old institutions, if it is not ordained by one man. Above all, it is necessary that there is one man alone who should give it the method, and from whose mind should proceed every order of this kind. Wherefore, a prudent organiser of a republic—and one who has a mind to act not on his own behalf but for the common good, not for his own posterity but for the common fatherland—must strive to have authority, alone. Nor will any wise intellect ever reprehend any extraordinary action he uses to order a kingdom, or constitute a republic. It is requisite that, though the deed accuses him, the result will excuse him; and when it is good, like that of Romulus, it will always excuse him: because he who is violent in order to spoil things is to be reprehended, not he who is violent to repair them.[29]

The doctrine of expediency is here unambiguous: but it is for a special case, the founder of a state or, as previously discussed, a regenerator. What about all the other individuals involved at some time in their lives in political decisions: the soldiers, ambassadors, magistrates, officers of every kind, and even the people themselves? On their political morality Machiavelli is, once again, clear. Necessity extends to everybody forced to act on behalf of the safety of his native land. When faced by such decisions "there must be consideration neither of what is just nor unjust, neither what is compassionate nor cruel, neither what is praiseworthy nor ignominious; on the contrary, setting aside every other consideration, one must follow to the utmost that resolution which will save the life and maintain the liberty of the native land".[30] So the picture is complete. Political morality depends on prevailing circumstances: but in corrupt times a state of emergency is likely to be permanent; and in emergencies all means are legitimate for the good purpose of maintaining the integrity of the native land. The extension of *necessitas* could go no further; and it has not done so from Machiavelli's day to this.

That Machiavelli considered himself a realist in political matters, and that he was, indeed, a realist within a well-defined tradition—of which he represents the extreme statement—is evident. How realistic a realist he was, in more absolute terms, is another matter. In one respect he certainly qualifies for the title.

It is not possible to deny that political affairs have generally been managed, from the earliest times to the present day, in a "machia-vellian" fashion. Even the ancients had grown weary of men of affairs and statesmen, so called, staggering about from one ex-pedient to the next; perpetually overwhelmed by unforeseen circumstances; their energies absorbed in trying to outwit each other; deceiving the populace in whose name they rule; gaining office by promises they cannot fulfil; having no idea which course of many to adopt; and being engaged, for the most part, in no other activity than hanging on to power. Lies, hypocrisy, self-justification, vilification, and ruthlessness were universal. So they were in Machiavelli's day. And it is hard to escape the con-viction that contemporary experience would scarcely encourage him to change his mind on this matter.

On the other hand, Machiavelli's realistic vision of the political affairs of his own day was flawed by ideas impossible of realisation. We may dismiss the vision of a messianic warrior conjured up in *The Prince*, because, for Machiavelli himself, this was clearly only an academic possibility. The inconsistencies within the *Discourses* are more serious. Machiavelli's view of mankind is, in general, pessimistic. Yet he appears to believe that there are states in which civic rectitude and genuine patriotism can flourish. The German cities are a unique modern example; Sparta was an ancient one; and the Roman republic was the supreme instance in history. Ex-planations, consistent with pessimism, could have been found for the existence of such states; and in the *Discourses*, as elsewhere, Machiavelli does find them. Yet, thoughtlessly and emotionally, he assumes an unnecessary stance by arguing in favour of the government of the populace as against the rule either of the few nobles, or the single prince. The people, he says, are less ungrateful than princes; they are better judges of men's suitability for office; they are more prudent and stable; their voice "not without good reason" has been likened to the voice of God, since they can so readily discern the evil and the good which is to befall them; and, though they have less aptitude in the framing of laws than has the single great man, they are more able to sustain laws once formu-lated.[31] All this is patently at variance with what Machiavelli says elsewhere, and with his own experience. He is the victim, here, of enthusiasm. He is supposed to be arguing the superiority of the mixed constitution: that the healthy state will comprise regal and aristocratic, as well as popular, power. To place such a belligerent stress upon the superiority of the populace is to argue for democracy; and this Machiavelli could not have intended. He is, seemingly, incapable of maintaining a balanced position. He is so keen to be dynamic, so desirous of saying daringly different things, that he puts himself into a completely false position. The real limitations on Machiavelli's realism may be seen then, not so much in his general comments on political morality which are still depressingly apposite, but rather in faulty argumentation—often the result of enthusiasm—whereby he undermines his own conclusions by inconsistencies and implausibilities.

Machiavelli's best insight into the nature of government in the *Discourses* comes, not when he is concerned to exaggerate the merits of the populace—which he never believed in—but when he is discussing the ways in which a prince, taking over hostile territory, must deal with popular demands for the restoration of freedom.

> He will find that a small part of them wish to be free in order to rule; but all the others, who are numberless, desire liberty in order to live securely. Because in all republics, in whatever way they are constituted, there are never more than forty or fifty citizens who attain positions of authority [*gradi del comandare*]: and because this is a small number, it is easy to secure oneself against them either by doing away with them, or by giving them a share in such honours, according to their stations, that they are for the most part contented. Those others, for whom it is enough to live securely, are easily satisfied, by the making of institutions and laws wherein, together with his own power [that is, the prince], the general security is comprehended.[32]

The fact is, Machiavelli implies, that the majority of people do not decide anything; they do as they are told; unless they are directed, they can achieve nothing positive. He says as much elsewhere in the *Discourses* when stressing how useless is a multitude without a head: though here one is in difficulties over Machiavelli's terminology.[33] The *popolo* is not necessarily the same as *la moltitudine* and this, in turn, is often to be distinguished from *una moltitudine*. These are, qualitatively as well as socially, on a descending scale in Machiavelli's estimation. But, however these terms may be interpreted, the role assigned to the people in government, despite Machiavelli's inapposite eulogy, is insignificant. Real power is always in the hands of a few. It had been no different in ancient Rome.

It is important, none the less, to remember that the *Discourses* are not Machiavelli's last word either on republics, princedoms, the people, the multitude, or the mob. This honour belongs to the *Florentine History*, and here Machiavelli, dealing with the history of his own nation and his own city, is a good deal less sanguine about everything: there is no good government in contemporary Italy; and there is no element of *virtù* to be discovered in any extant social stratum. The last remnants of ancient spirit had disappeared with the extinction—by the mean-spirited, greedy, inept, and cowardly populace—of the old nobility. In ancient Rome the rivalry between nobility and people had been productive of great things; in Italy it had led only to faction, ruin, and corruption.[34] Neither *The Prince* nor the *Discourses* represent Machiavelli's truly realistic thinking about politics and history. They are marred by enthusiasm. So, too, is the *Art of War* which in some ways—despite its assertion that the security of states rests ultimately on force of arms—remains as Machiavelli's most idealistic and most conventional creation. It is in the *Florentine History* that Machiavelli's realism is starkest: not that the work is without errors and distortions of judgement and fact; but that Machiavelli's realisation of modern corruption is most complete and most hopeless. There are no more Cesare Borgias grotesquely garbed as failed messiahs; and no appeals to obviously inadequate and uninterested members of the Medici family, to restore health either to Italy or at least to Florence.

Instead we have the remote figure of Theodoric who is really but a variation on the theme of ancient *virtù*—this time in barbarian guise. And there is, too, Machiavelli's fantastic, and barely-substantiated, delineation of Michele di Lando, a humble wool-comber, who came to the fore during the insurrections of 1378. Michele is depicted as virtually the saviour of Florence: but it is only at this point that Machiavelli's yearning for a long-vanished civic spirit betrays him into romantic hero-worship. The weakness is, however, transient, and even helps to make the sequel more despairing. Michele receives his due reward from a grateful republic: he is banished, and passes once and for all from Machiavelli's narrative.[35] And thereafter Florence continues its degraded passage through time. Every party, every class, every group, has its own axe to grind. The whole story is one of short term expedients, evasion, dishonesty, and violence. All-destructive human ambition is rampant throughout the history. Necessity informs every action. There is no long-term planning; no vision by statesmen of creating a stable society; merely endless faction fighting and conspiracy.

The *Florentine History* is a fascinating but weary work, for in it we can see political expediency, as diagnosed by Machiavelli, operating without any of Machiavelli's own ideals for renovation. And probably the most bitter indictment of political activity, in all Machiavelli's writings, is to be found in this book. There is no passage stranger or blacker than the speech Machiavelli puts into the mouth of an anonymous leader of the plebs during the Florentine tumults of 1378. Years of party strife and class discontent had culminated in an outbreak of violence which gathered momentum throughout the summer. The mass of the workers, who had many genuine economic grievances, were exploited in disputes between parties: but, as Machiavelli says, "let no one initiate a revolution in a city in the belief that he can then stop it at his pleasure, or regulate it in his own way".[36] The violence quickly got out of hand and riots ensued. The discontent of the lower classes grew worse, now intensified by fear of retribution for the arson and robbery in which they had been involved. Nocturnal assemblies took place as the artisans debated the best mode of procedure; and here one of the most fiery and experienced tried to arouse his fellows by analysing, in grim language, their present predicament and their only possible course of action.[37]

If, he says, it were merely a question of deciding now whether or not to take up arms, rob and burn houses, and plunder churches, he would perhaps be of the opinion that it were better to prefer tranquil poverty to dangerous gain. But arms have already been taken up, evils have been perpetrated, so that their present consideration is not whether to lay arms aside but how to secure themselves from the consequences of their crimes: "I certainly believe that, when other things do not teach us, necessity may do so." All other classes and interests in the city are uniting against them, so that there seems only one course to be pursued: in order to be pardoned for their previous errors, they must commit new ones, doubling their sins, multiplying the acts of arson and robberies, and involving as many other people as possible in these deeds, for "where many err, no one is punished; little faults are punished, but great and serious ones are rewarded; and when many suffer, few seek vengeance, because general injuries are borne with more patience than private ones".

The speaker then turns from these immediate matters to more general social and moral issues. The advantages of increasing violence, he says, are certain; for their enemies are both disunited and rich; and "their disunity will give us victory, and their riches, when they become ours, will support us". As for antiquity of blood, he says, this should deceive no one; all men are equally ancient; and, stripped bare, all look the same. It is only poverty and riches which make any difference. Some, for reason of conscience, have repented what has been done and wish to refrain from further acts of violence; but these faint-hearts are to be condemned, for neither conscience nor infamy should frighten them:

Because those who conquer, in whatever way they do conquer, never incur shame for having done so. And of conscience we ought to take no account; because where there is—as in us—

fear of starvation and of imprisonment, one cannot and must
not have any fear of Hell. If you will but take note of the way
men proceed, you will see that all those who attain to great
riches and great power have done so either by fraud or by
force: and those things which they have usurped, either by
deceit or by violence, they make honest under the false title of
"profit", in order to conceal the ugliness of their acquisition.
And those who, either through scant prudence or too much
stupidity, shun these methods are always smothered in servitude and poverty; because faithful servants are always servants,
and good men are always poor; none ever escape from servitude other than the faithless and the bold, and none ever escape
from poverty but the rapacious and the fraudulent. God and
Nature have put all the fortunes of men in their midst; and these
are open more to theft than to industry, and more to bad than to
good arts; so it comes about that men devour one another, and
the less capable always come off worst. One ought, therefore,
to use force when opportunity offers; and no greater opportunity could be offered to us by Fortune, the citizens being
disunited, the Signory hesitant, the magistrates frightened; so
that they might easily be overcome before they unite and take
courage; whence either we shall become rulers of the whole
city, or have so great a part of it that not only past errors will be
forgiven us, but we shall have the power to threaten it with new
outrages. I admit that this course is bold and dangerous; but
where necessity forces us, boldness is deemed prudence, and in
great matters spirited men never take account of danger;
because enterprises commenced with danger are always finished
with reward, and one never escapes from a danger without
danger. Moreover, I believe—where one sees prepared prison,
torture, and death—that we should fear keeping quiet more
than trying to make ourselves secure; because in the first case
the evils are certain, and in the other they are doubtful. How
many times have I heard you complain of the avarice of your
superiors, and of the injustice of your magistrates! Now is the
time not only to free yourselves from them, but to become so
superior to them that they will have more to complain of and

fear from you, than you from them. The opportunity which is brought to us by the occasion is fleeting; and, when it has fled, one seeks to recapture it in vain. You see the preparations of your adversaries; let us anticipate their plans; and those of us who first take up arms will without doubt triumph, with the ruin of their enemy and with their own exaltation: and thus honour will result for many of us, and security for all.

This speech seems to me to be the most remarkable passage that Machiavelli ever wrote. And its historical context serves to heighten its effect. All the most extreme maxims of *The Prince* and of the *Discourses* are here, but with redoubled force, for now they are put into the mouth of a lowly worker who seems motivated solely by class interest; and there seems to be no question here of a state being created, or of some kind of spiritual regeneration. All we have is an attempt by one man to explain how his class might evade the consequences of their own violence, and gain both wealth and power at the expense of more favoured citizens. He preaches the most unashamed doctrine of necessity to be found anywhere in Machiavelli. His comments on human nature, on greed, ambition, and class exploitation are equally bitter. And it is all for self-preservation—not for the good of the state. But nothing is straightforward here, and the setting is typical of the *Florentine History*. It is totally ambiguous. The plebs are nowhere in the book accorded the least word of approval; they have, in this instance, just indulged themselves in an orgy of destruction and violence; and here they are being encouraged to commit further excesses. However, at the same time, we know that they have been exploited by the upper classes; that they have been duped by the Gonfalonier and others; and that they have been encouraged to perpetrate their crimes in the furtherance of party interests which, ultimately, can do them no good whatsoever. They are starving and desperate. Imprisonment, torture, and death are the likely fates for many; while increasing exploitation and misery is all that the future holds for the rest. What does it all mean?

François de Belleforest, the French historian and scholar,

included this speech amongst many others from the *Florentine History* in his monumental compilation, *Harangues militaires*, which was published at Paris in 1573: and his most significant marginal comment comes at that point when the orator claims that all who have acquired riches and power have done so through force and fraud. "This opinion", says Belleforest, "reveals well the humours of Machiavelli who has instructed a prince in tyranny, and beyond all scruple of conscience."[38] But this is not the point of Machiavelli's remark about force and fraud, nor is it the point of the speech as a whole. It is clear, from the nature and context of the oration, that Machiavelli is neither inviting our approval nor disapproval; neither our sympathy nor our disgust. Despite the hard aphorisms—concerning the force of necessity, the honour accorded to success however achieved, the pretences of the powerful, the hollowness of conventional piety, the relativity of virtue to circumstances, the danger of inaction, and the transience of opportunity—Machiavelli is not saying that people ought to behave in this way. He is saying —as the plebeian spokesman himself says at the beginning of his harangue—that this is how people do think and do act through force of circumstances. It is neither right nor wrong. It is inevitable. Necessity has its own laws.

8

Fortuna *and* Virtù

OF THE NUMEROUS antitheses and polarities in Machiavelli's
work, two are especially noteworthy—Fortune and *virtù*, *virtù*
and corruption—for between them they comprise the totality of
human experience. On the level of individual aspiration Machiavelli himself, in one of his more statistical moods, tells us that
Fortune is the arbiter of one half of our actions, but that she still
leaves us to direct "the other half, or thereabouts". With regard
to states, their life cycle, like man's, consists of birth, growth,
maturity, decay, and death; with a condition of *virtù* as their high
point and of corruption as their end. After corruption and dis-
solution the process could, theoretically, begin anew; though
generally it would already have been interrupted by some
extraordinary external force. The connection between the two
polarities is that individual *virtù* may react favourably on the
state; while a healthy state will both display a corporate *virtù*,
and encourage this quality in its citizens; and this, in turn, may
result in the favours of Fortune.

Most commentators have felt obliged to struggle with an interpretation of these terms, and the present chapter must needs add
to the "usual fog of words about the concepts of '*virtù*' and 'Fortuna'" so scathingly dismissed by Ridolfi in the preface to his *Life
of Machiavelli*. Ridolfi goes on to say that he has tried to write the
book he has always wanted to read (was there ever a scholar who
did not?), in which Machiavelli's own deeds and own words
"would speak for themselves".[1] One can only reply, in self-
justification, that *Fortuna* and *virtù* are among Machiavelli's own
words, and that they are employed with extraordinary frequency.

It may be possible to compose a narrative of Machiavelli's life without discussing these terms: it is impossible to avoid them when discussing his ideas.

"He who does not fear Fortune is not very wise." So wrote Lodovico il Moro, the man who, according to Machiavelli, had brought ruin upon his countrymen by inviting the French into Italy. He painted these words on the walls of his dungeon at Loches as he waited for death to release him from a hopeless bondage.[2] A thousand years earlier at Pavia, another prisoner, Boethius, wrote that a wise man should be no more troubled by adverse Fortune than a valiant captain should be dismayed by the noise of battle, for difficulties are but the means whereby the one may extend his glory, the other increase his wisdom: "for which cause *Virtus* is so called, because it hath sufficient strength to overcome adversity".[3] Lodovico the politician sickened and died in his cell, thoroughly humbled by Fortune. Boethius the philosopher was murdered in his dungeon, but Fortune allowed his *Consolation of Philosophy* to survive and be admired thereafter. In the last resort neither had been able to overcome the fickle goddess, who merely chose to humble the one and grant posthumous fame to the other. But their respective attitudes—either to accept the tyranny of Fortune with resignation, or to battle against her by the exercise of virtue—represent two general responses to the unpredictable, gratuitous, and irrational aspects of all human affairs which have remained constant throughout history. In March 1513 Machiavelli himself, luckier than Lodovico or Boethius, was released from prison, merely suffering from limbs dislocated by torture: and he, too, had a word to say about Fortune. He had turned his face to her and loved himself for his own bravery in bearing pain. More than that, he was determined to win her favour by his own efforts. The works which resulted from these efforts, Machiavelli's slow progress back to recognition, and the last treacherous blow administered to him by Fortune, we have already seen. But what more can we learn about this force, and about its apparent antithesis, *virtù*, which loom so large throughout his writings?

One thing is clear. It would be naïve to attempt a reconstruction

of any general theory held by Machiavelli on this subject—
because he had no such theory. Fortune and *virtù* occur in his
writings in as many guises as are possible for any pair of nouns.
They appear both as substantive and as metaphorical forces; they
are used colloquially and technically; they appear in trivial and in
portentous contexts. No neat and clear-cut solution can be reached
about them; and all that one can do is to examine some of the
most striking instances where these terms are employed, to
demonstrate how, in different ways, they were important for
Machiavelli.

Fortune in its simplest sense appears early in Machiavelli's
political writing. In September 1500, during his first mission to
France, Machiavelli and della Casa, suffering badly from lack of
funds, wrote to the Signory that they would "prefer to be at the
discretion of Fortune in Italy rather than in France".[4] More
significantly Fortune appears in Machiavelli's second mission to
Cesare Borgia, where he writes frequently concerning the Duke's
extraordinary fortune which served to maintain his government.[5]
In a letter dated 20 November 1502, Machiavelli reported how,
when under pressure from the Duke to commit Florence to an
engagement, he had pointed out that "good and ill fortune do not
always remain on the same side". And one year later, to the very
day, Machiavelli wrote from Rome regarding how the Duke's
former henchmen had deserted him, being unwilling to share
the evil fortune which had overtaken him.[6] At this point, in his
legations, Machiavelli regarded Cesare's fall as largely due to his
own blunders—an attitude maintained in the *Decennale Primo* of
1504: though subsequently, in *The Prince*, Cesare was to become
the victim of Fortune's malignity. In the *Decennale Primo*, Fortune
is represented simply as a rather perverse goddess able to dominate
men as the fancy takes her: she injures Florence wilfully; and she
chooses not to put an end to the Italian wars.[7] The oppressive
power of Fortune is already clear to Machiavelli: but he, as yet,
expresses it in simple terms. Greater complexity was to come with
the reversal of his own fortune in 1512; with the overthrow of the
republican régime which he had served so faithfully; and with the
restoration of the long-banished Medici.

Shortly before his imprisonment, Machiavelli had been ponder-ing, in his *Ghiribizzi*, the ways in which men's affairs vary, and had concluded that the reason for this was their inability to adapt to changing circumstances: a man who could understand the times and vary his actions accordingly could, he thought, always enjoy good Fortune. Unfortunately men cannot do this; and Fortune "varies and commands men and holds them under her yoke". Machiavelli discusses the same subject in similar vein, but at greater length, in an undated verse composition, the *Capitolo di Fortuna*.[8] Here he writes that many consider the goddess to be omnipotent because all men, sooner or later, feel her power. Her palace is filled with as many wheels as there are ways for men to fulfil their aspirations; but she is fickle and unstable, now aiding the wicked, now punishing the good, now turning kingdoms and states upside down, as the fancy takes her. Curiously, the more successful a man is the less gratitude he shows the goddess: all the evil that befalls man is attributed to her doing, whereas the good is always put down to his own virtue. Amongst all the throng in her palace, Audacity and Youth fare the best; but Fear lies impotent on the ground, while Punishment and Envy make war upon him. Opportunity [*l'Occasion*] alone takes its pleasure amongst the wheels, which are turned night and day by Sloth and Necessity—the former spoiling the world, the latter putting it once again in order.

There, within her palace, Fortune stores power, honour, riches, and health, to bestow upon those whom she fancies; and servi-tude, infamy, disease, and poverty, to inflict upon those whom she dislikes. The luckiest people are those who choose a wheel which happens to please her, because good and ill success depend upon whether your inclinations accord with Fortune. But even this cannot be relied upon, for suddenly she might reverse your wheel in mid-course and, because man cannot change his character or give up the disposition bestowed upon him by the heavens, he finds himself abandoned as the wheel revolves. Thus "a man who could leap from wheel to wheel" would always be happy: but this ability is denied by the secret power [*per occulta virtù*] which governs us, so that everything changes with its course. Nothing in the world is eternal for Fortune wills it so, in order that her power may the more easily be recognised. And in view of all this it is difficult to understand Machiavelli's next piece of advice that man should take Fortune "for his star", and, as far as is possible, should accommodate himself, every hour, to her variation. Since we are denied this power by Fortune herself, what is the point?

Machiavelli continues the poem with an interesting description of the historical paintings which adorn Fortune's palace, depicting her greatest triumphs. We see the greatness of the Egyptian kings; the Assyrians who with Fortune's aid supplanted them; then the Medes, followed by the Persians, the Greeks, and a succession of powerful states each of which was, in turn, overwhelmed: "here is shown how fine they were, how lofty, rich, and powerful; and how, in the end, Fortune gave them as prey to their enemies". The high and godlike deeds of the Roman Empire are also represented, and then "how the whole world was smashed to pieces with its ruin". Fortune is then likened to a rapid torrent which destroys everything; adding to this part, diminishing that; altering its banks and its bed; making the earth tremble as it passes; and overturning the affairs of the world with its furious onrush. Occasionally one might see, amidst these paintings in the palace, the deeds of an Alexander or Caesar, suggesting that Fortune is pleased with those who push and jostle her: but even of these, the former failed in his object, and the latter was slain by assassins. The whole series of paintings shows only that Fortune can raise men from humble origins, and then dash them down again—as an eagle may carry a tortoise, then drop it to the ground, so that the fall may smash open its shell. "We see, at last, that few men in days gone by, have been fortunate: and they were the ones who have died either before their wheel reversed itself or, in turning, has carried them to the bottom."

These verses constitute Machiavelli's fullest and most despondent view of the power of Fortune over human affairs, and they anticipate (or echo) many passages scattered throughout his writings. We see his belief that were man able to adapt himself sufficiently he could always be revolving on the right wheel at the right time: an idea adumbrated in the *Ghiribizzi*, reiterated in *The Prince*, and pessimistically set forth in the *Discourses*.

There are two reasons why we cannot change our ways: one is that we cannot oppose that to which Nature inclines us; the other is that, having prospered greatly with one method of procedure, a man cannot possibly be persuaded that he could do well by acting otherwise: whence it comes about that in one man Fortune varies, because she changes the times, and he does not change his ways. The ruin of cities likewise comes about through not altering the institutions of republics with the times . . . but they are slower [than individual men] because they have more trouble in changing, since it is necessary that the times should be such as move the whole republic; for this a single man, altering his own way of proceeding, is insufficient.[9]

The idea that men always blame Fortune for failure, but themselves appropriate all credit for success, is another which appears in the *Ghiribizzi* and in *The Prince* where the Italian magnates are said to have lost their territories, not through the fickleness of Fortune, but through their own sloth. And it occurs again in the *Florentine History*, when Machiavelli writes that Rinaldo degli Albizzi, finding his advice rejected after the exile of Cosimo de' Medici, imputed the misfortunes of his party to heaven itself, "rather than to the ignorance and blindness of men".[10]

The *Capitolo di Fortuna* also makes clear the relationship between Fortune and the process of political progress and decay, with a passing but significant reference to the activities of sloth and necessity. These are the two historical compulsions mentioned in *L'Asino*, *The Prince*, and, again, in the *Florentine History*: sloth causing debility and discord; necessity encouraging activity and *virtù*. Similarly, the triumphal paintings, showing the progress and translation of empires, is a striking analogue both to the historical sequence described in the introduction to the second book of the *Discourses*, where power passes from one empire to another; and to the historical account of *virtù* in the *Art of War*. All three sequences culminate with Rome; and end, with the fall of that empire, amidst confusion and ruin.

Noteworthy, too, is the likening of Fortune's activities to the onrush of a swollen torrent sweeping all before it. This is the simile employed in the twenty-fifth chapter of *The Prince*, where Machiavelli deals specifically with the power of Fortune over human affairs and how far men may withstand her: "I liken her to one of those destructive rivers which, when enraged, floods the plains, destroys trees and buildings, takes up the soil from one place and deposits it elsewhere; everybody flees before them, everybody yields to their onrush, without being able anywhere to withstand them". In *The Prince*, however, Machiavelli continues on a more optimistic note. Just as the effects of flood may be mitigated if men have prepared defences, barriers, and canals during fair weather, so Fortune demonstrates her power where *virtù* has not been ordained to resist her; turning her force in directions where embankments and dykes have not been raised to check her.

In the *Capitolo di Fortuna* there is nothing about such preparations which might enable man to cope with the power of Fortune. Yet there are hints both that Fortune is not omnipotent, and that her favour may be won by certain qualities. Amongst the varied crowd who throng her palace, the best showing is made by Audacity and Youth, whereas Fear takes a frightful beating and can accomplish nothing; while, in the painting, Alexander and Caesar are depicted as having enjoyed some success because Fortune likes those who "jostle, shove, and pursue her".[11] But most significant of all is an enigmatic tercet near the beginning of the poem: Fortune's natural power dominates every man, "and her reign is always violent if some yet greater *virtù* does not quell her" [*Se virtù eccessiva non l'ammorza*].[12] The possibility of triumphing over adversity is still left open: if only barely.

One of the principal difficulties posed by Machiavelli is that terms such as Fortune and *virtù* have such extended and multiform meanings. He never makes up his mind, even within one short work, either on the exact nature of Fortune, or the extent of its power. Sometimes the word represents little more than sheer chance, even though, on other occasions, Machiavelli will use the more exact words *caso* or *sorte*.[13] Sometimes Fortune is depicted as an elemental force—the flood which either sweeps all before it, as in the *Capitolo di Fortuna*, or which may be partly controlled, as in *The Prince*. Sometimes she is personified as a pagan goddess who ruthlessly wields her power, and deliberately makes or breaks men in order to demonstrate her supremacy. It is for this reason, writes Machiavelli, that many of those who have performed great deeds in this world have sprung from humble origins, because Fortune wishes "to show to the world that it is she who makes men great, not prudence". So she demonstrates her power at that time in their lives when prudence cannot possibly have any significance. The brilliant career of Castruccio Castracani exemplifies this aspect of Fortune; while her perversity is manifested by Castruccio's end when, on the brink of total success, his life was taken from him by Fortune who had been "growing envious of his glory".[14]

On other occasions, however, Machiavelli is less pessimistic, and depicts Fortune as susceptible to persuasion or to human influence. The most famous instance of this is again in the twenty-fifth chapter of *The Prince*, where Machiavelli develops an idea, also alluded to in the *Capitolo*, concerning the success possible for audacity, youth, and activity. The chapter begins, as we have seen, with the metaphor of the flood. It continues by arguing that people attain success by different methods according to the nature of the times, and that men very rarely have the ability to change their mode of behaviour to suit changing circumstances. The example of Pope Julius II is taken to demonstrate how his impetuosity, being in accord with the times, led to success. But, stresses Machiavelli, had circumstances arisen necessitating caution rather than impetuosity, Julius would have been ruined. So Machiavelli concludes by reiterating his thesis that Fortune is changeable and men steadfast, so that the latter are only successful when their predominant characteristics are in tune with the times. Then, as a kind of tailpiece he adds that:

it is better to be impetuous than cautious, because Fortune is a woman, and it is necessary if you wish to keep her under, to beat her and knock her about. And it is seen that she lets herself be overcome more by these methods than by those men who go about it more coldly: and, therefore, like a woman, she is the friend of young men, because they are less cautious, more savage, and command her with more audacity.

This, in its way, is a perfect example of a wandering argument in which Machiavelli is carried away by changing metaphor and by his failure to attach any precise meaning to his favourite words. It could, of course, be argued that, psychologically, such imprecision is more faithful to the realities of human experience than any more careful definition could ever be. Clearly, it is true that Fortune is sometimes like a flood; that sometimes one can prepare for unforeseen eventualities by prudent preparation; that varying circumstances do necessitate flexible behaviour; and that, perhaps, on the whole, daring might be more efficacious than caution. As a general emotional response to the vagaries of Fortune, this chapter might be deemed artistically satisfying. On the other hand it does wander: and this is not merely on the level of metaphor. Once again we have a typical Machiavellian disjunction. There are, surely, more ways of responding to circumstances than either impetuosity or caution. And bold, decisive action—which is really what is required by many of the dire political problems envisaged by Machiavelli—is neither the same as impetuosity, nor is it irreconcilable with caution. To plunge into danger without calculating the risks involved is, in fact, playing into Fortune's hands. Such temerity is merely trusting to luck: it is an abdication of human responsibility for action, and cannot legitimately be regarded as an exercise of *virtù*.

There is, however, a more general reason which induced Machiavelli to end his twenty-fifth chapter on a positive note. Were Fortune not susceptible to bold human activity, the whole point of *The Prince* would be lost, for it is Machiavelli's contention that, here and now, an Italian leader could be effective. However, in the final chapter, which is concerned to inspire the prince with the zeal requisite for driving barbarian invaders from Italy, Fortune undergoes an even more curious metamorphosis than hitherto. Machiavelli takes up a point made earlier, when Moses, Cyrus, Romulus, and Theseus were cited as leaders who owed the greater part of their achievements to *virtù*, while owing to Fortune nothing but opportunity. Now at the end of *The Prince* Machiavelli maintains that the abject condition of the children of Israel, of the Persians, and of the Athenians had been "necessary" in order that the *virtù* of Moses, Cyrus, and Theseus, might be revealed; just as the even greater degradation of Italy is "necessary" so that *virtù* of an Italian spirit might be discovered. Both Opportunity and Necessity had been active within the palace of Fortune; and the idea that Necessity acts as a spur to *virtù* is one of the more constant of Machiavelli's themes with, as we have seen, devastating implications for conventional morality. But an extraordinary change now comes over the text of *The Prince*. Without warning, we leave the pagan portals of the goddess Fortune and find ourselves faced with an arcane allusion to some leader who, though unnamed, is evidently Cesare Borgia, whose activities had been such as to make the Italians think that he was sent by God for their "redemption". This, indeed, is a divine epiphany; and God now strides about confidently as Machiavelli waxes less and less coherent and more and more messianic. Italy, he says, "pleads with God that he might send someone who will redeem her from this cruelty and these barbarous insolences". In whom could Italy place more hope than in the house of the Medici who have both *virtù* and Fortune, as well as the favour of God and the Church? Only consider the actions of the great leaders just named: true, they were all marvellous men; "nevertheless they *were* men, and each of them had less opportunity than the present, because their enterprise was no more just than this, nor easier, and God was no more a friend to them than to you". Machiavelli now quotes Livy to the effect that a necessary war is a just war, and that arms are holy when there is no other hope but in arms. Italy is ready and willing to follow. Moreover:

extraordinary things, beyond example, have been brought about by God: the sea has divided; a cloud has shown you the way; the rock has poured forth water; it has rained manna; everything has concurred in your greatness; the rest you must do yourself. God does not wish to do everything, in order not to take from us free will [*libero arbitrio*] and part of that glory which belongs to us.

God had last performed this particular set of miracles for the benefit of Moses himself; and the juxtaposition of Livy and *Exodus* to encourage the Medici is one of Machiavelli's most delightful inspirations. But it doesn't help clarify his argument.

Fortune, it will be seen, is still mentioned—with *virtù*—as an attribute of the Medici who are favoured by God and the Church. But God has usurped the major role of Fortune. It is now God who shows favour; God who gives opportunity; and it is, above all, God—not Fortune—who leaves something for men to do for themselves. This, presumably, can only be the same "half, or thereabouts" which, in the twenty-fifth chapter, had been left to men by Fortune also in order not to extinguish completely man's "*libero arbitrio*". Now God, like Fortune, is unwilling to take away man's "*libero arbitrio*": and this should surely be read as "free will"—not as the "free choice" favoured by some critics. Machiavelli, paying the penalty for slipshod thinking, lax terminology, and passion, has slipped from a conventional and inadequate personification of the fickle goddess Fortune into an equally conventional and inadequate personification of God. In one sense the slip is understandable, since both are equally undefined, and have been allotted similar functions. But it indicates, once again, Machiavelli's failure to control metaphor.

In general terms, however, one may say this: that, for Machiavelli, Fortune usually represents that part of human affairs where men's own efforts prove either of little or no avail: where, either through the operation of sheer chance, or providence, or God himself, the most carefully-laid plans may be upset by accidents, sudden illnesses, death, and an infinitude of unpredictable circumstances. Nevertheless, Machiavelli recognises that the world is not quite total chaos; that there is sufficient consistency in human affairs to make plans and activity worthwhile; that it is not beyond reason to assume that circumstances may develop along certain lines rather than along others; that accidents do not happen all the time to everybody; or, at the very least, that fortuitous occurrences are not always so dire that plans are perpetually void. It is possible, therefore, to work towards a preconceived end which, if circumstances do not change completely, may even be attained. Machiavelli's observation of politics had suggested this: and it had been confirmed by the study of history, where Machiavelli felt able to discern recurring patterns of behaviour and political change. There is a sphere in politics, as in all human life, where effort may be effective. People in the past had determined the course of events by the exercise of that mysterious quality, virtù, the only positive factor in human affairs.

The idea that Fortune, whether as a personification or abstraction, might be tamed or at least won over by certain positive human qualities had its origins in antiquity. That bravery or daring might win Fortune's favour was a commonplace in Rome; and Terence, Virgil, Livy, and Seneca, all used this expression almost proverbially.[15] A more subtle argument may be found in Cicero's Paradoxes, where only the wise man is said to be free, while every fool is a slave; for the wise man, acting righteously, fulfilling his civic duties, and acting according to judgement and reason rather than passion, may be deemed master of Fortune herself. Plutarch was even more critical of Fortune and argued for the predominating influence of wisdom in human affairs: for if wisdom were to be attributed to Fortune "let us ascribe justice and sobriety to Fortune also, aye, and let us put down to Fortune stealing and picking pockets and lewdness, and let us bid farewell to argument, and throw ourselves entirely on Fortune, as if we were, like dust or refuse, borne along and hurried away by a violent wind". Juvenal, too, asserted that man fashions his own Fortune, for Virtus leads him to a life of peace: "if we have wise foresight, thou Fortune, hast no divinity: it is we that make thee a deity, and place thy throne in heaven". These are the ideas which we find also in Claudian for whom Virtus "mocks at Fortune"; and again in Boethius where Virtus, gentle and contemplative, may enable man to frame for himself whatever Fortune he pleases.[16]

In the Middle Ages and the Renaissance, the notion that it is possible for man to dominate at least part of his fate, and that he should certainly not sit down under adversity, was almost as widely accepted as the rigid fatalism to which it was opposed. Sometimes, as with Dante, the idea has political connotations. He suggests that human failure and, in particular, the corruption of Florence was due to each man's natural aptitude being out of step with his Fortune.[17] This is very akin to Machiavelli's view that were men sufficiently adaptable they might enjoy continual success; though Dante's attitude is less flexible and personal than Machiavelli's. It belongs more to the tradition wherein everything has its preordained place; where misfortune results from upsetting the system; and where a wise universal monarch may instruct and guide his subjects so that they find themselves in the right position at the right time. Petrarch, in a more contemplative, and less dynamic, vein, devoted a whole treatise—along the lines indicated by Cicero and Plutarch—to the argument that the dominion of Fortune may be overcome through the exercise of virtue.[18] For Leon Battista Alberti *virtù*, while retaining the moral implications of earlier writers, also embodies ideas of strength as well as wisdom in its successful combat with Fortune.[19] That the whole idea was becoming a cliché is shown by Bembo's unoriginal and immensely popular *Gli Asolani*, where he expresses his view that a properly educated man should rather trample evil fortune underfoot and make a jest of its games, than submit basely to its whims, "weeping and complaining like a well-spanked little boy". Even if he has not learned how to defend himself from a woman's blows—"for Fortune seems to be a woman if we are to believe the gender of the word itself"—it would be far more in accord with man's freedom to admit his own weakness rather than put the blame for his failings upon another.[20]

More apposite still are the ideas expressed in a play performed at Rome, on 2 January 1501, as part of the entertainments for the marriage between Lucrezia Borgia and Alphonso d'Este, son of Ercole, Duke of Ferrara.

First appeared a boy in woman's clothes who represented

virtù, and another in the character of Fortune. They began to banter each other as to which was the mightier, whereupon Fame suddenly appeared standing on a globe, which rested on a float, upon which were the words, "Gloria Domus Borgiae". Fame, who also called himself Light, awarded virtù the prize over Fortune, saying that Cesare and Ercole (Caesar and Hercules) by virtù had overcome Fortune; thereupon he described a number of the heroic deeds performed by the illustrious Duke of Romagna. Hercules with the lion's skin and club appeared, and Juno sent Fortune to attack him. Hercules, however, overcame Fortune, seized her, and chained her; whereupon Juno begged him to free her, and he, gracious and generous, consented to grant Juno's request on the condition that she would never do anything which might injure the house of Ercole or that of Cesare Borgia. To this she agreed, and, in addition, she promised to bless the union of the two houses.[21]

The importance of this entertainment is obvious. Virtù has shed all its contemplative connotations and its association with moral virtues. It even transcends the classical proverb that Fortune favours the brave. Now virtù is simply military prowess and strength of arms: the activist qualities which Machiavelli was to praise in The Prince, as being able not merely to help man agree with Fortune but rather to dominate her. Virtù earns, for those who possess her, the light of fame: and she overcomes Fortune, forcing her to promise future favours. And, finally, one of the heroes, whose virtù had triumphed, is that very Cesare Borgia soon to impress Machiavelli, on first acquaintance, as a very splendid and magnificent prince:

in war he is so bold that there is no great enterprise that does not seem small to him, and to gain glory and territory he never rests or knows danger or weariness: he arrives at a place before anyone has heard that he has left the place he was in before: he wins the love of his soldiers, and has got hold of the best men in Italy. These things make him victorious and formidable, and are attended with invariable good fortune.[22]

Subsequently, as we know, Cesare dwindled in Machiavelli's estimation: only to grow even greater, as the Florentine pondered upon the qualities which might enable a man to achieve political success.

As one would expect, since Fortune itself is manifested in an almost infinite variety of circumstances, so the human qualities requisite for meeting her demands are similarly varied; and Machiavelli complicates matters by using only one word to indicate the entire spectrum of effective human behaviour. Moreover, though separating private from public morality, he employs the same word to indicate what he regards as correct behaviour in either sphere.

Virtù may indicate conventional moral virtues: either set in opposition to vices such as gluttony or dissipation; or being used to indicate a traditional virtue such as prudence.[23] More dramatically, it may stand for qualities—piety, humanity, charity, good faith—which would lead to political disaster; as the virtues which, in certain pressing circumstances, become vices. It may be equated with the civic *Virtus* of the Romans—the quality which led ancient generals, citizens, and legislators, to "wear themselves out on behalf of their fatherland"; or it may even be equated with the Christian virtue of fortitude, enabling a warrior to bear hardship honourably.[24] Sometimes, *virtù* is associated with goodness, as in Machiavelli's characterisations of Pope Leo X, Theodoric, and Piero de' Medici; or as in Michele di Lando's "courage, prudence, and goodness".[25] And, on one occasion at least, we find Machiavelli thinking about the relationship between Fortune and *virtù* in terms which would have been acceptable to Cicero, Plutarch, and Boethius himself. This passage is prompted by Camillus's words, "the dictatorship did not elate my spirits, nor did exile depress them". From this Machiavelli concludes:

> that great men are always the same in every Fortune; and if it varies, now raising them up, now oppressing them, these men do not change, but always hold their minds firm, and so conjoined to their mode of life, that one can easily recognise that in each case Fortune has no power over them. Weak men

govern themselves otherwise; because they grow vain and are intoxicated in good Fortune, attributing all the good that they have to that *virtù* which they have never evinced. Whence it comes about that they grow insupportable and hateful to all around them. Whence comes about the sudden alteration in their lot; and when they look it in the face, they fall into the other defect, and become cowardly and abject.

Machiavelli then transposes from the personal to more political vein. Rome is his example of a state which neither lost courage in defeat, nor became arrogant in victory; and Venice is an illustration of the exact opposite—a state which attributed its successes to *virtù* but collapsed through its own pusillanimity and incompetence as soon as "good luck" deserted it.[26]

Generally, however, *virtù* for Machiavelli does not imply conventional ethical values: though its traditional moral overtones lead him into one dialectical disaster. This is in the seventh chapter of *The Prince*, where he describes the sinister career of Agathocles, tyrant of Sicily. Machiavelli, having discussed princedoms obtained either by *virtù* or Fortune, invents a category whereby political success is attributable to neither. The category is wickedness [*sceleratezza*]: and he cites Agathocles as a man who, whatever the vicissitudes of Fortune, led a thoroughly evil life. Yet "he accompanied his villainies with such *virtù* of mind and body, that, devoting himself to the military profession, he rose through its ranks to be Praetor of Syracuse". Here, *virtù* seems to mean nothing other than outstanding ability and strength. It is divorced from all moral connotations. But the chapter is, allegedly, devoted to rulers who have come to power neither through Fortune nor *virtù*: and, sure enough, Machiavelli pursues this distinction, though it leads him into difficulties.

It cannot be called *virtù* to kill fellow citizens, to betray friends, to be without faith, without pity, without religion; such methods may gain empire, but not glory. Because, if one considers the *virtù* of Agathocles in entering into and extricating himself from dangers, and the greatness of his courage in supporting and overcoming adversity, one cannot see how he can be judged inferior to any most excellent captain; nevertheless, his savage cruelty and inhumanity, with infinite villainies, do not permit that he should be celebrated amongst the most excellent men. One cannot, then, attribute to Fortune or to *virtù* what was achieved by him without the one or the other.

We are well and truly in the toils of terminological debility. Nothing more clearly illustrates the danger of using one word to indicate several different, and even contradictory, qualities: and we struggle with Agathocles's "*virtù* of mind and body", which raised him to power but cannot be properly termed *virtù*, because *virtù*, accompanied by such cruelty, is really not *virtù*. Of course one can disentangle Machiavelli's meaning from all this, but the attempt to retain a moral implication for the word *virtù*, and the exclusion of Agathocles from the ranks of *virtuosi*, is both discrepant and arbitrary. It is all the more arbitrary in that it follows a chapter devoted principally to Cesare Borgia who was unable to triumph over the malignity of Fortune, despite extreme personal *virtù* consisting precisely in fraud, cold-blooded murder, and the ruthless and bloody sacrifice of his officer, Ramiro d'Orco, to placate public opinion. It is quite impossible to distinguish between Cesare and Agathocles, or, for that matter, Oliverotto da Fermo whose villainies are also regarded by Machiavelli as beyond *virtù*. The futility of this attempt to define *virtù* as superior military ability, and organising capacity, without evil overtones is heightened by the subsequent discussion of Hannibal who owed his successes to nothing other than his "inhuman cruelty which, together with his infinite *virtù*, made him always revered and terrible in the sight of his soldiers, and without which his other *virtù* would have been insufficient for this effect". On the whole, the attempt to associate the kind of *virtù*, which Machiavelli especially admires and recognises as politically effective, with more conventional ethical values is a failure. Artistically, the eighth chapter of *The Prince* is an excrescence which, unconvincing in itself, also vitiates the effect of Machiavelli's subsequent turning upside-down of conventional virtues, and his creation of a new political morality.

For Machiavelli the most usual meaning associated with the word, *virtù*, is one which, though now rarely encountered, was once current in English: the idea of strength, efficiency, power, or efficacy in particular circumstances for particular purposes. Thus an artist like Brunelleschi may be commemorated in Florence by a statue bearing testimony to his *virtù*: in other words to his outstanding artistic skill.[27] We may be told that the *virtù* of the Parthians—that is their special skill and strongpoint —lay in their archers.[28] We read that, under the Decemvirate, the Roman armies had the same *virtù* as previously, yet lacked the good spirit of earlier times; that the Latins had such a love for liberty that they could only be subjugated by a superior *virtù*; that a tyrant might have such *virtù*, being energetic and proficient in war, that he would be bound to enlarge his dominions; and that in certain states *virtù* lies in wealth and not in soldiers; while, in the *Capitolo di Fortuna*, Fortune herself becomes identified with the "secret *virtù*" which governs human affairs.[29]

Sometimes, moral virtues are explicitly excluded by the context, as, for example, in the brief account given in the *Florentine History* of Sixtus IV who, from humble origins, became Pope by his own *virtù*: "and this was the first pontiff who began to show how much a Pope could do, and how many things previously called sins could be hidden under papal authority".[30] A succession of frauds, broken promises, and murders, all went into the making of Castruccio Castracani's *virtù*: and his career also constitutes a striking statement of the bizarre equation underlying so much of the *Art of War* and the *Florentine History*: that plenty of bloodshed in battle equals *virtù*. But the clearest evidence that the distinction between *virtù* and wickedness is false lies in Machiavelli's frequent comparison between Scipio and Hannibal. This fascinated him as an instance of the way in which diametrically opposed methods might each achieve military success. Scipio was a commander who made himself loved for his "mercy, loyalty, and piety". Hannibal was feared for his "cruelty, treachery, and lack of religion". Yet both had *virtù* to a superlative degree. In these circumstances *virtù* can only be defined as the outstanding ability—moral or immoral, good or bad—requisite for success in determinate circumstances; and it is a quality which affects public affairs rather than private relationships.

The fact that Machiavelli's best examples of individual *virtù* —Castruccio himself in the *Life of Castruccio Castracani*; Cesare Borgia in *The Prince*; Alexander and Caesar in the *Capitolo di Fortuna*; and Hannibal and Scipio in the *Ghiribizzi*, *The Prince*, and the *Discourses*—all came to untimely ends is nevertheless indicative that Fortune always has the last word. Machiavelli sometimes realises the dangers to which such determinism could lead. How would it be possible to discover any rules for conduct, if everything must end up according to some arbitrary whim of Fortune?

This is, of course, the eternal difficulty of determinism, whether it be predestinarian or historicist, and Machiavelli only occasionally comes near to grappling with the problem. When he does, his answer is similar to that of many another thinker striving to maintain the validity of human action within a preordained divine pattern: men, though unable to oppose Fortune, may second her. Not knowing how things may turn out, they must carry on in hope, whatever Fortune may bring them.[31] Men struggle, therefore, because they do not know what is in store for them. Psychologically this makes sense: but it negates serious responsibility on the part of any individual or of any polity for its condition, good or bad. And it nullifies the exhortation uttered by Machiavelli in the very next chapter where he stresses the difference between modern and ancient republics. Every day, he says, one may see astonishing losses and gains, for, where men have little *virtù*, Fortune makes great show of its power: "and since Fortune is changeable, republics and states frequently change; and they always will change, till someone arises who is such a lover of antiquity that he regulates her so that she has no reason to demonstrate, at every revolution of the sun, how much she can do".[32] The problem remains: if Fortune does whatever she wishes, whenever she wishes, how can man take any initiative in seconding her, and how will the imitation of antiquity, or anything else, minimise her supreme power?

In trying to establish the meanings attached by Machiavelli to *virtù* and Fortune, one is not merely faced with inconsistencies but is also oppressed with the sense of proceeding in ever diminishing circles. Machiavelli, following Polybius, regards Rome as conclusive proof that *virtù* may lead to Fortune: for Roman success was due not to Fortune but to a sound constitution, good military institutions, and strong civic spirit. Like Polybius, Machiavelli becomes involved, without realising it, in a complex of unresolved difficulties due to the inadequacy of his analytical technique, to the limitations of his political vocabulary, and especially to his failure to define frequently-used terms. Fortune is very comprehensive; but what of Necessity which serves in Fortune's palace?

In *L'Asino*, Necessity appears as an alternative to *virtù* itself: it is one of the forces which encourages kingdoms to rise to greatness. In the *Capitolo di Fortuna*, it is even more important, putting the world in order when Sloth has ruined everything. At the very outset of the *Discourses* Machiavelli poses one of his fundamental antitheses: men work either through necessity or through choice; and where there is less choice so there is greater *virtù*.[33] Necessity is, in fact, the principal driving force in Machiavelli's view of political and military activity: people only do good through necessity; they only obey the laws and work together through necessity; princes only observe treaties through necessity and, as we have seen, they break them through necessity, too. People, driven by necessity, are very formidable in war; and "necessity makes *virtù*, as we have often said". Necessity, Machiavelli stresses, plays a vital part in human affairs and leads men to glory; "as some moral philosophers have written, man's hands and tongue—two most noble instruments for ennobling him—would not have worked perfectly, nor brought human activities to the height one can see they have reached had they not been driven forward by necessity". The ancient military commanders, says Machiavelli, recognised the *virtù* of necessity and the extent to which it made troops obstinate in battle; and he cites Livy to the effect that though two armies were equal in *virtù*, one had the advantage through being constrained by necessity, "the last and best of all weapons".[34]

Clearly, then, necessity stands in very close relationship to *virtù*; it encourages or even engenders it. On the other hand, *virtù* is merely a quality of limited efficacy. A ruler displays *virtù* when he recognises that it is "necessary" to do evil deeds to maintain his state, and acts accordingly; or when he finds it "necessary" to have recourse to the bestial mode of combat, and does so. It is "necessary to be a fox to discover snares, and a lion to terrify wolves"; though it is also "necessary" to disguise this characteristic. It is "unnecessary" to have the moral virtues; but "very necessary to seem to have them". The ruler may be forced, in order to maintain his state, into actions contrary to faith, charity, humanity, and religion, but he must needs have a mind disposed to turn according to the command of the whims and the variations of Fortune, and, when so "necessitated", to do evil. And of all the qualities conventionally regarded as virtues, there is nothing "more necessary" than to appear religious. Necessity is, as we have seen, the foundation of Machiavelli's realism, and of the perverse virtues which make up the new political *virtù*. But this *virtù* is only manifested in terms of an effective response to such necessity. Even on the level of great states we are going round in circles: Rome's greatness was due to *virtù* not Fortune, because its civil and military organisation was such that, in the circumstances, it was bound to lead to success. Necessity leads to *virtù*; *virtù* leads to favourable Fortune; favourable Fortune provides opportunities; Necessity demands that opportunities be seized because they are only fleeting; *virtù* is requisite if one is to seize an opportunity; and opportunity when taken results in success. But in the last resort Fortune may step in at any time and kill the most brilliant leader, or ruin the greatest state.

We can go round in an endless series of incompatibilities because Machiavelli never makes a serious attempt to define his terms. His polarities are rarely true polarities. His precision is only seeming, not actual. Fortune is merely the totality of inexplicable forces operating on human affairs; necessity is a more immediate manifestation of these forces; and *virtù* too easily becomes a label which Machiavelli sticks on to any quality which is politically effective, and of which he therefore approves. They are not categories of marked usefulness in the description and analysis of complex political activity: but Machiavelli prefers to keep his most important conceptions on the level of metaphor which might as easily change according to the dictates of emotion, or literary effect, as to the requirements of consecutive argument.

Machiavelli's was not a truly analytical mind. His responses both to the dominion held by Fortune over human affairs, and to the strength of mind and body displayed by some very few great men, were intuitive. Deeply moved by his experiences and observations, Machiavelli wrote what he felt; and his appeal, under the guise of intellectual analysis, is really to the emotions. He was like that to the very end of his life; and among the last of his official writings is a letter to the Signory, reporting on the progress of military preparations to cope with the impending Imperial onslaught:

> it is said that men ought to make *virtù* of necessity; but if to *virtù* necessity be added, it comes about that *virtù* greatly increases, and becomes insuperable. Your Lordships and this city, with *virtù* alone, have up to now defended and saved Lombardy and the Romagna: it is impossible that now, necessity being added to *virtù*, you should not save yourselves.[35]

In the event, the Florentine government collapsed for, though the necessity was dire, the *virtù* was not forthcoming. Machiavelli knew that this would be so: but he desperately wished it otherwise. And—since we are moving here in a world of sententious maxims—one might say that, though necessity might be the mother of *virtù*, in Machiavelli's case the wish was father to the thought.

9

Method

OF ALL THE topics most commonly debated by students of
Machiavelli, those concerning his morality, method, and style,
have generally been deemed the most significant. Already in the
sixteenth century one may find references to each of these features
of his work: though, of course, the emphasis given to each aspect
has varied with the times and the principal preoccupations of the
age. Early discussion of Machiavelli centred more on morality
than on anything else. A little later matters of method came to be
seriously discussed; while admiration for purely literary qualities
is a more modern phenomenon. Machiavelli was well aware that
he was going to cause trouble by making necessity so necessary
to subsequent political thinkers: and his deliberate attempt to
transvaluate all political values has, justifiably, provided fuel for
debate ever since. However, he deemed this question of morality
but a corollary to his fundamental purpose which was the con-
struction of a new two-way method involving the reading of
history for practical lessons in politics, and the practising of
politics according to precepts gained by reading history. This was,
in Machiavelli's own view, his great gift to contemporaries and to
posterity; and it has certainly attracted the attention of serious
commentators. However, it is doubtful whether either his
challenging maxims or his historical method would have continued to attract the attention of modern readers were it not for
his brilliant prose style. For Machiavelli was not a systematic
thinker; nor, as I have tried to argue, was he an especially original
one as far as his material or ostensible methods were concerned.
But he was an artist of the highest order, both in his use of

language and in his imaginative adaptation of conventional themes and forms to say dramatic, startling, and arresting things; and, intuitively, to summarise in a few words some disturbing psychological or political insight.

The debate on his morality, amorality, or immorality, continues unabated. Discussion concerning the historical method, and the attempt to arrive at political truth by inductive reasoning, is still largely unresolved. But on Machiavelli's qualities as a prose writer there is general agreement. Everybody says that he was a great literary stylist, and many believe him to be the greatest Italian prose writer of all time. That it is still an exciting experience to read Machiavelli—and that he is especially refreshing to return to after a dusty trudge back into fifteenth-century treatises on the duties of kingship, or forwards into the theology-dominated political squabbles of the sixteenth and seventeenth centuries—is undeniable. The general acceptance of Machiavelli as one of the world's greatest writers makes it especially difficult to raise a dissenting voice. But it seems to me that—whatever the literary merits of Machiavelli's style—as a vehicle for the conveying of ideas and, more to the point, for presenting arguments about ideas, that style is not flawless. As Machiavelli himself says, "it seems that in the actions of man . . . bad should always be associated with good, and it so easily grows up with that good that it seems impossible to avoid the one while wanting the other".[1] And, ironically, the features which, above all else, give his prose its power and impact, are those which most devastatingly undermine not merely the presentation of his arguments but the very nature of his thought. Machiavelli is a very fine writer. The price for this gift to posterity is some very poor thinking.

When the word *method* is mentioned in connection with Machiavelli, one's mind immediately reverts to those belligerent and optimistic statements, set at salient points in all his major works. He will write of things as they are, not as they ought to be: he will use his years of practical experience, and his wide reading of affairs both ancient and modern, to discover permanently valid truths; history remains fundamentally the same, for men's passions are the same: we can learn rules for modern political conduct from the juxtaposition of ancient and modern *exempla*. This is supposed to be Machiavelli's new *method*, his "untrodden path". He says so himself: frequently. But it was not new: his own use of the technique was not methodical; and, properly speaking, it does not constitute Machiavelli's method at all.

That the idea of using history as a fund of material from which to draw forth supposedly practical lessons was not original to Machiavelli should hardly need demonstration. It was common throughout the Middle Ages, the Renaissance, and comparatively recent times: indeed, there are some political philosophies which still employ this method. It was already archaic in Machiavelli's time, and Guicciardini's comment on such attitudes is as fresh now as the day he scribbled in his *Ricordi*: "How mistaken are those who quote the Romans at every step. One would have to have a city with exactly the same conditions as theirs and then act according to their example. That model is as unsuitable for those lacking the right qualities as it would be useless to expect an ass to run like a horse".[2] Similarly, systematic comparison between past and present was a technique widely employed, especially by Italian propagandists in the fifteenth century: and that it had a wider European currency may be seen from the work of Philippe de Commines whose *Mémoires*, written late in the fifteenth century, embody the general conception that both history and experience are of value to the practising politician. In military writing, too, the technique of garnishing the bare bones of Vegetius and Frontinus with present-day experience, culled from practising soldiers, may be seen exemplified in Christine de Pisan and other theorists long prior to Machiavelli. But this kind of discussion is hardly worthwhile. More to the point is to examine the connection between Machiavelli's style and his thought; and to study the principal modes of argument which properly constitute his method.

A great writer's style is compounded of many ingredients, and their full comprehension requires a meticulously detailed and subtle analysis. However, in so far as they affect Machiavelli's political and historical thought, the principal features of his prose are easily distinguished. One characteristic, his rigidly sequential

mode of presenting an argument, has been alluded to in connection with the *Florentine History*; and here it is only necessary to
emphasise that Machiavelli's favourite constructions begin with
because, or some similar conjunction—*thus, for, therefore, whence,*
and *hence*—and that these constructions mirror his clear-cut view
of historical causation.[3] Numa's religious foundations led to good
institutions; good institutions to good fortune; and good fortune
to Rome's continued successes. Where there are good soldiers
there is good government; and good government means good
fortune. States always go from good to bad, and from bad to
good: because *virtù* brings forth tranquillity; tranquillity, laziness; laziness, disorder; disorder, ruin; ruin, order; order, *virtù*;
virtù, glory and good fortune. And so it goes on. For Machiavelli
history moves in recurrent patterns. With sufficient study one
may amass the data requisite for prophecy: for things always
happen *because* and *thus*.

Another aspect of Machiavelli's writing which, though important, admits of little comment, is the fondness for aphorisms
which he shared with many of his contemporaries. Aphoristic
style has always been common among political theorists and
philosophers: but it was particularly cherished in the Renaissance
—an age which delighted in epigrams and witty conceits; in the
bringing to light of ancient wisdom compressed within classical
inscriptions; and in solving the allusive mysteries of visual imagery
and hieroglyphics. There is a peculiar attraction in the pithy
sentence which conveys an idea in the minimum space with
maximum effect: and Machiavelli was very good at writing
them. However, such facility has its drawbacks. The "truths"
may not follow from the evidence on which they are based;
they may be more "effective" than accurate; and because they are
striking, they may give undue prominence to an idea felicitously
expressed, but ill-conceived. The aphorism, by its nature, tends
to favour the more extraordinary notion, especially one which
depends on unlikely juxtaposition. It works best when extreme.
And this quality is particularly marked in Machiavelli.

Long ago, Burd, in his introduction to *The Prince*, criticised
Innocent Gentillet—a later sixteenth-century political polemicist,

and author of one of the longest discursive attacks on Machiavelli ever penned—for his method of refuting the Florentine. Gentillet's procedure is to extract from Machiavelli some maxim or general theorem to stand at the head of a chapter; to enlarge it, by drawing forth its full implications; and then to disprove it at great length. "Now," says Burd, "there are few writers to whom such a method of treatment would not be fatal; but it is especially unfair in this case, where the selections are made from two only of Machiavelli's works"—that is *The Prince* and the *Discourses*.[4] This is true, as far as it goes. It is unfair to attack isolated phrases from but part of a writer's *Oeuvre*. Burd does not, however, take into account that *The Prince* and the *Discourses* are Machiavelli's principal theoretical works on political affairs; that they are compounded of arguments starting and finishing with forceful theorems; that these theorems are frequently extreme in tone; and that they are truly representative of Machiavelli's views, and beg for the kind of abuse hurled at them by Gentillet and others. Machiavelli loved extravagant statements; and even Guicciardini, himself no political innocent, felt obliged to comment on one of Machiavelli's more brutal suggestions in the *Discourses*, that one should not take "as an absolute rule what the author says, who was always extremely partial to extraordinary and violent methods".[5]

Another stylistic trait, bearing directly on Machiavelli's thought, is the remarkable limitation of his political vocabulary. There has been endless debate concerning the meaning of words such as *necessità, fortuna, ordini, corruzione*, and above all, *virtù*, which recur throughout his work, often in combination with one another and frequently being repeated several times within a very short space. In assessing a writer, avowedly concerned with real-istic political analysis, one should at least question the case for unqualified admiration when it becomes difficult to establish with any precision what his ideas really were. It is true that one can establish a whole series of reasonable synonyms to use as a frame of reference for these terms: some of these should have emerged already in the course of this book, and, more especially, in the last chapter. But that it is necessary to devise such schemes,

METHOD   243

and that they rarely meet with complete approval from other readers, suggests that, whatever the literary effect of repeating the word *virtù* half a dozen times in the space of a short paragraph, this constitutes an intellectual weakness not a virtue. Particular words are made to carry too many meanings and, always, they are key words which clearly have great significance for Machiavelli himself: but this significance is emotional, not intellectual. Thus, while it is not at all difficult to grasp the general tenor of a passage, it remains impossible to attach precise meanings to many of Machiavelli's statements. Paradoxically, the strong, qualitative words give an impression of diamond-hard, uncompromising thinking, while, in fact, blurring ideas and keeping them perpetually out of focus.

A somewhat similar spurious precision is imparted to Machiavelli's work by another stylistic feature which merits more detailed attention because, unlike the love of aphorisms and the limitations of technical vocabulary which he shared with many predecessors and successors, it is—though not unique to Machiavelli—decidedly idiosyncratic and intimately related to his ideas. On this it is, perhaps, best to begin where *The Prince* itself begins:

> All states, all dominions, which have had and now have rule over men, have been and are either republics or princedoms. Princedoms are either hereditary, whereof the family of their lord has been long time ruler, or they are new. The new are either entirely new, as was Milan to Francesco Sforza, or they are as members joined to the hereditary state of the prince who acquires them, as is the kingdom of Naples to the King of Spain. These dominions, thus acquired, are either accustomed to living under a prince, or are used to being free; and they are acquired either with the arms of others or with one's own, either by fortune or by *virtù*.

It is thus that Machiavelli introduces the material comprising the first nine chapters of his book. A series of neat alternatives delimit the area of study. Everything is either one thing or the other; never a combination of differing qualities. Machiavelli will not acknowledge that states might be complex rather than simple; that a princedom might be elective, not hereditary; or, if hereditary, that it might be only recently so; and that it might be acquired by a combination of forces, or by both fortune and *virtù*. Moreover, since, according to Machiavelli himself, *virtù* can help create fortune, the terms are not mutually exclusive even within *The Prince* itself. This is typical of the way in which Machiavelli writes and thinks. He loves the strong antithesis of a completely disjunctive sentence which is, perhaps, the most marked quality of Machiavelli's prose.[6] The technique is, of course, an ancient tradition in logic, but Machiavelli most frequently uses it, as in the passage cited, divorced from the syllogistic apparatus of the logician. Often his practice is more akin to the medieval literary *débat* than to anything else. Many of his questions—such as whether the people or princes are more ungrateful; whether *virtù* or fortune was the cause of Rome's greatness; whether it is better to take the offensive or remain on the defensive—are wholly artificial, and so much depends on circumstances as to be unanswerable. The technique was to become, in Machiavelli, a stylistic mannerism which degenerates into a grave weakness: for it is used as the basis of merely assertive, not logically structured, arguments.

The disjunctive style seems to have come early to Machiavelli. It appears in his *Discourse on the Affairs of Pisa*, written during his very first year of office, where he writes that the troublesome city could be taken "either by force or by love"; and, having decided on the former, he debates whether it should be "either by assault or by starvation". We may find it in his Legations, as in his diagnosis of the French king and his advisers who had seen that "where force is necessary neither chalk nor reputation will suffice"; and who had "consideration only for those who are either well armed, or who are prepared to pay".[7] In his analysis of the negotiations between Cesare Borgia and the tyrants of the Romagna, Machiavelli writes that "on the one hand they talk of a treaty of amity, and on the other hand they make preparations for war"; and he perceived that there was, in the Duke, "a desire rather of revenge against those who have imperilled his state, than a désire or disposition of peace". He learned from Cesare himself that it is better to perform a service of one's own freewill than to be compelled to it; and subsequently replied that the Florentine Signory on the one hand could not contract an engagement of importance with Cesare, nor on the other did they dare offer him a trifling one.[8] Machiavelli's assessment of the motives of the Spanish cardinals and Cesare Borgia at the Papal election of 1503 was that "the latter needs to be re-established, and the former want to be enriched". Of his own financial difficulties at the Court of Rome, Machiavelli complained to the Signory that nowadays men "labour to get ahead, and not to go behindhand"; and in November 1503 he reported, as a general opinion, that the Venetians' attack on Faenza would serve them "as a door that will either open all Italy to them, or that will lead to their own ruin".[9] Not all of these examples are strictly disjunctive; but they give a good idea of the love for antithesis which was to become so characteristic of Machiavelli. Perhaps one other early example may help to make this point clear. In his *Provision for Infantry*, dated December 1506, Machiavelli writes that since Florence had learned through long experience "indeed with great expense and danger . . . how little hope it is possible to place in foreign and hired arms, because when they are numerous and of high repute they are either unendurable or suspected, and if they are few and without reputation, they are of no use, these signors judge it well that she should be armed with her own weapons and with her own men".[10] This is especially interesting since the same idea was to be expressed in *The Prince* in substantially similar terms: "mercenary captains are either capable men or they are not; if they are, you cannot trust them, because they always aspire to their own greatness, either by oppressing you, who are their master, or others contrary to your intentions; but if the captain is not skilful you are ruined in the usual way".[11]

Now there is obviously nothing intrinsically wrong with this style. It makes lively reading, and it may be used to delimit topics for discussion in a concise and clear way. This is true of the

opening chapter of *The Prince* where, despite flaws in the antitheses, there are some genuine alternatives offered for consideration. Similarly, in Chapter XII, Machiavelli uses the device to
introduce subsequent chapters. A prince defends his state either
with his own arms, or mercenaries, auxiliaries, or mixed; and
Machiavelli devotes attention to each of these in turn. In the
Art of War, too, the many instances of this sentence structure
almost always introduce a discussion of real alternatives, and are
only rarely employed for dramatic effect—as at the end of Book
Four, where the strongest necessity encouraging *virtù* in battle is
that where soldiers must either "conquer or die".[12] Elsewhere,
however, the device all too often degenerates into a cliché of
thought involving extremes, not genuine alternatives. Examples
of this are legion; but several must be cited because they help
throw certain of Machiavelli's attitudes into high relief. We are told
that in conquered territories "men ought to be either well treated
or crushed, because they can avenge themselves of lighter injuries,
of more serious ones they cannot". To take over great states,
such as France, presents insuperable difficulties: for there are so
many lords there that they can neither be satisfied nor exterminated. Those who become princes from humble origins must
do so either by *virtù* or fortune. In examining princedoms it is
necessary to consider whether a prince has sufficient power to
support himself in case of need, or whether he always depends
on outside help. Mercenary captains are either excellent in arms or
not.[13] Slowness in arriving at decisions results either from weakness in spirit and strength, or through the "malignity of those
who have to deliberate".[14]

Machiavelli also has a liking for antitheses covering all possibilities by simply being positive and negative. He does this to
initiate a more detailed examination of one or both extreme
terms; but once the device has been noticed it becomes uncomfortably obtrusive. It is not intellectually stirring to be told that
territories acquired by a prince are "either of the same country
and language, or they are not": that nobles must be regarded in
only one of two ways, "they either shape their course to your
fortunes or they do not": or that warring neighbours are of such

a character that, if one of them triumphs, you have "either to fear him or not".[15] Nor is it illuminating to read that the ancient Romans captured cities "either by assault or by surrender", and that surrenders were either "voluntary or forced".[16] The truth is that Machiavelli enjoys making distinctions and rules. It had become an habitual manner of self-expression; and we see it throughout his writings—though less in the *Art of War*, and less still in the *Florentine History*, than in *The Prince* and the *Discourses*. We can see Machiavelli almost parodying his own style in the *Mandragola* where Callimaco admonishes the foolish Nicia: "Well then, judge, either you have faith in me or you have not; either I can tell you of a sure cure or I cannot. On my side, I'll give you the medicine. If you have faith in me, you will accept it. Then if, a year from today, your wife doesn't have her own son in her arms, I bind myself to pay you two thousand ducats".[17]

It will already be apparent, from the few examples so far adduced, that the disjunctive technique, however facile, is no surface adornment to Machiavelli's style, but is organic to his presentation of material. It represents, perfectly, his way of regarding political affairs. In Machiavelli, antitheses are not only part of the structure of an argument. They also represent, for the author, genuine and permanent polarities: force or fraud; *virtù* or fortune; *virtù* or corruption; praise or blame; entirely good or entirely evil; love or fear. There are rarely any intermediate qualities, because Machiavelli does not think in such terms. That he does not think in them is obvious. Why he does not is less explicable, but probably stems in part from his years of observation as a diplomat and as a civil servant. He had been brought close to the reality of things, and had come away feeling that human behaviour does veer from one extreme to another. When, for example, people strive for their liberty they are afraid of those in power, and then, when they gain the upper hand, the others have cause to fear them: "it is as if it were necessary either to injure or be injured".[18]

Equally fundamental is Machiavelli's innate love of dramatic statements which arrest the attention and shake up all one's preconceptions. He is always more the artist striving for effects rather than a serious political analyst: and the disjunctive statement is one of the most simple devices for riveting a reader's attention. In political terms this finds expression in the throwing together of diametrically opposed modes of behaviour: either you treat conquered subjects well or you crush them; either you satisfy dissident elements, or you exterminate them. But even extreme severities may be well or ill used, not only according to circumstances but according to the manner of their application.

> Those may be called well used (if of evil it is permitted to speak well) which are done all at once, for the necessity of securing oneself, and are then not persisted in: but are turned, as much as possible, to the advantage of one's subjects. Those are ill used which, though they may be few in the beginning, increase with time rather than disappear. Those who observe the first method can, with the aid of God and of men, find some remedy for their state, as did Agathocles; it is impossible for the others to maintain themselves.[19]

It is this habit of thought and expression which leads Machiavelli to argue so violently against middle courses in political action. For him there are only two methods of fighting: by the laws proper to men, or by the force proper to beasts.[20] Sometimes the former will not suffice, so that it is necessary to resort to the latter; and here again we find that force itself is sub-divided. According to circumstances one may need to vary between the lion and the fox—force and fraud. But whatever course is necessary, it must be employed whole-heartedly. As Machiavelli puts it in the *Discourses*, "it is necessary, therefore, either never to injure anyone, or to inflict the injuries at one go, and then to reassure men and give them ground to expect peace and security".[21] The Romans themselves, says Machiavelli, avoided middle courses and preferred extremes. Government consists in the art of so controlling subjects that they can neither injure you, nor have cause to do so. This may be accomplished either by removing all possible means whereby they might do harm, or by so benefiting them that they have no reason to be discontented. Such action is exemplified by the Romans' treatment of the Latin cities: "subject peoples should either be treated well, or wiped out".[22]

The Romans knew what they were about. The majority of modern princes and republics do not. In politics you must be prepared to do evil. If you prefer a life of virtue, you should not be in politics at all. Most men, however, prefer to adopt middle courses which are most damaging, "because they do not know how to be entirely bad or entirely good", and Machiavelli illustrates this theorem with an astonishing misinterpretation of a fairly recent occurrence, where his love of the melodramatic reaches its apogee. According to Machiavelli, when Pope Julius II had gone to Perugia in 1506 to expel Giovampagolo Baglioni, the tyrant, he hurried thither without awaiting his army, regardless of the fact that Giovampagolo was there with a strong body of troops. The Pope thus placed himself in the hands of his enemy. Yet he was able to emerge from the situation not only unscathed but with his foe humbly suppliant.

The rashness of the Pope and the cowardice of Giovampagolo were observed by the prudent men who were with the Pope; and they could not understand whence it came about that the latter [Giovampagolo] had not—to his eternal fame—overwhelmed his enemy at one stroke, and enriched himself with booty: for accompanying the Pope were all the cardinals, with all their fine things. One could not believe that he abstained either through goodness or through conscience holding him back. No pious consideration could enter the breast of so violent a man, who had taken his sister for himself, and had killed his cousins and nephews in order to rule. But it was concluded that it came about because men do not know how to be "honourably" evil, or perfectly good: and when a wicked deed has grandeur in itself, or is in some way noble, they do not know how to set about it.

Thus Giovampagolo, who cared nothing about being incestuous and a public parricide, did not know how—or, to put it better, did not dare—when presented with a favourable opportunity, to undertake an enterprise which would have left an

eternal remembrance of himself, for being the first to show
prelates how little esteem merit those who live and rule as they
do. And he would have done something whose grandeur would
have overcome every infamy and every danger which could
have arisen from it.[23]

In fact, the situation at Perugia had been a good deal more
complex than Machiavelli depicts it; Giovampagolo had had little
choice in submitting, and, as a matter of fact, did rather well by
so doing.

In the autumn of 1506 Machiavelli had been on his second
legation to Rome and he had summarised the episode then with
another antithesis: "once Giovampagolo said that there had been
two ways for him to save his state; the one by force, and the other
by humility and by trusting the friends who counselled him to
it". Giovampagolo, wrote Machiavelli, had not been willing to
employ the first course, but had adopted the second; though
Machiavelli could only conclude that the Pope came to no harm
through Giovampagolo's "good nature and humanity".[24] However, by the time he came to write about the incident in the
Discourses, Machiavelli must have known that Baglioni had
already been outmanœuvred before the Pope's visit to Perugia;
but the detail of politics is sacrificed to the grandiloquent
gesture, terminating a typical Machiavellian antithesis between
good and bad. The conception of a Papal abduction, or even
assassination, is a remarkable one; though it is difficult to believe
that it was seriously intended by Machiavelli. Yet, if not seriously
intended, why is it used to exemplify an important general
theorem about political morality? Obviously because Machiavelli,
already swept away by his personal animus against Julius, in-
stinctively employs it as an effective device. It makes good copy;
but as an argument it is void.

Perhaps the best example of Machiavelli's disjunctive manner,
both in style and method, is an observation on recent Florentine
politics combined with more general theorems concerning
political behaviour, expressed in the same dramatic manner as
the denunciation of Baglioni. The theme is really an elaboration of

the same idea: that when doing evil it is necessary to be thorough: with the further implication that if you cannot be evil at all you should not be in politics. The matter is first raised in the sixth chapter of *The Prince*. Machiavelli, having embarked on the subject of those who become princes not through fortune but through their own *virtù*, juxtaposes Moses, Cyrus, Romulus, and Theseus—though he ironically refrains from discussing Moses in detail since he was the "mere executor of God's will" and had "so great a preceptor". These great men owed nothing to fortune but the bare opportunity of showing their metal: Moses finding the Israelites enslaved; Romulus coming to found Rome by chance; Cyrus living at the time when the Persians were discontented with the government of the Medes; and Theseus finding the Athenians dispersed. Did these innovators, asks Machiavelli, posing characteristically extreme alternatives, rely on themselves or on others? Did they have to resort to prayer, or were they able to use force? The answer is forthright: anybody who has to rely on prayer alone must fail; hence "all armed prophets triumph, and the unarmed are ruined". People are fickle, and, though easily persuaded, are with difficulty held firm in that persuasion. Nevertheless, when they cease to believe, "one can make them believe by force". Had Moses and the others not been armed they would have failed, "as happened in our time to Girolamo Savonarola who was ruined in his new constitutions, when the multitude began not to believe in him; and he had no way to hold firm those who had believed, nor to make the unbelievers believe". The idea is made even more specific in the *Discourses* where Machiavelli makes the point that those who wish to do good works in a republic have first to extinguish the envy of their rivals and opponents. Again there is an "either . . . or". It may be that so grave a crisis will arise in the state that men will be compelled to obey the citizen of greatest *virtù*, despite any antipathy they may feel for him. The alternative to this is itself disjunctive: rivals may either be removed by violence or in the natural order of things; but where death does not come about naturally there is no remedy left but to encompass their demise by any means possible.

He who reads the Bible sensibly, will see that Moses, wishing his laws and ordinances to go ahead, was forced to kill innumerable men who, moved by nothing other than envy, were opposed to his plans. Friar Girolamo Savonarola recognised this necessity very clearly; and Piero Soderini, Gonfalonier of Florence, likewise recognised it. The former (that is the Friar) could not overcome the difficulty through not having the requisite authority, and through not being well understood by his followers who did have the authority. Nevertheless, it was not neglected by him: and his sermons are full of accusations against the wise of the world, and of invectives against them: for thus he called the envious, and those who were opposed to his ordinances. The other, Soderini, thought to extinguish this envy, with time, with goodness, with his fortune, and by benefiting others. Seeing himself to be very young, and with so many new favours gained by his method of procedure, he thought to overcome however many might oppose him through envy, without any scandal, violence, or tumult. And he did not know that time cannot wait for anybody, that goodness is not enough, that fortune changes, and that malice finds no gift which placates her. So both the one and the other of these two came to ruin; and their ruin was caused by their not knowing how, or not being able, to overcome this envy.[25]

So we have a series of alternative possibilities resolved by leaving no other recourse but extreme action. To temporise or compromise is to invite disaster. The only solution, to kill off one's enemies, is a "shocking" one. And Machiavelli enhances the shock by incorporating Moses into his argument, depicting him as yet another ruthless, bloodstained politician. The effect is impressive, both in *The Prince* and in the *Discourses*; everything is simple, clear-cut, and neat. Yet, paradoxically, it is at the same time vague and generalised. There is no serious analysis here of the situation faced in Florence by either Savonarola or Soderini. It is true, perhaps, that neither man was as effective as he might have been with more decisiveness, ruthlessness, and, when necessary, violence. But the practical difficulties of eliminating all potential rivals by killing them off "before doing anything else" are not even hinted at. The whole thing, like the regret at Baglioni's faint-heartedness when he might have assassinated the Pope, is a grand gesture, but historically dubious.

I have discussed the disjunctive style at some length in order to demonstrate that Machiavelli uses it, consciously or unconsciously, more as a technique to facilitate argument by assertion, than as a means of initiating any rigorously logical process. Style is, of course, a natural expression of a man's manner of thinking, though, in Machiavelli's case, it is hard to resist the conclusion that on some occasions he was at the mercy of his own flow of fine words. He was, too, at the mercy of his love of dramatic statements and violent contrasts. What, in fact, is the so-called "Machiavelli method"—this juxtaposition of ancient and modern historical exempla—other than an instance of this? It is less profitably read as a serious attempt at inductive reasoning (the sifting and comparison of evidence till it yields some general truth) than as yet another simple confrontation between ancient *virtù* and modern corruption. It is true that not every ancient example is favourable, and that not every modern example is bad: we have Caesar as well as Cesare Borgia. Nevertheless, in the main, Machiavelli's view of history is as disjunctive as his syntax. And it is as facile.

Machiavelli thought either with his pen or with his heart. And he would, I hope, have approved the form of that sentence, if not its content. I have borrowed the technique as a convenient way of passing from a consideration of stylistic mannerisms which are related to Machiavelli's thought, to a consideration of the way in which personal enthusiasms and antipathies similarly moulded his arguments. The terms of my antithesis, like those of Machiavelli, are neither mutually exclusive nor comprehensive. Machiavelli's pen frequently ran away with him precisely because he was involved emotionally in what he was saying. Nor would it be fair to suggest that his political judgements are invariably literary or emotional rather than analytical. None the less the general point remains valid: because analysis was not his strong point; because his manner of argument is idiosyncratic and follows rules other than those of logic; because he himself claimed to be employing what is now termed an inductive method; and because some modern critics have largely agreed with his own estimate, while others, though finding flaws in his application of induction, are inclined to think that he made a genuine attempt. An examination of several typical arguments—some great, some small—in Machiavelli's work might help towards clarifying the issue.

One preliminary observation must be made. Machiavelli's treatment of source materials—for the comparatively recent history of Florence and the rest of Italy; for the reconstruction of the Roman military machine; and for the study of ancient institutions—has already been examined. That it does not accord with modern methods is patent. His adherence to classical authority is slavish, and his use of more recent historians highly selective and unilinear. But, granted that these attitudes were typical of his age and long after, is there still a possibility that Machiavelli used his sources in an inductive manner? The first of many difficulties comes from the fact that, especially in the *Discourses*, the sources are uncollated and are not used comparatively. That is—despite employing both a number of historians on specific points, and Polybius for more general ideas—Machiavelli is largely following only one source, Livy, which he uses as the basis for political comment: and Livy is, on the whole, a narrative historian who presents his material from a consistently Roman standpoint and suggests underlying political motivation in a rudimentary fashion. A commentator seeking to explain, out of Livy, the how and why of Roman history has the choice of an almost infinite variety of interpretations. In the sense that Machiavelli takes particular incidents and builds thereupon a general theorem of political behaviour one might, stretching many points, call it an inductive process: but to use the term of such a procedure is to render it almost meaningless. There can only be true induction if the commentator is working from a more complex source than Livy, or, better still, is willing and able to evaluate a variety of sources in order to establish the most likely sequence of events and their most feasible explanation. The feebleness of an argument which erects each of its general theorems upon a few ambiguous examples, culled from one narrative, is obvious. However, leaving aside this objection to Machiavelli's use of historical data, there remain other more fundamental flaws in his method.

The essence of induction is that a conclusion should emerge from the sifting of sources: but in Machiavelli we find a tendency to impose conclusions upon evidence, or at least not to see that his material might yield several different interpretations. A few examples may suffice to make the point. In the *Discourses* Machiavelli is much exercised to prove the probity of the Roman plebs in the early non-corrupt days of the republic. One instance he cites is a particular edict of the Senate to the effect that troops should pay into the public treasury one-tenth of the booty each had seized from the Veientes, in order to fulfil a vow taken by their commander, Camillus, that this proportion should be donated to Apollo. The edict excited such furor that it was quickly revoked, and the booty was not called in. Yet for Machiavelli this occurrence demonstrates the trust in the plebs entertained by the Senate who were convinced that everybody would bring in their fair share; and, "one sees" also "how the plebs had not the slightest thought of acting fraudulently with regard to the edict by donating less than they ought".[26] One might equally well interpret so vague an incident as indicating that the Senate deemed an edict necessary to ensure that the plebs *would* pay up; and that the edict was revoked because the selfish plebs had no intention of fulfilling their commander's vow by donating anything to the Gods.

Elsewhere in the *Discourses*, Machiavelli, arguing that the religion introduced by Numa kept the Romans obedient to the Gods and encouraged them in the ways of civic rectitude, cites the story of the indictment of Lucius Manlius by Marcus Pomponius, the plebeian Tribune. Before the trial Lucius's son, Titus, threatened to kill the Tribune if he did not swear to withdraw the charge. Poor Marcus was compelled to take an oath to this effect, and "out of respect for having taken the oath, he withdrew the accusation". Thus, says Machiavelli, did a Tribune "put aside the hatred he had for the father, the injury that had been done to him by the son, and his own honour, in order to obey the oath he had taken".[27] A reader less concerned to praise Roman rectitude might well wonder whether Titus's threat to kill Marcus was at all relevant to the outcome.

Another example of the *non sequitur* style of argument is Machiavelli's discussion of whether it is better in battle to await the enemy's attack and then, having borne it, to take the offensive, or to attack them first with fury. The test case selected is the battle waged by two Consuls, Decius and Fabius, against the Samnites and Tuscans. Decius was an impetuous commander, and launched a fierce assault; whereas Fabius was more inclined to hold back till the enemy had weakened.

> Hence it is seen, from the way things turned out, that Fabius's plan worked much better than did Decius's. The latter exhausted himself in his first assaults so that—seeing his company nearer to flight than anything else—in imitation of his father, he sacrificed himself for the Roman legions, to acquire by death that glory which he could not obtain by victory. Learning of this, Fabius, in order not to acquire less honour by being alive than his colleague had gained by dying, pushed forward all the forces which he had reserved for such a necessity: whereby he won a most happy victory. Hence one sees that Fabius's mode of procedure is more reliable and more worthy of imitation.[28]

It seems extraordinary that any thinking person could write this sort of thing. Why is it not possible to attribute Fabius's success solely to the fact that Decius's attack had weakened the enemy? Upon whom would the enemy have wasted their first strength had Decius not engaged them? But Machiavelli seems reluctant to draw more than one conclusion from "evidence", and that frequently the least plausible.

Sometimes, indeed, he even cites evidence as a conclusive proof of one point of view, when it obviously corroborates the exact opposite of what he is saying. A particularly bad instance of this is in the chapter devoted to proving that princes and republics should be satisfied with victory. Machiavelli begins by citing examples in which states—having either been victorious in war, or, on the other hand, having been offered favourable terms of peace—have refused to be content in the hope of gaining more, and have, as a result, come to grief. He ends, however, by adducing the example of Hannibal who, having been recalled to Carthage to face the Roman invasion, was not ashamed to sue for peace when he recognised that his country, if defeated, would be reduced to slavery: "if then Hannibal, who was so *virtuoso*, and had his army still intact, preferred peace to war . . . what should a man do who has neither the *virtù* nor the experience of Hannibal?"[29] But this has nothing whatever to do with the matter in hand. For Hannibal was constrained to fight despite the fact that he recognised the situation as hopeless. Indeed, since the Romans had already enjoyed several victories over the Carthaginians and thereby reduced Hannibal to a state where he had to sue for peace, the whole affair is a decisive argument against Machiavelli's main contention. For the Romans, not satisfied with their past victories, tried for more: and they triumphed completely.

Another weakness, similar to this, is Machiavelli's frequent failure, when drawing one of his general conclusions, to take account either of a complete story or of numerous other historical instances which would have invalidated his theorem—or would have led to different conclusions. Guicciardini was especially quick to notice these matters; and one example may serve as representative of his astute criticism. Machiavelli asserts that one should not stake the whole of one's fortune except on the whole of one's army and that, as a consequence, it is frequently harmful to defend passes or difficult positions. Guicciardini does not comment on the obviously incomplete nature of Machiavelli's discourse which takes no heed of the possibility that, in defending passes, the whole of one's fortune is not necessarily risked. But he does point out that several instances might be adduced where the defence of a difficult position has been beneficial; that the Swiss failure to stop the French crossing the mountains in 1515, cited as evidence by Machiavelli, had nothing to do with their subsequent defeat; and that the example of Hannibal, also used by Machiavelli, was irrelevant since the Romans were not in a position to defend the Alpine passes even had they wished to; while, had they been able to do so, it might well have been to their advantage. "In fact," says Guicciardini, "this example can be turned round completely, for as Hannibal in the crossing of the Alps suffered greatly from attacks by the natives, how much worse off would he have been if he had also had to face the Romans there!"[30]

These are not unusual examples in Machiavelli's writing: though they are more marked in the *Discourses* than elsewhere. One could go on and on citing further instances of such fallacies. Guicciardini himself started this mode of criticism, probably even before the *Discourses* were published; and it makes good sport, trying to spot the *non sequiturs* or the non-starters. Nevertheless, there are other objections to Machiavelli's method, more serious than his tendency either to impose one particular interpretation upon episodes suggestive of several or to arrive at conclusions by selecting only that evidence which seems to support them. The clearest indication that Machiavelli's induction is a spurious procedure is this: that when his sources do not fit a preconception, he is prepared to misrepresent or even falsify them so that they do.

The most flagrant sustained instance of this is in the *Florentine History*, where Machiavelli is concerned to provide historical corroboration for his theoretical condemnation of mercenary troops. To do this he misses no opportunity to attack and ridicule the practice of warfare in fifteenth-century Italy: campaigns are always ineptly and feebly waged; victory, when obtained, is always unexploited; defeats are never disastrous; and battles are always bloodless. We have seen how Machiavelli deliberately disregards his sources for such battles as Zagonara and Molinella, claiming that in the first there were but three fatalities, and those by sheer chance; and that, in the latter, no one was killed at all.[31] Ammirato pointed out that at Molinella there were about three hundred fatalities; and Sir Charles Oman, noticing this, defends Machiavelli on the grounds that "when twenty thousand men meet, and part with a loss of three hundred men between them, we can only say that Machiavelli's sneers are practically, if not literally, justified".[32] The point is well taken, and it must be conceded that, on the whole, a battle such as Molinella argues a good deal more discretion than valour on the part of the combatants. But the episode does expose Machiavelli's technique of hyperbole. The small total of three hundred men killed should be support enough for the accusation that the fighting was hardly serious; but the case thus presented would not be startling enough. It is much more effective to assert that only horses were killed and that the conflict was, from the human point of view, harmless. And, being more effective, this becomes Machiavelli's historical truth, regardless of the fact that it misrepresents his sources. Battles are either very gory indeed, or bloodless. They cannot be anything in between.

Another bad example of deceit, or self-deception, occurs in the second book of the *Discourses*, when Machiavelli is establishing the complete superiority of infantry over cavalry. One of his examples is that of Crassus and Mark Antony in Parthia where, he says, the Roman infantry were able to wage many successful battles against the innumerable mounted troops of the Parthians —despite the suitability of the terrain for cavalry engagements. Crassus, Machiavelli admits, was killed; but this was more the result of treachery than force, for the Parthians never dared to attack him openly, but played a waiting game.[33] This is not at all the truth of the matter. The Romans had very mixed fortunes against the Parthians, suffering several reverses at the hands of the enemy cavalry and mounted archers. Crassus, in fact, died when his army was routed at Carrhae in 53 B.C. The extent to which Machiavelli has distorted the story may be judged from the *Art of War* where, taking a more general view, he gives a completely different version of the campaign. He excuses himself for confining his discussion of warfare to Europe, but points out the totally different practice of the Romans, with their strictly disciplined infantry, and the Parthians with their looser and more irregular cavalry tactics. Their respective successes depended entirely upon the terrain, so that in the large open plains of Parthia the Roman army, "heavy and slow, by means of their armours, and their orders, could not overrun it, without their grievous hurt (those that defended it, being on horseback most expedite) so that they were today in one place, and tomorrow distant fifty miles. Hereof it grew, that the Parthians might prevail with their chivalry only, both to the ruin of the army of Crassus, and to the peril of the same, of Marcus Antonius."[34]

Consider also another instance from the same chapter in the *Discourses* where Machiavelli cites the action fought by Marcus Regulus Atilius against the Carthaginians in 255 B.C. Here the Roman general is represented as being prepared to sustain an attack, not only by cavalry but also by elephants, with infantry alone. His defeat, says Machiavelli, was due not so much to the fact that "the *virtù* of his infantry was not great enough, as to the fact that he had not such confidence in them to believe that they would overcome that difficulty". The logic of this is inextricable. If Regulus did not have confidence in his infantry, how is it possible to argue that he was prepared to wage the battle as though he did have confidence in them? And, more to the point, Machiavelli omits all mention of the fact that the Carthaginian force, led by the Spartan general Xanthippus, by virtue of its cavalry, was able to overwhelm a Roman army twice its size. Again a more judicious comment is found in the *Art of War* where, to support his contention that an army beaten in one situation may reverse the result by different tactics in different terrain, Machiavelli cites Regulus's defeat as a straightforward victory by cavalry and elephants. Instances such as these are indicative of the way in which Machiavelli assesses his evidence as a particular literary context dictates; and how he interprets the same historical example in different ways to suit the argument of the moment.[35]

It will by now be evident that the majority of Machiavelli's false inferences, *non sequiturs*, misrepresentations, and errors of judgement, are largely the result of certain emotional preconceptions. It is his hatred of mercenary troops, based on his Italian experiences, which leads him to so blind a condemnation of cavalry. It is his determination to establish the total superiority of ancient warfare which leads him to view modern battles only in terms of ancient ones: so that he could not see what was already manifest in the Italian wars—that the power of artillery was revolutionising the art of war, and that cavalry was long to continue as a vital force. It is his distrust of princes and nobles which leads him into the toils of a defence of popular government when he should be extolling the virtues of the people only in conjunction with monarchical and aristocratic power. In all these examples, too, we can see another feature of Machiavelli's style and method. It is not merely that his incapacity to recognise the validity of middle courses, or combinations of disparate qualities, results in a refusal to discuss the merits of a balanced strategy combining infantry, cavalry, and fire power; or in his failure to write sensibly on the mixed constitution he is supposed to favour. It is also that he seems almost psychologically impelled to take up these stances because they are diametrically opposed to common conceptions. Everybody, he asserts untruthfully, believed in the superiority of cavalry: he must maintain that of the infantry. Everybody was saying that the invention of firearms would revolutionise warfare and invalidate the military practice of the ancients; he must, categorically, maintain the exact opposite. Everybody believed that the generality of the people were untrustworthy and incapable of government: he must argue not that princes and nobles were as bad as the people (a possibility he does, in fact, raise himself) but that the people were far superior in judgement, honesty, and effectiveness. That his own estimate of human nature, and his study of the role of the people in Roman history, rendered this last opinion dubious seems not to have bothered him: no more than he allowed it to undermine the message of hope in *The Prince* where he depicts the corrupt, selfish, and short-sighted masses as eagerly prepared to do the bidding of a military saviour for the good of the fatherland. These are not inconsistencies in Machiavelli's thought. They are incapacities, and a good deal more serious.

There are other weaknesses in Machiavelli's dialectical method which merit attention, though they stand a little apart from the elements already discussed. These are what might be termed either bizarre arguments, where he makes assertions without seeing the curious implications of what he is saying; or wandering arguments, where he begins by discussing one point and finishes somewhere else. One of the former, his strange defence of blood-thirsty battles and brutality in the *Art of War*, has been discussed elsewhere.[36] It is, perhaps, paralleled by a chapter in the *Discourses* where Machiavelli discusses the failing whereby, in times of peace, republics tend to pass over able men and choose less worthy citizens for office. For this he prescribes two remedies: one is to keep the citizens poor so that "by riches without *virtù* they can corrupt neither themselves nor others"; the other is to be constantly ready for war so that, like the Romans in their early days, there is always need for citizens of repute and a place for men of *virtù*. In such a situation worthless men cannot gain honour since their ineptitude soon becomes obvious: "but other republics which are not constituted like that, and which make war only when necessity constrains them, cannot defend themselves against such inconveniences".[37] It is possible to see what Machiavelli means, but the implications of his argument are unhappy. He seems to suggest that to wage war only when necessary is a bad thing. Is it then a good thing to wage war when there is no necessity to do so? As a matter of fact, this would seem to be the general purport of the *Discourses* as a whole, where continuous Roman expansion is depicted as a necessary condition of the republic's survival. But this, like the condemnation of Christianity in the *Art of War*, is badly thought out—or rather, it has not been thought out at all.

Of wandering arguments the *Discourses* furnish several examples illustrating the lack of control already noticed many times in the course of comment on Machiavelli's other works. One of these, in the first Book of the *Discourses*, is interesting as an illustration both of Machiavelli's limited political vocabulary, and his love of refuting commonly-held tenets.[38] Machiavelli is arguing that the multitude [*la moltitudine*] is more wise and more constant than a prince, and he criticises Livy and other historians who argue that nothing can be more futile and more inconstant than the multitude. Machiavelli begins reasonably by pointing out that the failings attributed to the multitude could be attributed to all men, and especially to princes of whom history records but few wise ones. All men do wrong to an equal extent when there is nothing to prevent them; but the common opinion that the people [*i popoli*] when in power are fickle, mutable, and ungrateful, could just as well apply to princes if one were considering neither as having respect for the laws. On the other hand, when comparing governments in which the laws are respected, we will find that the people are better than princes. It is here that Machiavelli wanders off to assert that the voice of the people has been likened to the voice of God; that the people are less ungrateful than princes; and that a prince who does whatever he wishes is mad [*pazzo*] whilst a people [*un popolo*] able to do whatever it wishes is not wise [*non è savio*]. The last part, in particular, shows the heavily-weighted language of this chapter which adduces scarcely any evidence for its series of assertions. Above all, it must be noticed that we begin by discussing the *multitude* and end up discussing the *people*— which is not, in Machiavelli, the same thing.

Again, in the third Book, Machiavelli is to be found struggling with a typical medieval debating point: should one place more trust in a good general with a weak army or in a good army with a weak general? He adduces several examples on both sides, but concludes in utter confusion. It seems certain, he says, that many good men may more easily discover one man and instruct him so that he becomes good, than vice versa. On the other hand, there are examples which suggest that a capable leader is able to train a rabble of slaves or peasants into an efficient fighting machine. Thus, despite his initial certainty, Machiavelli has moved to the opinion that the matter is evenly balanced: one good man can find another; but a good army without a head is likely to become arrogant and dangerous. So, Machiavelli concludes, "I believe that one should place much more confidence in a general who has time to train men and the wherewithal to arm them than in an arrogant army with a turbulent [*tumultuario*] leader appointed by itself".[39] The shift of ground is extraordinary. The argument begins as a debate between the relative merits of a good general with weak army or a weak general with good army. It ends as a decision in favour of a good general with favourable opportunities, as against an arrogant army with a riotous leader!

It is difficult, in a study of this kind, not to give an impression of selecting weaknesses in Machiavelli and crucifying him without regard for the rest of his work. But the examples discussed are typical, not unrepresentative, of Machiavelli's methods. With these categories of fallacy in mind, it should be easy to recognise similar instances which abound in his work—especially in the *Discourses* which are dialectically the weakest of all Machiavelli's writings. And, as a final example of the real Machiavelli method, it is worth considering his arguments concerning Christianity and paganism in the *Discourses*: because here it is possible to find nearly all the characteristics outlined in this chapter. Furthermore, these arguments, more than any others, led to Machiavelli's ill-repute in the sixteenth century and to a good deal of justified adverse criticism.

An appearance of piety is regarded, in *The Prince*, as the best aid to a ruler seeking to impose upon a gullible populace. Religion facilitates policy: and the idea is amply developed at several points in the *Discourses* where its relationship to the historical process of decay is also discussed. In the first Book Machiavelli devotes several chapters to the role of religion in Rome, establishing his position that the Romans were indebted less to Romulus than to Numa, for the latter introduced laws and religion which are of paramount importance in controlling the army and instilling civic rectitude: "where there is religion, arms may be easily introduced; but where there are arms but no religion that can be introduced with difficulty".[40] The false distinction and fallacious conclusion are apparent: why must we choose between the two founders in this crude fashion; or why may one not argue, as does Guicciardini, that since Romulus gave Rome its arms and institutions, the way was already prepared for Numa; and why, in this case, should Machiavelli assert that given good arms and institutions it is difficult to instil religion—since this is what did happen at Rome? There is worse yet to come. Machiavelli extends his argument to the general principle that religion is the best means for preserving a state from corruption, and that those who wish to maintain their state incorrupt should, above all else, keep unspoiled the observances of their faith, and always hold them in veneration: "because one can have no greater indication of the ruin of a province than to see divine worship despised".[41] Machiavelli's general point on the value of religion to the state may well be true; but it is not *because* lack of religious observances is a sign of corruption. The terms have been put back to front.

Religion, says Machiavelli, will keep states united. Prudent rulers should, therefore, encourage supernatural beliefs, even though they themselves deem them false; and it was for this reason that miracles were sedulously fostered at Rome. At this point Machiavelli digresses to a consideration of Christianity, which, he maintains, would have united Western Europe had it been maintained in its original form. But it had declined, principally through the corruption of the Church of Rome and the profligacy of the Papal court. The first debt owed by the Italians to their spiritual leaders was irreligion and evil ways. The second debt was that the Church had kept Italy disunited since, though without the power to make itself supreme, it was sufficiently strong to prevent any temporal ruler from achieving this. Thus the debasement of Christianity had disastrous results, quite the opposite of the religion of ancient Rome.

Machiavelli's main enthusiasm for paganism is that it could be manipulated by the state; and he cites several instances where the Senate and Consuls were able to cope with disturbances of Tribunes and plebs by appeals to their gross superstition. The odd thing is that Machiavelli, in citing these examples and approving of them, does not recognise that they reveal the stupidity, selfishness, and short-sightedness of the people whom he otherwise extols, and the wisdom of the nobility whom he always criticises. Nor does he remark that the manipulation of superstition could as easily be employed for bad ends as for good. The same is true of his subsequent comments on the interpretation of auguries, where he only sees it as a means of giving psychological reassurance to discontented or hesitant troops.

All this is, in any case, loosely argued and badly put together: but Machiavelli crowns his achievement with another astonishing blunder. To clinch his argument, he describes how the Samnites,

on the verge of total defeat by the Romans, had recourse to
religion.[42] They decided to make a final effort; and, because they
knew that victory depended on instilling in the minds of their
soldiers an obstinate determination in battle, they decided to
revive one of their ancient blood sacrifices. Accordingly, a
solemn and terrifying ritual took place when, after the sacrifices,
the officers stood between the dead victims at flaming altars and
vowed never to abandon the struggle against the Romans. Then
the soldiers were called, one by one, to stand in the midst of the
centurions and swear never to reveal what they had just seen.
Then, with monstrous and terrible oaths, they vowed to carry
out any orders issued by their generals, never to abandon the
battle, and to kill anybody they saw taking flight. Some troops,
terrified by all this, were unwilling to take the oath, and were
promptly killed by the centurions who stood by with naked
swords in their hands. And so the vows were made. The outcome
was fearfully anticlimactic. The Roman general shrewdly observed that the Samnites would be fearful not only of their
enemy but also of the Gods and of their fellow citizens; and they
were, in fact, easily defeated by Roman *virtù* and by the fact that
fear engendered in previous defeats was greater than the obstinacy
engendered by their religion and the vow. All this, one would
think, is striking evidence as to the inefficacy of the whole
business; but Machiavelli blithely concludes that it was resorted
to because the Samnites had no other recourse than religion to
recover their lost *virtù*; "this fully attests how much confidence
one can have by means of religion, well employed"! And if this
seems a bizarre conclusion, bear in mind that in the second book
of the *Discourses* Machiavelli extols the blood sacrifices of the
ancients whose religion, unlike Christianity, encouraged men's
fierce and courageous spirit. And, one might ask, resulted in
what? The Samnites' defeat? In any case, Machiavelli goes on to
argue that the modern lack of *virtù* is not, after all, due to the
pusillanimity of Christianity, but only to its false interpreters.
And he concludes that, on further reflexion, it was not even the
false interpreters of Christianity who extinguished *virtù*, but rather
the overwhelming success of the Roman Empire itself.[43]

Machiavelli's discussion of religion is a perfect example of his methods at work. We have the love of daring assertions; the false inferences; the misrepresentation or distortion of evidence; the wandering argument; and a shower of general inconsistencies. The only thing lacking is a clear use of the disjunctive structure. But even here one might say that Machiavelli was caught on the horns of his own dilemma. On the one hand there is his wish to extol ancient practice in everything, together with his desire to shock conventional Christian thinkers. On the other there is a nagging awareness that the corruption he so laments may have been the logical outcome of that very greatness he admires in ancient Rome. For once he tries to get the best of both arguments; and the result is a farrago of nonsense. In many ways it is quintessential Machiavelli. It reads remarkably well; it looks decisive; and it engenders excitement and controversy. But it is, fundamentally, blurred thinking: out of focus, emotional, and naïve.

And yet, amidst the confusion, Machiavelli's understanding rises superior to his dialectic. For example, he puts his finger on two aspects of religion in general, and Christianity in particular, which, three centuries later, were to revolt thinkers as dissimilar as Marx and Nietzsche. Christianity had been, and continued to be, responsible for a depressing fatalism which enabled the unscrupulous to exploit an unthinking majority. It could, also, too easily be employed as a means of suppressing human aspirations, or of keeping people quiescent. Similarly, Machiavelli's diatribe against the Papacy and the Church of Rome is a valid assessment of the effects of corrupt religious institutions. Anyone, he writes, who should consider the gulf between the present practice of Christianity and its original institutions, would without doubt have to conclude that the Church was on the brink of "ruin or the scourge".[44] In October 1517, Luther nailed his ninety-five theses to the church door at Wittemberg. Neither the Pope, nor Machiavelli, nor—probably—Luther himself, realised it: but the scourge was at hand, and the Church of Rome could never be quite the same again.

The fact is that Machiavelli himself poses the greatest dilemma of all. On the one hand it is possible to dissect each of his arguments, and establish his failure to use evidence accurately or even sensibly: to show how his conclusions do not follow from the material he adduces, or that he avoids conclusions suggested by his examples: to demonstrate, in short, his inability to construct a sound argument. Yet, on the other hand, it remains true that his picture of political activity bears a closer resemblance to actuality than the structures of far more systematic thinkers, both before his time, and since. If one disregards the absolutist manner in which he states his conclusions, and considers them as indicative of usual—but not invariable—situations, many of Machiavelli's views are eminently sane. In his own day, the Italian states, for all the cleverness of their administrators and diplomats, were unable to organise themselves to cope with the invasion of foreigners intent only on loot; and the chess-board tactics of the condottieri had been found wanting when tested by serious opposition. More generally, it is impossible to deny that in politics those who pursue middle courses—that is the dilatory and the indecisive—are likely to prove failures; and that politicians frequently find it necessary to eliminate their opponents either by force or by fraud. It is, too, depressingly clear that those engaged in politics have had, and still have, a morality peculiarly their own; and that their behaviour is generally such that, in a private citizen, it would incur opprobrium and, very likely, dire retribution. To this day governments, whatever they choose to call themselves, still rest upon their ability to coerce their subjects by force—that is by the threat of punishment. While the floods of propaganda, broken promises, and vapid speechmaking, characterising every régime, everywhere, testify that fraud is still the major weapon of all astute politicians, whose cynical assessment of the gullibility of the populace has now attained such hideous proportions that even Machiavelli would have blenched before it. Religion is no longer the force it was, though it is still made to serve a turn or two: but its place has been taken by ideologies still parroting, amongst many other slogans, those empty cries of *libertà* and *bene commune* which echoed through the despondent pages of the *Florentine History*.

Machiavelli saw all these things, and much more, with terrible clarity. He recognised the total discrepancy between the imaginary polities of the system-builders and the way states really function; and between the ethics enjoined by political moralists and the cynical opportunism of practising politicians. But he did not see all this as a result of diligently applying his laborious and inexpert historical method. The study of the ancients provided a framework within which he attempted to express his views on political behaviour: but, though it became habitual with him, it was never an effective logical tool. The arguments Machiavelli adduces are, in a very real sense, extraneous to the majority of his dynamic conclusions. His perceptions came, not as a result of reading history, but from genuine observation of political activity; and they were not speculative, but rather intuitive. It is likely that his view of human affairs would have been little different had he never read a word of Livy. To this extent one may say that the historical method was not fundamental to Machiavelli's political observation; but that it was, rather, an elaborate and irrelevant superstructure.

Conclusion

CALLIMACO, IN THE *Mandragola*, had reflected that the worst thing that could happen to him would be to die and go to hell; and he reminded himself that many others had died before him, and that there were many worthy men in hell. Should he, therefore, be ashamed of going there too?

This passage may well have come to Machiavelli's mind as he lay on his own death-bed: and there is nothing inherently improbable in the story of his dream, set down a century later by the Jesuit, Etienne Binet:

> he had this vision a little before he gave up the ghost; he saw a parcel of poor people like beggars, tattered, half-starved, deformed, who stood confusedly, and were but few in number: and it was told him, that those belonged to paradise, of whom it was written, *Blessed are the poor, for theirs is the kingdom of heaven.* When these retired, there appeared an innumerable company of persons full of gravity and majesty; they looked like a senate, where state-affairs and very serious matters were treated of: He saw there Plato, Seneca, Plutarch, Tacitus, and others of the same condition: He asked who these venerable gentlemen were? and he was told, that they were the damned, and the souls reprobated by Heaven; for, *the wisdom of the world is enmity with GOD.* This vision being ended, he was asked, which of these companies he would be of? He answered, that he would rather be in hell with these great wits, to consult with them about state-affairs, than be with this vermin of scoundrels that had been shewn him. And

presently he died, and went to see how the state-affairs went in the other world.[1]

Whether the story be true or false, the majority of Machiavelli's early critics were agreed that, whatever the identity of his fellow-residents, hell had assuredly become his permanent address in the hereafter. Throughout the sixteenth and seventeenth centuries we find Machiavelli depicted as the very hand of the devil; as an "imp" of Satan; as "hell-bourne"; as a "damnable fiend" of the underworld; and as the "great muster-master of hell". John Donne went so far as to describe a vision of the netherworld in which Machiavelli, attempting to gain a place in Lucifer's innermost sanctum, was out-argued by Ignatius Loyola, founder of the Jesuits. And it was even possible for Samuel Butler to suggest, facetiously, that "Old Nick" himself took his name from "Nick Machiavel".[2]

This hellish reputation has resulted in a noteworthy philological curiosity. No other writer, apart from Plato, has made a greater impact upon the English vocabulary: not Homer, Aristotle, Virgil, or Livy; not Dante, Petrarch, or Boccaccio; not Hobbes or Locke, Hegel or Marx, Jung or Freud. Not even Shakespeare himself has earned a comparable entry in that mighty thesaurus of English words and phrases, the *New English Dictionary*. *Machiavel, Machiavellize, Machiavellian, Machiavelline, Machiavellism, Machiavellist*: these are but some of the contorted forms in which the unfortunate Florentine's name has passed into the common currency of the English language. And they all indicate something unscrupulous, evil, and base.

One would think it no longer necessary to demonstrate that this is a travesty of Machiavelli, both as a man and as a thinker: though it is still common to see critics defending him against ancient accusations, and frequently over-compensating in the process. Much of the trouble arises simply from a confusion between Machiavelli and Machiavellism: between what the man himself wrote, and how later generations interpreted him. The history of Machiavelli's reputation constitutes an interesting and important study: but it has nothing whatever to do with an understanding of the writer's ideas, capabilities, and limitations.

In one sense Machiavelli is to blame for his posthumous misfortunes. He loved to say shocking things in a shocking fashion, distorting his argument, and overstating his case in order to achieve an effect. He had done this with particular energy in *The Prince*; and the continuing popularity of this book has largely coloured posterity's view of its author. It is not only the shortest of Machiavelli's major works; it is also the simplest, the crudest, and the one which makes the least demands upon a reader, while offering the quickest return in terms of drama and excitement.

The strange thing is not that so many sixteenth-century commentators were scandalised by *The Prince*, but that so vast an edifice of scholarship has since been erected upon the foundation of this slight, *ad hoc*, text, written to impress the Medici by a clever, and rather daring, reversal of a hallowed literary tradition. *The Prince* is still the core of most modern Machiavelli study: though it is now more usual to consider it in comparison with the *Discourses*. The relationship between these two works has become a major preoccupation: but attempts to treat them as ideological antitheses, or, alternatively, to establish their essential homogeneity, help perpetuate the feeling that they are the most important key to Machiavelli's thought. Concentration upon *The Prince* and the *Discourses* also accounts for the ease with which some critics have generalised about Machiavelli's ideas and have imposed an arbitrary system upon them. It further explains the cloudy arguments about Machiavelli's theory of the state—when he obviously never had one; about his historical theory—when he never really worked out more than a rudimentary and largely unnecessary schema; and about his science of politics—when his political thought was so clearly dominated by emotional responses.

The only way to dispel this miasma of exaggerated responses, misconceptions, and misrepresentations, is to study Machiavelli's works, as far as possible, in their entirety. The *Legations* constitute a vital clue to the evolution of Machiavelli's ideas: and it could well be argued that in the correspondence arising from the second mission to Cesare Borgia, and in that relating to the first Roman mission, we have before us Machiavelli's first political master-piece, compounded of sharp observation, verbal wit, vivid charac-terisation, and dramatic intensity. Certainly, even *The Prince* seems subdued by comparison both with the hair-raising letters describing the events leading up to, and succeeding, the murders at Sinigaglia, and with the icy survey of Cesare's declining fortunes in Rome. There is brilliance, dynamism, and acuity, as well as crudity, in *The Prince*; grandeur of conception, as well as confusion, in the *Discourses*; a comprehensive summation of a long tradition in the *Art of War*; and, despite ambiguity and technical uncertainty, a compelling subtlety and realism in the *Florentine History*. No one can even begin to understand Machia-velli without studying all these works: and studying them free of prejudice both of good or ill, and unfettered by the accreted jargon of those who seek to impose a system upon such diverse writings.

Machiavelli was no systematiser. The only homogeneity in his writings is that provided by a number of basic preconceptions resulting, not from speculation, but from bitter experience. His dialectic was marred by a technique inadequate for the demands he made upon it, and by a temperament unsuited to systematic and dispassionate analysis. But his political insights are not less true because he was unable to sustain them by logical argu-ment. His observations upon the limited mental horizons of politicians, upon the mechanical nature of political activity geared to no other purpose than self-perpetuation, and upon the violation—in the name of the state—of every human decency, remain as true today as when he wrote them. There is nothing in contemporary politics which could possibly induce Machiavelli to change his mind: and the five centuries which have passed since his birth would merely serve to provide him with more, and better, historical data to corroborate his views.

Notes

ABBREVIATIONS USED*

A.W. = Machiavelli, *Art of War*, trans. Peter Whitehorne (ed. London, 1905).

Burd = Machiavelli, *Il Principe*, ed. L. Arthur Burd.

D. = Machiavelli, *Discourses*.

Detmold = *Machiavelli, Historical, Political, and Diplomatic Writings*, trans. Christian E. Detmold.

F.H. = Machiavelli, *Florentine History*.

Gilbert, *Chief Works* = Machiavelli, *The Chief Works and Others*, trans. Allan Gilbert.

Gilbert, *Forerunners* = Allan Gilbert, *Machiavelli's Prince and Its Forerunners*.

Letters = Machiavelli, *Lettere*, ed. F. Gaeta.

Letters = Machiavelli, *The Letters . . . A Selection* trans. Allan Gilbert.

M.C. = Machiavelli, *Tutte le opere*, ed. Mazzoni and Casella.

Op.F.P.M. = Machiavelli, *Le Opere*, ed. Fanfani, Passerini, and Milanesi.

P. = Machiavelli, *Il Principe*.

Ridolfi = R. Ridolfi, *The Life of Niccolò Machiavelli*, trans. Cecil Grayson.

Villari = Pasquale Villari, *The Life and Times of Niccolò Machiavelli*.

INTRODUCTION

1. The programme is fully described in *Quarto centenario di Niccolò Machiavelli. Discorso di Atto Vannucci, e relazione de Efisio Contini, Segretario della commissione promotrice* (Florence, 1869).

2. *Prose e versi letti da alcuni studenti dell'università di Padova pel quarto centenario di Nicolò Machiavelli* (Padua: F. Sacchetto: 1869).

Alessandro Marin's contribution is at pp. 23–34.

1. MACHIAVELLI'S POLITICAL EXPERIENCE

1. *Lettere*, pp. 29–33: *Letters*, pp. 85–9.

2. *Lettere*, pp. 28–9.

3. *Libro di Ricordi di Bernardo Machiavelli*, ed. C. Olschki (Florence, 1954).

*For full details see Bibliography, pp. 288–92.

276   MACHIAVELLI: A DISSECTION

4. The following sentences from Cecil Clough, *Machiavelli Researches* (Naples, 1967), p. 10, are typical: "The phrase 'all' was *no doubt* an exaggeration, since the rights were *probably* vested in only some of the branches of the family, *probably* descendants of Filippo already mentioned; *perhaps* those concerned were those who had similar rights over the Church of Sant'Andrea and elsewhere, *though this is not certain*. The significance of the minute is that Niccolò, son of Bernardo, *appears to have been* taking the lead in the dispute, and that Dolfin's letter of introduction was *probably* to the same Niccolò, and concerned with the same dispute at a later stage".
The italics are mine.

5. *Decennale Primo*, ll. 16–30: *M.C.*, p. 800.

6. For examples see J. R. Hale, "War and Public Opinion in Renaissance Italy", *Italian Renaissance Studies*, ed. E. F. Jacob (London, 1960), pp. 94–122.

7. Francesco Guicciardini, *History of Italy and History of Florence*, trans. Cecil Grayson, ed. John Hale (London, 1966), pp. 19–20.

8. For this characterisation of Soderini, in the manner of Machiavelli, see Filippo de' Nerli, *Commentari dei fatti civili occorsi dentro la città di Firenze dall' anno 1215 al 1537* (Trieste, 1859), i, p. 176.

9. Detmold, iii, p. 5.

10. Ibid. pp. 19, 26.

11. *Op.F.P.M.*, iv, p. 10.

12. *Decennale Primo*, ll. 523–50.

13. See pp. 132–5.

14. See pp. 144–6.

15. Detmold, iv. pp. 5–6.

16. Luca Landucci, *A Florentine Diary from 1450 to 1516* trans. Alice de Rosen Jarvis (London, 1927), p. 218.

17. Detmold, iv. p. 59.

18. This *Discourse* is printed in *Op. F.P.M.*, vi, pp. 330–5.

19. Detmold, iv. pp. 104, 150. Ridolfi, who so delights in exposing the archival gaucheries of his predecessors, asserts (p. 102) that "the letters of this legation are almost all written by Machiavelli and in his own hand. Vettori merely signed them, alone, simply adding at most a few lines in his own hand". This view, based upon intuition and not evidence, has been convincingly disposed of by Rosemary Devonshire Jones, "Some Observations on the Relations between Francesco Vettori and Niccolò Machiavelli during the Embassy to Maximilian I", *Italian Studies*, xxiii (1968), pp. 93–113.

20. Francesco Guicciardini, *Istorie d'Italia* (Florence, 1818–19), iii, p. 225.

21. Landucci, *A Florentine Diary*, p. 235.

22. Detmold, iv. p. 214. Cf. *Capitolo dell' ambizione*, ll. 166–8: *M.C.*, p. 853.

23. Detmold, iv, p. 221.

24. Ibid., pp. 235, 259.

25. Ibid., pp. 271, 274.

26. Ibid., p. 276.

27. *D.ii.27*: *M.C.*, p. 184[a].

28. Cited by Villari, ii, p. 21.

29. Detmold, iii, pp. 388, 398; iv, pp. 111, 171, 309.
30. Detmold, iv, p. 326.
31. Detmold, iii, pp. 447–51.
32. Ibid., pp. 461, 466, 471, 475, 480.
33. Ibid., pp. 147, 158, 170, 208.
34. Ibid., pp. 222, 226, 258.
35. Ibid., p. 259. P.7; M.C., p. 16[b].
36. Detmold, iii, pp. 192, 261–2, 270.
37. Gerber, i, p. 38, argued, on the basis of the handwriting of the autograph MS., that this narrative may have been written after The Prince. More recently, Allan Gilbert, Chief Works, i, p. 163, has suggested that it could be a draft for a projected section of the Florentine History—thus putting it among Machiavelli's last writings. Ridolfi, pp. 64, 272, with the exclamation mark which is his chief critical tool, rejects Gerber: but offers no reasonable explanation for the discrepancies, nor for the literary tone of the fragment. The same dating is, incidentally, probably true of two other works allegedly written at about this time: On the Method of Dealing with the Rebels of the Val di Chiana; and Words on the Raising of Money. The first of these has been regarded as an early instance of the historical method later to be employed by Machiavelli in his discursive writings—though it clearly depends on an idea worked out in the Discourses; and the latter has been interpreted as an early statement of Machiavelli's belief in the power of arms and virtù over Fortune. But the only evidence for early composition is the fact that the subject matter of these short pieces concerns events about the year 1503. We have come to a pretty pass if the dating of historical works can only be determined by subject matter.
38. Detmold, iii, pp. 158–60, 169, 178–9, 182, 216.
39. Ibid., p. 269.
40. Ibid., pp. 171, 210.
41. Detmold, iii, p. 202; iv, p. 323.
42. Detmold, iii, p. 300: Decennale Primo, ll. 472–4.
43. Detmold, iii, pp. 304–6.
44. Ibid., pp. 318–21.
45. Ibid., pp. 335–6.
46. Ibid., pp. 349–50, 354, 358, 360, 367, 369.
47. Ibid., pp. 297, 300, 307.
48. Ibid., pp. 313, 333–4.
49. Ibid., pp. 349, 364, 369, 372, 386.
50. See pp. 61, 75.
51. Detmold, iv. p. 55.
52. Ibid., p. 69.
53. See Machiavelli's letter of 26 August 1513: Lettere, No. 138, p. 296: Letters p. 138.
54. Detmold, iii, p. 356.
55. Detmold, iv, p. 258.
56. D.i.27: M.C., p. 95[b].
57. Detmold, iii, pp. 74–80.
58. Ibid., pp. 83–84.
59. Ibid., pp. 100–101, 114, 125–8.
60. Detmold, iv, p. 249.
61. M.C., pp. 731–9.
62. M.C., pp. 730–1. Detmold, iv, pp. 419–20.
63. Op.F.P.M., vi, pp. 313–30.
64. Detmold, iii, pp. 462, 464.
65. Ibid., p. 133, for the advice to Louis: iv, pp. 51, 250, for the other references.

66. Detmold, iii, pp. 166, 332.
67. Detmold, iv, p. 34.
68. Detmold, iii, pp. 44, 47–9.
69. Detmold, iv, pp. 284–6.
70. Detmold, iii, p. 446.
71. *Opere di Niccolò Machiavelli* (Italia, 1813), vii, pp. 48–51: inaccurately rendered in Detmold, iii, pp. 483–4.
72. Detmold, iii, p. 410; iv, p. 129. Villari, i, p. 306.

2. EVOLUTION OF "THE PRINCE"

1. *Lettere*, No. 120, p. 232: *Letters*, p. 101.
2. *Lettere*, No. 122, pp. 234–5: *Letters*, p. 102.
3. *Lettere*, No. 124, pp. 239–40: *Letters*, p. 104.
4. *Lettere*, No. 126, p. 244: *Letters*, pp. 106–7.
5. *Lettere*, Nos. 130, 133, pp. 262–3, 271: *Letters*, pp. 121, 123.
6. *M.C.*, pp. 871–2.
7. *De principatibus* is the title given in Machiavelli's letter to Vettori of 10 December 1513: *Lettere*, No. 140, p. 304: *Letters*, p. 142.
8. *Lettere*, No. 119, pp. 228–31: *Letters*, pp. 96–100: *M.C.*, pp. 878b–80a.
9. *Lettere*, No. 140, pp. 301–6: *Letters*, pp. 139–44.
10. *Lettere*, Nos. 141, 142, pp. 306–13: *Letters*, pp. 144–8.
11. *Lettere*, No. 145, p. 323: *Letters*, pp. 153–4.
12. *Lettere*, No. 152, p. 343: *Letters*, p. 163.
13. *Lettere*, No. 160, p. 368: *Letters*, p. 183.
14. J. R. Hale, *Machiavelli and Renaissance Italy* (London, 1961), p. 160.
15. Cited in Burd, p. 171 n.
16. *Lettere*, No. 163, pp. 374–5: *Letters*, pp. 185–6.
17. An important account of the political circumstances underlying the composition of *The Prince* is in Cecil H. Clough, *Machiavelli Researches* (Naples, 1967), pp. 27–78: though this includes a good deal of argument based merely upon sequences of hypotheses.
18. *P.*20: *M.C.*, p. 42a–b. *Lettere*, No. 140, pp. 305–6: *Letters*, p. 144.
19. *M.C.*, p. 3.
20. *P.*15: *M.C.*, p. 30b.
21. *P.*11: *M.C.*, p. 24b.
22. *P.*14: *M.C.*, p. 29a.
23. Gilbert, *Forerunners*, is invaluable on this subject.
24. Cf. *Lettere*, Nos. 157, 159, pp. 359, 364: *Letters*, pp. 175, 178.
25. See pp. 201–2. The first critic to argue the inutility of Machiavelli's advice was Reginald Pole about 1539. See his *Apologia ad Carolum Quintum* in *Epistolarum Reginaldi Poli* (Brescia, 1744–57), i, pp. 147–8.
26. *P.*19: *M.C.*, p. 38b.
27. *P.*23: *M.C.*, p. 47a.
28. On *virtù* and fortune, see pp. 216ff.
29. *P.*26: *M.C.*, p. 51b. The reference is to Petrarch, *Canzone*, 16, ll. 13–16: "*Virtù* against rage shall take up arms, and the combat will be brief; because ancient valour, in Italian hearts, is not yet dead".
30. See pp. 36–7.
31. *Lettere*, No. 135, p. 279: *Letters*, pp. 128–9.

32. *Lettere*, No. 138, p. 292: *Letters*, pp. 133–4.

33. *Lettere*, No. 138, p. 296: *Letters*, p. 138.

3. The "Discourses"

1. R. Riccardi, "Zibaldone", printed in Alvisi's ed. of Machiavelli's *Lettere familiari* (Florence, 1883), p. xiv.

2. See Cecil H. Clough, *Machiavelli Researches* (Naples, 1967), pp. 79–107, for an interesting—if too hypothetical—discussion of the text of the *Discourses*.

3. *P.2: M.C.*, p. 5ᵃ. For the view that the *Discourses* were started before *The Prince* see Federico Chabod, *Machiavelli and the Renaissance* (London, 1958), p. 31 n.2; Ridolfi, Chapter XIV n. 10. For the strange, and unnecessary, suggestion of a missing treatise, see Felix Gilbert, "The Composition and Structure of Machiavelli's *Discorsi*", *Journal of the History of Ideas*, XIV (1953), pp. 136–56. For more general arguments based upon an idealised view of Machiavelli's evolution as a republican, see Hans Baron, "Machiavelli: the republican citizen and the author of *The Prince*", *English Historical Review*, LXXVI (1961), pp. 217–53. All these views are presented in an extraordinarily doctrinaire manner, unwarranted by the exiguous evidence.

4. *D*.ii.1; iii.19; iii.42: *M.C.*, pp. 138ᵇ, 229ᵃ, 257ᵃ.

5. For the events between 1513 and 1517 mentioned in the *Discourses*, see L. J. Walker's ed. (London, 1950), ii, pp. 262–4.

6. See F. Gilbert, "Composition and Structure"; C. H. Clough, *Machiavelli Researches*.

7. See pp. 219–20.

8. Villari, ii, pp. 265–72. Felix Gilbert, "Bernardo Rucellai and the Orti Oricellari", *Journal of the Warburg and Courtauld Institutes*, XII (1949), pp. 101–31. See also F. Gilbert, "Composition and Structure", pp. 150–3.

9. Gilbert, *Chief Works*, ii, p. 929 n. 6. Cf. *Lettere*, No. 140, p. 304.

10. See Burd, pp. 240–1n., for a convincing argument on Machiavelli's use of Livy concerning Nabis. But since the passage in question, which is not integral to the chapter, could have been added at any time—even after the composition of the *Discourses*—one is no further on.

11. *M.C.*, pp. 3ᵃ, 55ᵃ, 266ᵃ.

12. *M.C.*, p. 56ᵃ.

13. *M.C.*, pp. 56ᵇ–57ᵃ.

14. *M.C.*, p. 55ᵇ.

15. *M.C.*, p. 196ᵃ.

16. See the chronological table in Walker, ii, pp. 222–64.

17. *M.C.*, pp. 135ᵃ–137ᵃ.

18. Francesco Guicciardini, *Considerations on the "Discourses" of Machiavelli* in *Francesco Guicciardini: Selected Writings*, ed. and trans. C. & M. Grayson (London, 1965), pp. 107–8.

19. See especially *D*.i.39; iii.43.

20. On Polybius see Kurt von Fritz, *The Theory of the Mixed Constitution in Antiquity: a Critical Analysis of Polybius' Political Ideas*

(New York, 1954). Such is the similarity of temperament and terminology between Polybius and Machiavelli, that this penetrating and meticulous book seems to me more illuminating than the majority of studies devoted to the Florentine.

21. See, for example, J. H. Hexter, "Seyssel, Machiavelli and Polybius VI: the Mystery of the Missing Translation", *Studies in the Renaissance*, III (1956), pp. 75–96.

22. See C. C. Bayley, *War and Society in Renaissance Florence: the "De Militia" of Leonardo Bruni* (U. of Toronto, 1961), pp. 178–240.

23. Walker, i, pp. 61–63.

24. *The General History of the Wars of the Romans by Polybius*, trans. Hampton (London, 1812), pp. 17–18.

25. Ibid., p. 19.

26. Ibid., pp. 401–2.

27. Ibid., p. 395.

28. *D.i.2: M.C.*, pp. 60^a–61^b. Cf. *F.H.v.1: M.C.*, p. 499^a: States "if they are not overwhelmed by some extraordinary force" will complete the cycle of *virtù/* corruption.

29. *D.ii.1; iii.17: M.C.*, pp. 137^a–9^a, 226^b.

30. *D.i.37: M.C.*, pp. 105^b–7^b.

31. *D.iii.24: M.C.*, p. 235^b.

32. *D.i.18: M.C.*, p. 87^b.

33. *D.i.37: M.C.*, p. 107^a.

34. *D.i.6; ii.9; ii.32; M.C.*, pp. 67^b, 151^b, 192^a.

35. *D.i.6; iii.37: M.C.*, pp. 76^b, 251^b.

36. *D.iii.1: M.C.*, pp. 193^b–6^a.

37. *D.iii.22: M.C.*, p. 232^b.

38. *D.i.17: M.C.*, p. 86^a.

39. *D.i.18: M.C.*, p. 88^{a-b}. Cf. *D.i.55: M.C.*, p. 127^b.

40. *D.i.55: M.C.*, p. 128^b. It should be noted, however, that Machiavelli was favourably impressed by the Emperors from Nerva to Marcus—a mere hundred years. See *D.i.10: M.C.*, p. 75^b.

41. *D.i.55: M.C.*, p. 127^a.

42. *L'Asino*, V. ll. 58–63: *M.C.*, p. 830.

43. *D.i.12: M.C.*, p. 78^a.

44. *D.ii.2: M.C.*, p. 141^{a-b}.

4. A LITERARY INTERLUDE

1. Ridolfi, Chapter XVI n. 19, pp. 302–3.

2. Ridolfi, introduction to *La Mandragola di Niccolò Machiavelli* (Florence, 1965).

3. *Lettere*, No. 170, p. 383.

4. *M.C.*, pp. 817–40.

5. *L'Asino*, II. ll. 85–90.

6. Ibid., III. ll. 76–80.

7. Ibid., IV. ll. 139–42.

8. Villari, ii, p. 362.

9. *L'Asino*, V. ll. 38–9. Cf. *D.i.37: M.C.*, pp. 105^b–6^a.

10. *L'Asino*, V. ll. 79 ff. Cf. *F.H.*, v.1: *M.C.*, op. 498^b–9^b.

11. *P.12*, 25.

12. *L'Asino*, VI. ll. 52–7.

13. Ibid., VII. ll. 40–2, 100–105.

14. John Addington Symonds, *The Renaissance in Italy* (London, 1897), v, pp. 143–7.

15. Ridolfi, pp. 172–5.

16. Ridolfi, *La Mandragola*, p. 8.

17. Gilbert, *Chief Works*, ii, p. 775.

18. *La Mandragola* is printed in *M.C.*, pp. 693–726.

19. *La Mandragola*, V.6; III.3.

20. Ibid., IV.2.

21. Ibid., III.12.

22. Cf. *L'Asino*, I. l.99.

23. *La Mandragola*, I.3. Cf. *D*.iii.6: *M.C.*, p. 204ᵃ. Cf. also *H.F.*, ii.32: *M.C.*, p. 431ᵃ.

24. *La Mandragola*, III.2.

25. Ibid., I.1.3.

26. Ibid., IV.1.

27. Ibid., II.3.

28. Ibid., III.4.

29. Ibid., III.9.

30. Ibid., III.11.

31. Ibid., IV.6.

32. Ibid., V.1. Cf. *F.H.*, i.17: *M.C.*, p. 392ᵇ.

5. THE "ART OF WAR"

1. My quotations, cited as *A.W.*, are from *The Art of War*, trans. Peter Whitehorne, 1560, reprinted in the Tudor Translations series (London 1905). I have modernised the spelling: and I give page references to the ed. of the *Art of War* in Mazzoni and Cassella.

2. *A.W.*, p. 121: *M.C.*, p. 314ᵇ.

3. *Lettere*, No. 178, pp. 396–7.

4. For the former view, see Sir Charles Oman, *A History of the Art of War in the Sixteenth Century* (London, 1937), pp. 93–7. For the latter view, see the intro. to *The Art of War*, ed. Neal Wood (Indianapolis, New York, Kansas City, 1965), especially p. xxxiii. It is a pity that Wood saw fit to revise and reprint the Ellis Farneworth translation which—unlike Whitehorne's tough and literal version— is so pleonastic and wildly inaccurate as to be completely misleading.

5. *A.W.* p. 30: *M.C.*, p. 268ᵃ. Cf. for a similar metaphor concerning the sun and the shade, *D*.ii.30: *M.C.*, p. 188ᵇ.

6. On the early printings of these authors, see Maurice J. D. Cockle, *A Bibliography of Military Books up to 1642* (London, 1900), Nos. 1, 3, 17.

7. See L. Arthur Burd, "Le fonti letterarie di Machiavelli nell'Arte della Guerra", in *Atti della Reale Accademia dei Lincei*, Ser.V.iv (1896), Pt.1, pp. 187–261.

8. On Valturius and Cornazano, see Cockle, Nos. 501, 505. On French treatises and their relation to Latin and Italian sources, see G. Dickinson, intro. to *The "Instructions sur le Faict de la Guerre"* (London, 1954), pp. xcii– cix, cxvi–cxxv.

9. Ridolfi, p. 178, has the "marvellous innovations". For Egidio Colonna, see C. C. Bayley, *War and Society in Renaissance Florence: the "De Militia" of Leonardo Bruni* (U. of Toronto, 1961), pp. 181–2. Bayley's study is of considerable importance for the light it throws upon the military mentality of fifteenth-century Italy.

10. Bayley, p. 183.

11. Bayley, p. 233.

12. W. H. Woodward, *Vittorino da Feltre and Other Humanist Educators* (Cambridge, 1921), p. 115.

13. See Bayley, pp. 219–25.

14. For more qualified approval of Biondo, and a consideration of his limitations, see Denys Hay, "Flavio Biondo and the Middle Ages", *Proceedings of the British*

Academy, xlv (1959), pp. 97–128.

15. *A.W.*, pp. 13–15: *M.C.*, pp. 265–6.

16. *A.W.*, pp. 93–5: *M.C.*, pp. 300[b] –1[b].

17. *A.W.*, pp. 95–6: *M.C.*, p. 302[a].

18. See, for some examples, H. Weissinger, "Renaissance Theories of the Revival of the Fine Arts", *Italica*, (1943), pp. 163–70. See also H. Weissinger, "The Renaissance Theory of the Reaction against the Middle Ages as a cause of the Renaissance", *Speculum*, xx (1945), pp. 461–7. Machiavelli himself has something to say on this subject: see *D.ii.5*: *M.C.*, p. 146[b], for his opinion that Christianity destroyed ancient history, poetry, and art.

19. See pp. 51–3.

20. *A.W.*, p. 97: *M.C.*, p. 302[b].

21. *A.W.*, p. 162: *M.C.*, p. 333[a].

22. *A.W.*, p. 98: *M.C.*, p. 303[b].

23. *A.W.*, p. 117: *M.C.*, p. 312[a].

24. *A.W.*, p. 225: *M.C.*, p. 363[b].

25. *A.W.*, p. 227: *M.C.*, pp. 364[b]–5[a].

26. *A.W.*, p. 43: *M.C.*, p. 275[a].

27. *A.W.*, p. 80: *M.C.*, p. 293[b].

28. *A.W.*, pp. 74–5: *M.C.*, p. 290[b].

29. *A.W.*, pp. 34, 43: *M.C.*, pp. 270[a], 275[b].

30. *A.W.*, p. 47: *M.C.*, p. 277[b].

31. *A.W.*, p. 54: *M.C.*, p. 281[a].

32. *A.W.*, p. 46: *M.C.*, pp. 276[b]–7[a].

33. *A.W.*, pp. 46–7: *M.C.*, p. 277[a–b].

34. *A.W.*, p. 231: *M.C.*, p. 367[a–b].

35. *A.W.*, p. 63: *M.C.*, pp. 284[b]–5[a].

36. Cf. *P.26*: *M.C.*, p. 51[a–b].

37. *A.W.*, p. 70: *M.C.*, p. 288[a–b]. Cf. *D.ii.18* where Machiavelli had employed identical arguments and phraseology.

38. *A.W.*, p. 75: *M.C.*, p. 291[a].

39. *A.W.*, p. 97: *M.C.*, p. 303[a].

40. *A.W.*, p. 117: *M.C.*, p. 312[b]. The reference is, presumably, to *D.ii.17*.

41. Felix Gilbert, "Machiavelli: the Renaissance of the Art of War", in *Makers of Modern Strategy*, ed. E. M. Earle (Princeton, 1944), pp. 16–18. Cf. *The Art of War*, ed. Wood, p. xxi.

42. *A.W.*, pp. 111–12: *M.C.*, p. 309[a–b].

43. Machiavelli had said most of this before in *D.ii.17*. For the passage in the *Report on the Affairs of Germany*, see *M.C.*, p. 743[a–b].

44. Villari, ii, p. 306.

45. Hampton's *Polybius* (ed. of London, 1812), pp. 217–18.

46. Christine de Pisan, trans. William Caxton, *The Book of Fayttes of Armes and of Chyualrye*, ed. A. T. P. Byles (E.E.T.S., 1932), pp. 25–8.

47. Ibid., p. 291.

48. The following list—doubtless very incomplete — includes eds. of Vegetius published separately or together with other military classics. (I) Printed in Italy: Rome, E. Silber, 1487; Pescia, R. de Orlandis, 1488; Rome, E. Silber, 1494; Venice, Bernadino di Vitale, 1524; Venice, Gregorio di Gregorii, 1525; Venice, Comin da Trino, 1540; Venice, G. Giolito, 1551. (II) Printed in France: Paris, G. Marchand, 1488; Paris, P. le Noir, 1527; Paris, C. Wechel, 1532; Paris, C. Wechel, 1535 (two eds.); Paris, C. Wechel, 1536; Paris, A. Wechel, 1553; Lyons, F. Raphel-

engium, 1592). (III) Printed in Germany: Augsburg, G. Zainer, c. 1470; Cologne, N. Gotz, c. 1475; Augsburg, J. Wiener, c. 1475; Erfurt, H. Knappen, 1511; Augsburg, H. Stainer, 1529; Cologne, E. Cernicornus, 1532; Augsburg, H. Stainer, 1534; Cologne, M. Cholinum, 1580, Frankfort, 1616. (IV) Printed in the Low Countries: Utrecht, N. Ketelaer & G. Leempt, c. 1475; Antwerp, Plantin, 1585; Leyden, Plantin, 1607; Antwerp, Plantin, 1607. (V) Printed in England: London, T. Marshe, 1572.

49. Oman, pp. 93-4.

50. See for example, *The Art of War*, ed. Wood, p. xxxiv.

51. Christine de Pisan, *op. cit.*, p. 80.

52. *A.W.*, pp. 231-2: *M.C.*, p. 367[b].

53. A good idea of the range and scope of such material is provided by Cockle's *Bibliography of Military Books*.

54. See, for example, the articles of the tournament at Smithfield, 1467, in S. Bentley, *Excerpta Historica* (London, 1831), pp. 180, 208, at Sandricourt, 1493, in A. Vayssière, *Le pas des armes de Sandricourt* (Paris, 1874), pp. 3-4; and at Milan, 1507, in Jean d'Auton, *Chroniques de Louis XII* (Paris, 1889-95), iv, p. 303.

6. The "Florentine History"

1. *M.C.*, pp. 747-63.

2. On the *Life of Castruccio Castracani*, see Villari, ii, pp. 282-8; Ridolfi, pp. 181-2.

3. *Lettere*, No. 177, pp. 394-5.

4. *Op.F.P.M.*, iv, pp. 105ff.; Gilbert, *Chief Works*, i, pp. 101-15.

5. Gilbert, *Chief Works*, i, p. 108.

6. Ibid., pp. 113-14.

7. *Lettere*, No. 194, p. 417: from Machiavelli to Francesco Guicciardini, dated 30 August 1524.

8. Gilbert, *Chief Works*, iii, p. 1028.

9. *F.H.*, *Proemio*: *M.C.*, pp. 378[b]-9[a].

10. *F.H.*, *Proemio*: *M.C.*, p. 380[a].

11. *Thucydides*, trans. B. Jowett (Oxford, 1881), i, p. 15.

12. *F.H.*, iv.28: *M.C.*, p. 493[a-b]. Cf. Giovanni Cavalcanti, *Istorie Fiorentine*, ed. F. Polidori (Florence, 1838-39), i, pp. 503-6. See also Villari, ii, pp. 419-20.

13. For the unrevised version of this speech, see *Op.F.P.M.*, ii, pp. 40-1.

14. *F.H.*, iv.26: *M.C.*, p. 490[a-b].

15. *F.H.*, iv.27: *M.C.*, pp. 491[a]-2[b]. Cf. *D.i.33*: *M.C.*, pp. 101[b]-102[a], for a similar view of Uzzano and the Medici.

16. *F.H.*, ii.35: *M.C.*, p. 435[a-b].

17. See Wallace K. Ferguson, *The Renaissance in Historical Thought* (Cambridge, Mass., 1948).

18. *F.H.*, v.1: *M.C.*, p. 498[b]. Cf. pp. 117-8.

19. *F.H.*, viii.29: *M.C.*, p. 614[b].

20. *F.H.*, iii.5: *M.C.*, pp. 446[b]-7[b].

21. *F.H.*, v.1: *M.C.*, pp. 499[a-b].

22. Ibid.

23. *F.H.*, ii.34, 36, 40: *M.C.*, pp. 433[a], 437[a], 441[b].

24. *F.H.*, ii.42: *M.C.*, p. 443[a].

25. *F.H.*, iii.1: *M.C.*, pp. 443[b]-4[b]. This nostalgia for the vanished military caste, and contempt for

the upstart merchants who supplanted them, has a long history extending back to Boccaccio. See C. C. Bayley, *War and Society in Renaissance Florence etc.* (U. of Toronto, 1961), pp. 206 ff.

26. Significant references to the people, though not in the order discussed, are as follows: *M.C.*, pp. 433[b], 435[b], 443[a], 450[a], 463[b], 470[b], 472[a], 507[b], 548[b]–9[a], 590[a].

27. *F.H.*, i.4–6: *M.C.*, pp. 383[b]–4[b]. There is, besides Theodoric, the extraordinary figure of Michele di Lando who rises, like a saviour, from the people. See p. 211.

28. *F.H.*, vii.8: *M.C.*, p. 569[a].

29. *F.H.*, iv.1: *M.C.*, p. 472[b].

30. *M.C.*, pp. 426[a], 437[a], 472[a]. 492[a].

31. *F.H.*, ii.1: *M.C.*, p. 408[b].

32. *P.*12; *D.*i.4; *D.*iii.31; *A.W.*, pp. 13–15; *Discorsi sull'ordinare la milizia* in *Op.F.P.M.*, vi, p. 330; *Discorso sopra il provvedere danari* in *Op.F.P.M.*, vi, p. 279.

33. *F.H.*, i.39: *M.C.*, p. 407[a]–[b].

34. *F.H.*, vi.1: *M.C.*, p. 530[a]–[b]. Cf. *D.* ii.6: *M.C.*, p. 147[b]. And cf. *A.W.*, p. 162: *M.C.*, p. 333[a].

35. There were technical reasons for the changes in fortification and its efficacy which Machiavelli had recognised in the Seventh Book of the *Art of War.*

36. *F.H.*, v.33: *M.C.*, pp. 527[a]–8[a].

37. *F.H.*, vii.20: *M.C.*, pp. 577[b]–8[a]. On Machiavelli's sources see Villari, ii, pp. 426, 432. Cf. also Machiavelli's account of the Battle of Zagonara in 1424: *F.H.*, iv.6: *M.C.*, p. 475[b]. Here he writes that in a battle celebrated throughout Italy, only three men were slain:

and those because they fell into the mud and were drowned. See Villari, ii, p. 415; Burd, pp. 270–1n.

38. *F.H.*, viii.23: *M.C.*, p. 610[a]–[b].

39. *F.H.*, i.9, 11, 14, 23, 24, 30; ii.10; vii.22; viii.11, 17, 28: *M.C.*, pp. 387[a]–8[a], 389[a], 391[a]–[b], 397[a]–[b], 398[a]–[b], 402[a]–[b], 415[a]–[b], 579[a], 599[b], 604[b], 613[a].

40. Papal brief, cited in Ridolfi, p. 213.

41. Machiavelli's *Report* on the fortifications of Florence is published in *Op.F.P.M.*, vi, pp. 364–70. It has been translated in Gilbert, *Chief Works*, ii, pp. 727–34.

7. REALISM

1. Reginald Pole, *Apologia ad Carolum Quintum*, in *Epistolarum Reginaldi Poli* (Brescia, 1744–57), i, pp. 136–7.

2. See A. H. Gilbert, *Machiavelli's Prince and Its Forerunners* (Duke U. Press, Durham, N. Carolina, 1938).

3. See Burd, pp. 282–3n.

4. See, for one important example of this attitude at work, Felix Gilbert, "Florentine Political Assumptions in the Period of Savonarola and Soderini", *Journal of the Warburg and Courtauld Institutes*, xx (1957), pp. 187–214.

5. Gaines Post, *Studies in Medieval Legal Thought: Public Law and the State, 1100–1322* (Princeton, New Jersey, 1964), p. 308 n. 141.

6. Ibid., p. 263.

7. Ibid., p. 277.

8. Cited in Gilbert, *Forerunners*, p. 83.

9. Aristotle, *Politics*, III. 13.xvii–xx (1284b), Jowett's trans.

10. Ibid., III. 13.xxii (1284b).

11. See Gilbert, *Forerunners*: and Felix Gilbert, "The Humanist Concept of the Prince and *The Prince* of Machiavelli", *Journal of Modern History*, xi (1939), pp. 449–83.

12. Cited in Gilbert, *Forerunners*, p. 127.

13. *Politics*, V. 10.xxxii–xxxv (1312b).

14. Cited in Gilbert, *Forerunners*, p. 127.

15. Ibid., pp. 112–13.

16. Ibid., pp. 104–5.

17. Ibid., p. 124.

18. *Politics*, V. ll. iv–xxxiii (1313a–15b).

19. Girolamo Savonarola, *Tractato . . . circa el reggimento & gouerno della Citta di Firenze* (Florence, c. 1498).

20. Ibid., *Tractato secondo*, Chapter II.

21. Cited in Gilbert, *Forerunners*, pp. 137–8.

22. *D*.iii.6: *M.C.*, p. 201^a.

23. *F.H.*, ii.36–7: *M.C.*, pp. 436^a–40^a.

24. *D*.i.9, 29, 40; *D*.ii, Preface, 20: *M.C.*, pp. 73^a, 96^b, 113^a, 136^b, 172^b.

25. *M.C.*, pp. 283^a, 326^a.

26. *M.C.*, pp. 430^a, 432^a, 453^a, 480^b, 484$^{a–b}$, 511^a, 585^a.

27. *D*.iii.29: *M.C.*, p. 240$^{a–b}$.

28. *D*.i.17: *M.C.*, p. 86^a.

29. *D*.i.9: *M.C.*, pp. 72^b–3^a.

30. *D*.iii.41: *M.C.*, p. 256^b.

31. *D*.i.29, 58; iii.34: *M.C.*, pp. 98^a, 131^b–2^b, 248^b.

32. *D*.i.16: *M.C.*, pp. 84^b–85^a.

33. *D*.i.44, 57.

34. See pp. 178–9.

35. Michele di Lando's career is extravagantly described in *F.H.*, iii.16–18: *M.C.*, pp. 459^b–61^b.

His scurvy treatment at the hands of Florence is in *F.H.*, iii.22: *M.C.*, p. 465^a.

36. *F.H.*, iii.10: *M.C.*, p. 452^a.

37. *F.H.*, iii.13: *M.C.*, pp. 455^a–7^a.

38. François de Belleforest, *Harangues militaires* (Paris, 1573), p. 1094.

8. "FORTUNA" AND "VIRTÙ"

1. Ridolfi, p. ix.

2. Julia Cartwright, *Beatrice d'Este* (London, 1903), p. 372.

3. Boethius, *The Consolation of Philosophy*, trans. "I.T.", revised H. F. Stewart (Loeb Classical Library, London, 1946), p. 359.

4. Detmold, iii, p. 86.

5. Ibid., pp. 159–60, 178–9, 182, 269.

6. Ibid., pp. 216, 334.

7. *Decennale Primo*, ll. 126–32, 523–24.

8. *M.C.*, pp. 845–9.

9. *D*.iii.9: *M.C.*, p. 215$^{a–b}$.

10. *F.H.*, iv.30: *M.C.*, p. 495^b.

11. *Capitolo di Fortuna*, ll. 73–75, 165.

12. Ibid., ll. 13–15.

13. See for example, *D*.ii.27; iii.31: *M.C.*, pp. 184^b, 244^b. Cf. *F.H.*, v.3: *M.C.*, p. 500^b.

14. *M.C.*, p. 759$^{a–b}$.

15. Terence, *Phormio*, I. iv.26; Virgil, *Aeneid*, X.284; Livy, VIII.29; Seneca, *Medea*, 159.

16. Cicero, *Paradoxes*, V; Plutarch, *Moralia*, "De Fortuna"; Juvenal, *Satires*, X.365–6; Claudian, *Panegyric on the Consulship of F. Manlius Theodorus*, 1–6.

17. Dante, *Paradiso*, VIII.139; *De Monarchia*, III.16.

18. Petrarch, *De Remediis Utriusque Fortunae*.

19. Leon Battista Alberti, *Della Tran-quillità dell'Animo*, III; *Della Fam-iglia*, "Proemio".

20. Pietro Bembo, *Gli Asolani* (Ven-ice, 1505), sig. e.iii^{r-v}.

21. Contemporary account cited in Ferdinand Gregorovius, *Lucrezia Borgia* (London, 1948), p. 142.

22. *Op.F.P.M.*, iv, pp. 8–15: passage trans. Ridolfi, p. 50.

23. *D*.ii.19: *M.C.*, p. 171^a. *L'Asino*, ll.$^'$37–9.

24. *D*.i.Proemio: *M.C.*, p. 56^{a-b}. *A.W.*, p. 35: *M.C.*, p. 271^a.

25. *P*.11: *M.C.*, p. 24^b. *F.H.*, i.4; iii.17; vii.23: *M.C.*, pp. 383^a, 461^a, 580^a.

26. *D*.iii.31: *M.C.*, pp. 242^b–3^b.

27. *F.H.*, iv.23: *M.C.*, p. 488^a.

28. *A.W.*, p. 114: *M.C.*, p. 310^b.

29. *D*.i.43; ii.2; ii.12: *M.C.*, pp. 114^{a-b}, 139^a–40^b, 156^a. *Capitolo di Fortuna*, ll.118–20.

30. *F.H.*, vii.22: *M.C.*, p. 579^a.

31. *D*.ii.29: *M.C.*, p. 187^b.

32. *D*.ii.30: *M.C.*, p. 189^b.

33. *D*.i.1: *M.C.*, p. 58^a.

34. *D*.iii.12: *M.C.*, pp. 219^a–21^a.

35. *Op.F.P.M.*, vi, p. 264.

9. METHOD

1. *D*.iii.37: *M.C.*, p. 251^b.

2. *Francesco Guicciardini: Selected Writings*, ed. & trans. C. & M. Grayson (London, 1965), p. 30.

3. See pp. 173–5.

4. Burd, pp. 53–4.

5. *Guicciardini: Selected Writings*, p. 92.

6. Federico Chabod, *Machiavelli and the Renaissance* (London, 1958), has a very generalised chapter on Machiavelli's method and style where he diagnoses what he terms Machiavelli's "dilemmatic tech-nique". Strictly speaking the technique is rarely "dilemmatic" which indicates a specific kind of disjunctive sentence: though, oc-casionally, Machiavelli does pose a genuine dilemma, as, for example, in *D*. iii.13.

7. For the Pisan *Discourse*, see *Op. F.P.M.*, vi, pp. 284–8. The opinion on the court of France is cited from Detmold, iii, pp. 82–3.

8. Detmold, iii, pp. 192, 195, 202, 216.

9. Ibid., pp. 295–6, 342, 345. Cf. January 1504, when Machiavelli writes that he will be bringing either perfect security for peace, or instructions for war (Ibid., p. 403); September 1506, when he writes that the Pope must "either carry out his first intention, or hastily adopt such other course as may seem best to him" (Det-mold, iv, pp. 46–7); July 1510, when he writes that Louis XII will either revenge himself on the Pope or lose all his Italian posses-sions (Ibid., pp. 233–4).

10. Gilbert, *Chief Works*, i, p. 3.

11. *P*.12: *M.C.*, p. 25^a.

12. Curiously, the example selected by Chabod, *op. cit.*, p. 28, from the *Art of War*, iv—"I say there-fore that battles are lost or won" —is not as ingenuous as it appears. In this instance Machiavelli is, in fact, introducing a discussion of the ways in which battles *are* lost or won.

13. *P*.3, 4, 6, 10, 12: *M.C.*, pp. 7^a, 11^a, 12^b, 22^a, 25^a.

14. *D.ii.15: M.C.*, p. 159^a.

15. *P*.3, 9, 21: *M.C.*, pp. 6^b, 21^a, 44^a.

16. *D.ii.32: M.C.*, pp. 190^b–2^a.

17. *Mandragola*, II.6: *M.C.*, p. 703^b.

18. *D.i.46: M.C.*, p. 116^b.

19. *P*.8: *M.C.*, pp. 19^b–20^a.

20. *P*.18.

21. *D.i.45: M.C.*, p. 116^a.

22. *D.ii.23: M.C.*, pp. 175^a–7^b.

23. *D.i.27: M.C.*, p. 95^{a–b}.

24. Detmold, iv, pp. 35–6.

25. *P*.6: *M.C.*, pp. 12^b–14^a. *D*. iii.30:
    M.C., pp. 241^b–2^a.

26. *D.i.55: M.C.*, p. 126^{a–b}.

27. *D.i.11: M.C.*, p. 76^b.

28. *D.iii.45: M.C.*, p. 259^{a–b}.

29. *D.ii.27: M.C.*, pp. 183^b–5^a.

30. *D.i.23: M.C.*, pp. 91^b–2^b. *Francesco Guicciardini: Selected Writings*,
    pp. 87–9.

31. See pp. 184–6.

32. Sir Charles Oman, *History of the Art of War in the Middle Ages*
    (London, 1924), ii, p. 309.

33. *D.ii.18: M.C.*, pp. 167^b–8^a.

34. *A.W.*, p. 71: *M.C.*, p. 288^b.

35. *D.ii.18: M.C.*, p. 168^{a–b}. *A.W.*,
    pp. 133–4: *M.C.*, p. 319^b. The
    passage as in the *Discourses* is
    somewhat ambiguous and might
    be differently rendered to suggest
    that, though Regulus's plan failed,
    it was not because the *virtù* of his
    infantry was insufficient for him to
    believe that they would triumph.
    But in this case one would simply
    be left with a Roman miscalculation—the general may have believed his infantry good enough
    for the job: but they weren't.

36. See pp. 139–41.

37. *D.iii.16: M.C.*, p. 225^{a–b}.

38. *D.i.58. M.C.*, pp. 130^a–3^b.

39. *D.iii.13: M.C.*, p. 222^a.

40. *D.i.11: M.C.*, p. 77^a.

41. *D.i.12: M.C.*, p. 78^a.

42. *D.i.15: M.C.*, pp. 82^a–3^a.

43. *D.ii.2: M.C.*, pp. 139^a–41^b.

44. *D.i.12: M.C.*, p. 79^a.

CONCLUSION

1. Etienne Binet, *Du Salut d'Origen*,
   cited in Pierre Bayle, *Dictionnaire*.

2. For a study of these and similar
   reactions to Machiavelli see my
   forthcoming book *The Reception
   of Machiavelli in Tudor England*.

Bibliography

I. MACHIAVELLI'S WORKS

1. COLLECTED EDITIONS

ITALIAN TEXTS

Tutte le opere storiche e letterarie di Niccolò Machiavelli, ed. Guido Mazzoni & Mario Casella (Florence, 1929). This is not really "tutte le opere", but it comprises all the major works, and many lesser ones, in very well edited texts: though modern scholarship does not regard them as definitive.

Le opere di Niccolò Machiavelli, ed. P. Fanfani, L. Passerini, & G. Milanesi (Florence, 1873–7). 6 vols. (incomplete).

Opere, ed. Antonio Panella (Rome, 1939). 2 vols.

Tutte le opere di Niccolò Machiavelli, ed. Francesco Flora & Carlo Cordiè (Milan, 1949, 1950). 2 vols. (incomplete).

TRANSLATIONS

The Historical, Political, and Diplomatic Writings of Niccolò Machiavelli, trans. Christian E. Detmold (Boston, 1882). 4 vols. Valuable in so far as it gives the only English translation of the bulk of Machiavelli's official correspondence—though rather inaccurately. The major writings included in this edition are loosely translated.

Machiavelli. The Chief Works and Others, trans. Allan Gilbert (Duke University Press, N. Carolina, 1965). 3 vols. A reliable translation which includes, as well as the major writings, the *Capitoli*, the *Decennali*, and several other works not otherwise available in English.

2. LEGATIONS

ITALIAN TEXTS

Legazioni e Commissarie, ed. S. Bertelli (Milan: Feltrinelli: 1964). 3 vols.

Opere, ed. Fanfani, Passerini, Milanesi, iii-vi.

TRANSLATIONS

Detmold, iii-iv.

3. LETTERS

ITALIAN TEXTS

Lettere, ed. Franco Gaeta (Milan: Feltrinelli: 1961).

TRANSLATIONS

The Letters of Machiavelli. A Selection, trans. Allan Gilbert (New York, 1961).
Also included in Gilbert, *Chief Works*, ii.

4. "THE PRINCE"

ITALIAN TEXTS

Il Principe, ed. Giuseppe Lisio (Florence, 1899).

Il Principe e discorsi etc., ed. Giuliano Procacci & Sergio Bertelli (Milan: Feltrinelli: 1960).

Mazzoni & Casella, pp. 1–51.

Il Principe, ed. L. Arthur Burd (Oxford, 1891). Invaluable. The text is now regarded as antiquated, but the annotations have yet to be surpassed.

TRANSLATIONS

Machiavelli's The Prince. *An Elizabethan Translation*, ed. Hardin Craig (University of N. Carolina Press: Chapel Hill: 1944).

The Prince, trans. Edward Dacres, 1640: reprinted in the series The Tudor Translations, xxxix (1905).

The Prince, trans. W. K. Marriott (Everyman's Library, London, 1908, and subsequent eds.).

The Prince, trans. George Bull (Penguin Books, London, 1961, and subsequent reprints).

Also included in Detmold, i, and Gilbert, *Chief Works*, i.

5. THE "DISCOURSES"

ITALIAN TEXTS

Il Principe e discorsi sopra la prima deca di Tito Livio, ed. G. Procacci & S. Bertelli (Milan: Feltrinelli: 1960).

Mazzoni & Casella, pp. 53–262.

TRANSLATIONS

The Discourses of Niccolò Machiavelli, trans. Leslie J. Walker (London, 1950). 2 vols. This translation took a thrashing from the critics when it first appeared: and indeed it is sometimes dangerously inaccurate. Nevertheless, it is of great value for its notes and indexes: and it remains—for historical purposes—the most useful edition yet published in English or Italian.

Also included in Detmold, ii, and Gilbert, *Chief Works*, i.

6. "MANDRAGOLA" & OTHER LITERARY WORKS

ITALIAN TEXTS

Il teatro e tutti gli scritti letterari, ed. Franco Gaeta (Milan: Feltrinelli: 1965).
La Mandragola di Niccolò Machiavelli, ed. Roberto Ridolfi (Florence, 1965).
Mazzoni & Casella, pp. 625–872.

TRANSLATIONS

The Literary Works of Machiavelli, ed. & trans, J. R. Hale (London, 1961). This
    includes *Mandragola*, *Clizia*, the *Dialogue on Language*, and *Belfagor*.
Gilbert, *Chief Works*, includes *Mandragola*, *Clizia*, *Belfagor*, and much of the
    verse.

7. THE "ART OF WAR"

ITALIAN TEXTS

Dell'arte della guerra, ed. Piero Pieri (Rome, 1937).
Arte della guerra e scritti politici minori, ed. Sergio Bertelli (Milan, Feltrinelli:
    1961).
Mazzoni & Casella, pp. 263–374.

TRANSLATIONS

The Art of War, trans. Peter Whitehorne, 1560: reprinted in The Tudor Trans-
    lations (London, 1905). This seems to me the most literal, yet most readable
    translation into English.
The Art of War, a revised ed. of the Ellis Farneworth translation, by Neal Wood
    (Indianapolis, New York, Kansas City, 1965). This is a travesty rather than
    a translation. It is so inaccurate as to be worthless for the study of Machia-
    velli's military thought.
Gilbert, *Chief Works*, ii, includes a reliable version.

8. THE "FLORENTINE HISTORY"

ITALIAN TEXTS

Istorie fiorentine, ed. Plinio Carli (Florence, 1927). 2 vols.
Istorie fiorentine, ed. Franco Gaeta (Milan: Feltrinelli: 1962).
Mazzoni & Casella, pp. 375–621.

TRANSLATIONS

Included in Detmold, i, and Gilbert, *Chief Works*, iii.
History of Florence (New York: Harper Torchbooks: 1960). This version first
    appeared in the Bohn Library ed. (London, 1886). It omits Machiavelli's
    important introduction, arbitrarily ignores the original chapter divisions,
    and is otherwise inaccurate.

II. BIOGRAPHY

Pasquale Villari, *Niccolò Machiavelli e i suoi tempi illustrati con nuovi documenti* (Florence, 1877–82). 3 vols. There were three subsequent eds. of this work, culminating in a posthumous ed. by Michele Scherillo (Milan, 1927). 2 vols. The first complete English ed. was that translated by Linda Villari as *The Life and Times of Niccolò Machiavelli* London, n.d.). 2 vols.

Oreste Tommasini, *La vita e gli scritti di Niccolò Machiavelli nella loro relazione col Machiavellismo* (Rome, 1883–1911).

Roberto Ridolfi, *Vita di Niccolò Machiavelli* (Rome, 1954). The English trans. of this biography, by Cecil Grayson (London, 1963), is a revised and corrected version superseding the Italian eds.

Ridolfi's biography is now generally regarded as the most satisfactory: and certainly it maintains a higher standard of accuracy than its predecessors, and is illuminating on the documentary evidence for Machiavelli's life. Nevertheless, it is marred by an extreme critical naïvety; by a kind of hero worship quite as distasteful as Villari's old-fashioned apologetics; and by an arrogance generally manifested in the notes by exclamation marks placed after statements (however reasonable) by authorities with whom the author disagrees.

Villari is still impressive as a single-handed attempt to discuss Machiavelli in the full context of Italian political and intellectual history, comparing Machiavelli's writings with those of his predecessors and contemporaries in each field of activity—political thought, historiography, and military theory.

Tommasini is a case apart. His work is vast, rambling, and appallingly inaccurate. Yet it is an absolute mine of information: and the mind boggles at the amount of material examined.

It is now fashionable to decry Villari and Tommasini: but for the historian of ideas their works are still invaluable.

III. BIBLIOGRAPHY

Adolph Gerber, *Niccolò Machiavelli. Die Handschriften, Ausgaben und Übersetzungen seiner Werker im 16. und 17. Jahrhundert* (Gotha, Munich, 1912, 1913). Since the appearance of this work, there has been much detailed study of the manuscripts and early editions of Machiavelli's writings. Nevertheless, until this research is adequately co-ordinated, Gerber's monumental volume remains essential to the student of Machiavelli.

Achille Norsa, *Il principio della forza nel pensiero politico di Niccolò Machiavelli, seguito da un contributo bibliografico* (Milan, 1936), gives a classified list of over 2,100 items relating to Machiavelli.

P. H. Harris, "Progress in Machiavelli Studies", *Italica*, xviii (March 1941).

Gennaro Sasso, "Recenti studi sul Machiavelli", *Rassegna di Filosofia*, i (1952).

E. W. Cochrane, "Machiavelli: 1940–1960", *Journal of Modern History*, xxxiii (June 1961).

For current work, see the annual bibliographies published in *Italian Studies* and *Studies in Philology*; and, more especially, since 1965, the annual *Bibliographie internationale de l'Humanisme et de la Renaissance*.

IV. CRITICAL STUDIES

It will be appreciated that books and articles on Machiavelli—both general studies and more detailed examinations of aspects of his work—may be counted by the thousand. It is doubtful that the normal human life span is sufficient to enable anyone to read them all. The following short list is merely intended as a suggestion for further reading, and comprises works which are either especially useful, interesting, provocative, or markedly representative of particular attitudes towards Machiavelli.

Felice Alderisio, *Machiavelli. L'Arte dello stato nell'azione e negli scritti* (Bologna, 1950).

Federico Chabod, *Machiavelli and the Renaissance* (London, 1958).

Cecil H. Clough, *Machiavelli Researches* (Naples, 1967).

Allan Gilbert *Machiavelli's Prince and Its Forerunners* (Duke University Press, Durham, N. Carolina, 1938).

J. R. Hale, *Machiavelli and Renaissance Italy* (London, 1961).

Luigi Russo, *Machiavelli*, 4th ed. (Bari, Laterza, 1966).

Gennaro Sasso, *Niccolò Machiavelli. Storia del suo pensiero politico* (Naples, 1958).

J. H. Whitfield, *Machiavelli* (Oxford, 1947).

Index